Wordsworth

For my Mother and Father

No Centaurs here, or Gorgons look to find,
My subject is of man and humankind.

Wordsworth:
romantic poetry
and revolution politics

JOHN WILLIAMS

Manchester University Press

Manchester and New York

distributed exclusively
in the USA and Canada
by St. Martin's Press

published by Manchester University Press, Oxford Road, Manchester M13 9PL, UK
and Room 400, 175 Fifth Avenue, New York, NY 10010, USA

Distributed exclusively in the USA and Canada
by St Martin's Press, Inc., 175 Fifth Avenue, New York, NY 10010, USA

British Library cataloguing in publication data
Williams, John
Wordsworth: romantic poetry and revolution politics.
1. Poetry in English. Wordsworth, William, 1770–1850 — Critical studies
I. Title
821'.7

Library of Congress cataloging in publication data
Williams, John, 1946–
Wordsworth: romantic poetry and revolution politics / John Williams.
p.   cm.
Includes bibliographical references.
ISBN 0–7190–3168–0
1. Wordsworth, William, 1770–1850—Political and social views.
2. Great Britain—Politics and government—1789–1820.
3. France—History—Revolution, 1789–1799—Influence.
4. Politics in literature.   5. Radicalism in literature.
6. Romanticism—England.
I. Title.   II. Title: Romantic poetry and revolution politics.
PR5892.P64W5   1989
821'.7—dc20   89–36254
CIP
ISBN 0–7190–3168–0

typeset by J&L Composition Ltd, Filey, North Yorkshire

printed in Great Britain
by Billings of Worcester

Contents

Preface

This book is primarily concerned to discuss the way in which the political state of affairs in Britain at the turn of the eighteenth century influenced the poetry written by William Wordsworth from the time of his earliest published work, through to the period immediately following his completion of the 1805 *Prelude*. In that respect I do not claim to offer a comprehensive reading of the poet's work. To some extent, my choice of poems for detailed discussion has been limited and controlled by a concern for and interest in political and ideological context, and the way it complements and informs Wordsworth's theories of what a poet should be. What I have been concerned to do is to indicate that what emerges from such a study can be of relevance ultimately to a discussion of the majority of his output.

It has long been accepted, of course, that Wordsworth sustained an intense interest in political matters, and that his writing constantly bears evidence of this fact. My particular interest lies in the extent to which his political views were the product of a tradition of British political dissidence that pre-dates the impact of French revolutionary political philosophy and action on the British political scene. In this respect there are some new things to say; there are poems that deserve re-reading, and fresh insights to be gained.

What emerges is, hopefully, a reading of Wordsworth that will add something to existing readings; that will not be seen to politicise his work at the expense of other equally important considerations; and that will put the nature of his continued 'radical' frame of mind after he had rejected the solutions offered by French Jacobin republicans into a clearer perspective.

Among the many people to whom I owe a debt of gratitude for making the eventual completion of this book possible are my colleagues at Thames Polytechnic, especially those on the editorial board of the journal *Literature and History*, who advised me in the course of preparing an article on Wordsworth and the Salisbury Plain poems. At the outset I was helped immensely by John Dixon Hunt and Gwyn A. Williams, and subsequently received valuable advice from Heather Glen. Latterly an army of long-suffering anonymous readers has provided detailed criticisms, almost all of which proved invaluable. I would also like to thank John Banks of Manchester University Press for his sensitive editorship. Most of all, I am grateful to my family and friends who have given unfailing support throughout the long period spent researching the field and rehearsing ideas, and in particular I have to thank my wife Anne for her encouragement and patience over many years.

Abbreviations

(i) *The Prelude*

All references to *The Prelude* come from *The Prelude 1799, 1805, 1850*, ed. Jonathan Wordsworth, M. H. Abrams, Stephen Gill, London: W. W. Norton (1979). The reference will show the book number if it is not clear from the text, page number(s), line number(s). Thus Book X, p. 316 lines 22–5 becomes X, 316:22–5. The same page- and line-numbering procedure is used where possible for all other references.

(ii) *Other texts*

References to the following works are given in the text:

Betz   *Benjamin the Waggoner by William Wordsworth*, ed. Paul F. Betz, Brighton: Harvester Press (1981).

DS   *Descriptive Sketches by William Wordsworth*, ed. Eric Birdsall, London: Cornell University Press (1984).

EW   *An Evening Walk by William Wordsworth*, ed. James Averill, London: Cornell University Press (1984).

EY   *The Letters of William and Dorothy Wordsworth, The Early Years 1787–1805*, arranged and ed. Ernest de Selincourt, 2nd edn rev. Chester L. Shaver, Oxford: Clarendon Press (1967).

Gill   *The Salisbury Plain Poems of William Wordsworth*, ed. Stephen Gill, Brighton: Harvester Press (1975).

HG   *Home at Grasmere Part First, Book First, of The Recluse by William Wordsworth*, ed. Beth Darlington, Brighton: Harvester Press (1977).

LB   *Wordsworth and Coleridge Lyrical Ballads*, ed. R. L. Brett and A. R. Jones, London: Methuen (1968).

MY   *The Letters of William and Dorothy Wordsworth: The Middle Years*, ed. Ernest de Selincourt, rev. Mary Moorman, Oxford: Clarendon Press (1969).

O&S I–III *The Prose Works of William Wordsworth*, ed. W. J. B. Owen and Jane Worthington Smyser, 3 vols., Oxford: Clarendon Press (1974).

PW   *The Poetical Works of William Wordsworth*, ed. E. de Selincourt and Helen Darbishire, 5 vols., Oxford: Clarendon Press (1940–49).

Reed   *Wordsworth, The Chronology of the Early Years 1770–1799*, Mark L. Reed, Cambridge Mass.: Harvard University Press (1967).

1
Wordsworth
and pastoral politics

Whither is Europe's ancient spirit fled?
Where are those valiant tenants of her shore,
Who from the warrior bow the strong dart sped,
Or with firm hand the rapid pole-axe bore?
Freeman and soldier was their common name,
Who late with reapers to the furrow came,
Now in the front of battle charged the foe:
Who taught the steer the wintry plough to endure,
Now in full councils check'd encroaching power,
And gave the guardian laws their majesty to know.
(Akenside, *Ode: To The Country Gentlemen of England*)[1]

Akenside's *Ode* is one poem among many which illustrates the profound influence that images of agrarian society had on eighteenth-century habits of thought. The reason for choosing this particular example is because the moral is expressed in unambiguously political terms. Akenside is giving voice to a commonplace assumption that the landed gentry make the best, and fiercest, patriots. Those who marshall their troops to reap the 'furrow', who are actively engaged in providing the sustenance for a prosperous nation, and who are themselves hardened by physical work, will be the ones most eager and best prepared to defend their country.

This chapter is primarily concerned with looking at the way the pastoral theme in eighteenth-century poetry was adapted from its classical models, to reflect and reinforce a variety of ideological assumptions that underpinned political evolution in England in the course of the century. A necessarily persistent backdrop for such poetry was landscape; in consequence the landscape habitually provided an analogue for the eighteenth-century political 'prospect', to a point where tension developed between what might be seen in fact, and what might be deemed suitable for the poet to describe if the required analogue was to be achieved.

A discussion of the issues involved is of great importance for a study of Wordsworth; still traditionally thought of as a nature poet, he was a man obsessed with political life whose poetry was in part a product of that obsession. It was Sara Coleridge who recalled 'How gravely and earnestly used Samuel Taylor Coleridge and William Wordsworth, and uncle Southey also, to discuss the affairs of the nation, as if it all came home to their business and bosoms, as if it were their private concern.'[2] Succeeding chapters seek to illustrate that Wordsworth's political convictions were rooted in an essentially eighteenth-century concept of society, and that his understanding of political 'radicalism' belonged equally within that context.

Among recent studies of the relationship between eighteenth-century pastoral ideology and reality, John Barrell's contribution has been of particular value, and his use of the visual arts (notably work by Lambert, Gainsborough, Moreland and Constable) has helped to identify a crucial area of potential embarrassment for both artist and writer when called upon to depict the English landscape.[3] The actual living conditions of agricultural labourers and their families were far from a confirmation of the idyllic image of rural life to be found, for example, in Claude Lorrain's much admired landscapes of Italy. As the century progressed, the attempt to exclude poverty from the rural landscape by presenting it as virtually uninhabited, or by poeticising the description of labour, became less and less convincing.[4]

The conventional manner in which pastoral literature sought to reconcile undeniable inequalities within society was by countering the material wealth of some of its members with the moral or spiritual advantages that could be claimed for the lowly peasant or villager:

> For him light labour spread her wholesome store,
> Just gave what life requir'd, but gave no more:
> His best companions, innocence and health;
> And his best riches, ignorance of wealth.
>   (Goldsmith, *The Deserted Village*, 1770)[5]

This was an acceptably poetic account for Goldsmith's cultured, metropolitan readership. For anyone with even the beginnings of a first-hand knowledge of agrarian society, however, it presented problems.

In the latter years of the century it begins to become apparent that questions of literary taste, judgement and convention, are frequently being prompted by concerns of a social and political nature. The work of John Langhorne and George Crabbe make this very clear. Wordsworth's response to the problem was in essence no less conservative and atavistic than that of his predecessors. Despite his strictures in the 1800 Preface to *Lyrical Ballads* on mid-eighteenth-century poetry, he himself remained a poet trained in and committed to eighteenth-century priorities in verse and political ideology.

At its simplest, a writer inspired by picturesque values in art sought evidence of a divinely inspired, unifying order in the variety of natural forms. Schooling one's response to the landscape in this way owed much to the teachings of seventeenth- and eighteenth-century Deism, where it had become no longer possible to conceive of God as revealed through religion. Nature had become the source of divine revelation, and in consequence 'Nature' and 'God' were often treated synonymously.[6] The landscape poet was committed to a piously foregone conclusion about the evidence of God's handiwork in nature throughout its infinitely variable forms; this assumption was in turn readily transferred to reflections on the nature of social and political order. Human society, with its vast differences of degree and privilege, was understood to have a place within the whole order of creation, and to offer the student of mankind an edifying microcosm of that creation.

In passages from *The Pleasures of Imagination* consistently reproduced in what had been a seminal anthology for Wordsworth as a schoolboy, Vicesimus Knox's *Elegant Extracts*,[7] Mark Akenside argued that 'the fair variety of all things' might only be understood in terms of 'the Almighty One' who created them, and that this was true both of the world we see around us, and of 'social life' where man is destined to fulfil many 'different labours'. In 'Tintern Abbey' Wordsworth surely registers a debt to Akenside when he describes 'that serene and blessed mood, / In which the affections gently lead us on ...' (LB, 114:42–3). Akenside's 'symmetry' becomes Wordsworth's 'harmony' (49); but unlike Wordsworth, Akenside goes on to relate his belief in an 'unbounded symmetry of things' quite specifically to the political order by recalling the fate of Julius Caesar at the hand of the patriot, Brutus:

> For lo! the tyrant prostrate on the dust,
> And Rome again is free! Is aught so fair
> In all the dewy landscapes of the Spring,

> In the bright eye of Hesper, or the morn;
> In Nature's fairest forms, is aught so fair
> As virtuous friendship? as the candid blush
> Of him who strives with fortune to be just?
> The graceful tear that streams for others' woes?
> Or the mild majesty of private life,
> Where peace with ever blooming olive crowns
> The gate; where Honour's liberal hands effuse
> Unenvied treasures, and the snowy wings
> Of Innocence and Love protect the scene?

The preservation of a sound paternalistic political system is the ultimate 'prospect'; our earlier guided tour 'through blooming walks, / Through fragrant mountains, and poetic streams', was for Akenside a necessary preparation for a political vision which surpasses 'all the dewy landscapes of the Spring'.[8] There is a movement here from the outward to the inward eye: 'the mind, especially the literary and historical imagination, completed the visual structures'.[9] Though Wordsworth argued with trends in eighteenth-century poetry, he remained ultimately bound to the eighteenth-century assumptions from which Akenside worked.

Wordsworth's mature philosophy of the 'one life' was in many respects a radical advance on Akenside's orthodox, Deistic understanding of 'the Almighty One', but his belief in the integration of aesthetic and political conviction, though severely tested in the early 1790s, remained the unshaken principle by which he judged the new French Republic of 1792, and found it wanting.[10] The onset of murder and apparent anarchy in France revealed the insufficiency of man to create a more just society when guided solely by his own capacity for reason and rationality.

The passage quoted above from *The Pleasures of Imagination* serves well to illustrate how Wordsworth modified Akenside's ideas without losing his commitment to a traditional pastoral ideology which sought an analogue for social order in the natural world, revealing by degrees the mind of an omnipotent creator whose ultimate purposes remained shrouded in mystery. For Akenside political perfection is the goal, and is described as *protecting* 'the scene', in one sense quite literally the idyllic landscape.

From its earliest stages of composition, we find that Wordsworth in *The Prelude* was concerned to re-examine the relationship between man's response to natural objects and his involvement with political activity. The result was effectively to reverse Akenside's order of precedence. A sound relationship to nature, to 'the operations of the elements, and the appearances of the visible universe', actually protects the political order (O&S I, 142:500–1). Reversal, however, is not a sufficient description of what has happened. By the time Wordsworth was beginning to compose *The Prelude* (1798–99), he had established in his own mind an important distinction between a love of natural objects for their own sake, and a more profound love engendered by a recognition of the permanent moral and spiritual truths with which natural objects were imbued. The latter should constitute the main object of our reverence.

In Book X of the 1805 version of *The Prelude* he produced a tortuous passage (380:381–400) which sought to reveal a distinction between the love of God, established through meditation on natural objects, and commitment to the social and political world, expressed through 'service'. They are distinct but related, the second arising from the first, and remaining in that secondary relationship to it. The man who aspires to leadership within society is responding to a 'second love', subservient ultimately to 'things which lie / At rest within the bosom of thy will' (380:394–96). In the 1798–99 text (to become Book II ll.203–37 in the 1805 version), Wordsworth had made a distinction between love of nature 'sought / For her own sake' and nature revered more profoundly as an expression of 'The unity of all' (19:237–42; 20:256). The Book X passage applies this distinction overtly to the issue of political activity and its proper motivation. He insists that an individual's commitment to 'eminence' as a social animal is to be understood as the fruit of an 'after worship' or a 'second love', trustworthy only in so far as it springs from a profound love of God. Where Akenside uses the word 'Nature' in terms of essentially visual experience, therefore, Wordsworth expanded the moral and spiritual dimension it already potentially carried.

The paternalistic rhetoric of political protest which became so closely allied to eighteenth-century landscape and topographical poetry, and which Wordsworth inherited, stems from the 'archaic and academic whiggism' of the dissident Whigs and Commonwealthmen of the late seventeenth and early eighteenth centuries.[11] The considerable influence of the Commonwealthmen and their more conservative Country Party allies on radical political theory in the

1790s is now thoroughly documented. The 'nucleus of the group', Albert Goodwin suggests, were Robert Molesworth, John Toland and William Molyneux.[12] Later generations took up the cause, and we find the names of Francis Hutcheson and Thomas Hollis figuring prominently, along with Thomas Gordon of the *Independent Whig*, and Richard Baron whose reputation as a 'republican' arose from his editions of works by Algernon Sidney, Ludlow, Nedham, and Milton's political writings.[13]

Mid-eighteenth-century 'republicanism' was obviously a very different proposition from that which emerged from the second revolutionary upheaval of 1792 in France, but at the same time it exercised a decisive influence on the political debate that gave birth to radical republicanism in this country in the 1790s. Hollis is a central, if still shadowy figure in the encouragement of mid-century republicanism, and the history of his publishing career and political correspondence encapsulates the seeming paradox of a political creed capable of both radical and reactionary evolution and interpretation:

His own political views were by no means original, being derived from Harrington ... he cherished the ideal of a state devoid of political factions but led by great men, willing to execute the wishes of the independent and propertied classes formulated in frequently held but not popularly elected assemblies – a dream which had also occupied the thoughts of Andrew Marvell and Henry Neville.[14]

In 1948 Zera S. Fink claimed that Wordsworth's politics could only be understood if we appreciate first his continuing allegiance to this paternalist tradition, a situation that arguably applied to a good many of Wordsworth's contemporaries.[15] The work of republishing 'Commonwealthman' texts which Hollis undertook meant that, by the time a new generation of radicals was beginning to emerge in Britain after the American War, the Commonwealthman heroes were still accessible and revered:

Hampden, Russell, Sidney; ye intrepid martyres to freedom! All hail to your ever glorious memory! Alas! how near was the page of our history to being again stained with the record of another bloody tragedy, similar to that which terminated your bright and honourable career![16]

The writer is Thomas Hardy, at the point in his *Memoirs* where he recalls the founding of the London Corresponding Society in 1792, and his own election as its first secretary. Preserving these names for posterity was seen as more than a duty owed to nostalgia, it constituted a contemporary statement of political belief, and we may gauge just how desperate the situation seemed to propagandists of the time from Francis Blackburne's Preface to his *Memoir* of Hollis (1780):

Among other causes which have prevented the justice due to the character of Mr. Hollis from having its free course, is the political fashion of the times. A subscriber to Lord Molesworth's political creed is not to expect applause in an age when the present doctrines of the majority are so loudly echoed through the land, and when the loyalty of the day is chiefly distinguished by execrations on the principles of Milton, Sidney, Locke and other patriot writers of past times.[17]

Evidence of this kind points to the perpetuation of a coherent Commonwealthman tradition of political dissent in the midst of a broad spectrum of eighteenth-century political protest.[18] With its leaders in exile from the ranks of the Establishment Whigs after 1688, the tendency was to elaborate a claim to political disinterestedness grounded in moral and spiritual virtue which they alone – from the vantage-point of political 'retirement' – were able to perpetuate. This became a jealously guarded cornerstone of their political philosophy.

The peculiar insistence thus preserved on the related nature of political argument and moral philosophy of the kind associated with Hutcheson, is an important reason why the presentation of pastoral landscapes and the social virtues associated with them, were associated with not just a general feeling of political unease, but with a more specific ideological context of dissent.[19] The perpetuation of Commonwealthman ideology was the chief route by which the political debates of the mid and late eighteenth century had come to be imbued with a powerful rhetoric of moral and spiritual conviction, and the traditionally conceived pastoral world in which the Commonweathmen eked out their political retirement became an analogue for their meritorious philosophy.

Not infrequently an attempt was made to give political conviction tangible, topographical substance in the laying out of an estate; William Pitt's landscaping of Stowe is one such instance. The aesthetic merit of such schemes was underpinned by the political principles they evinced, and topographical poetry which praised these prospects implicitly reinforced those principles. The rhetoric of pastoral thus came to overlap with a rhetoric that claimed precedence for moral and spiritual values in the conduct of public life. 'Nature', a concept embracing numerous degrees of meaning from abstract philosophy to concrete visual perception, provided an established common point of reference answering the needs of a debate to be carried on both at the level of moral and spiritual priorities, and at the same time in terms of pragmatic temporal concerns for liberty, property and the law.

Though the early Romantics began, therefore, to exhibit what is in one sense a new responsiveness to landscape, there was equally no radical shift from the basis of the political battlecry of Sidney in the *Discourses*: 'The Liberties of Nations are from God and Nature, not from Kings'.[20] Wordsworth's vision of the 'one life' that developed after his arrival with Dorothy at Racedown in 1795 was in keeping ideologically with the eighteenth-century political beliefs of his patron at that time, the Bristol merchant John Pinney. For such a man, it was only to be expected that a copy of Sidney's *Discourses* had its place on the shelves of his house at Racedown, while even more significant was the fact that one of Pinney's sons decided he needed it with him in London shortly after the Wordsworths had taken up residence in Dorset.[21]

Wordsworth's paternalism, his reiterated appeal through nature to a transcendent, unifying moral authority governing political action, his distrust of a professional soldiery and indeed military adventurism in general, all suggest the absorption of political principles rehearsed and fiercely debated in the shadow of the Glorious Revolution, when men like Molesworth and Walter Moyle had first seen fit to define their opposition to the Establishment Whigs by calling themselves Commonwealthmen. In the process, the history of England during Cromwell's protectorship was rewritten; as Goodwin has argued, 'republicanism' during the Interregnum was transformed in the hands of Molesworth and his allies into a dissident Whig ideology 'which had little or nothing to do with notions of a social or political equality but which reemphasised the right of collective resistance'.[22] While it passively advocated religious toleration, it totally opposed popery and French despotism, seeing both as a logical extension of its opposition to Jacobitism.

Subsequently, whether it was the War of the Spanish Succession, the Seven Years War, the American War or the French Revolution, successive generations of disaffected politicians and writers sought to insist that the principles they saw being violated were 'from God and Nature', and thus theologically immutable.[23] The fact that diametrically opposed political interests within this relatively limited ideological spectrum laid claim to the same rhetoric makes the specific heritage claimed by individuals all the more important.

The enthusiasm of Wordsworth for the pantheon of Commonwealthman heroes has been well documented.[24] During his time in France in 1792, the political works of Milton, Harrington, Ludlow and Algernon Sidney were available on the Paris bookstalls: they would also have been known to Beaupuy, the liberal aristocrat who befriended Wordsworth while he was at Orléans, and his revolutionary lectures to the young Englishman would have been laced with references to these men as much as with passages from Rousseau and the philosophes. Two other Englishmen who had been in France since the Fête de la Fédération of July 1790 were James Watt and Thomas Cooper; Wordsworth met Watt in 1792, and given the poor standard of his French, he would presumably have learnt as much about the ideals of the Revolution from him as from anyone. Watt and Cooper's understanding of the republican cause may be gauged from the fact that in the procession of 1790, they carried a British flag and held aloft a bust of Sidney, the Whig martyr of 1683. The movement towards a far more radically populist revolution with the rise to power of Robespierre in 1792 increasingly isolated the English fellow-travellers, along with French liberals like Beaupuy, whose position may be understood by comparison with the more famous Lafayette.

Despite Wordsworth's apparently wholehearted defence of the Revolution and of the execution of the French King in his *Letter to Llandaff* of 1793, the sympathy and generosity which John Pinney extended to him in the years immediately following his return from France, suggests the existence of evidence within his work that he held true to basic Commonwealthman principles. Pinney was a veteran of the 1770s campaign to support the American colonists in the period leading up to the American War, a time when Commonwealthman rhetoric gained a new lease of life in the pamphleteering and political journalism of the nation. The poetry Pinney and his sons had seen was *An Evening Walk* (1788–93) and *Descriptive Sketches* (1792–93), and they clearly must have struck them as evidence of the young poet's sound political principles.

The copy of Sidney's *Discourses* on the shelves at Racedown Lodge was, as we have seen, a political manual still being made use of by Pinney's eldest son. By way of exchange for the *Discourses*, Wordsworth was sent William Crowe's *Lewesdon Hill* (1788),[25] a landscape poem, the politics of which illustrate well the integration of eighteenth-century pastoral poetry with Commonwealthman ideology.

William Crowe was born in Berkshire in 1745.[26] He was brought up in Winchester and went to Winchester College as a 'poor scholar', and from thence to New College, Oxford. Crowe's reputation for eccentricity has tended to mask the controversial aspects of his career and writing. His experience of academic life would have been not unlike that of Wordsworth while he was at Cambridge; the latter's impecunious background committed him to the often demeaning existence of a sizar.[27]

In 1782 Crowe was presented with the living of Stoke Abbas in Dorset, a tiny village beneath the hill of Lewesdon, only a few miles away from Racedown. In 1784 he was elected Public Orator at Oxford University. The living of Stoke Abbas, which he exchanged in 1787 for Alton Barnes in Wiltshire, was clearly conceived of as a sinecure, though Crowe, a great walker, did spend some time there, even if it was primarily upon Lewesdon rather than in the church.

Like John Pinney, Crowe belonged to a political generation nurtured in its radical views by the American War of Independence, distanced from the Establishment from the outset by his social background, and deeply suspicious of the morality of imperialism highlighted by the colonial crisis. Crowe applied his anti-war sentiments, grounded in a well-established tradition of political dissent, to the issue of war with revolutionary France in 1793. In the same year, Oxford prepared to welcome Portland as Chancellor of New College, and a collection of verse to be recited on the occasion survives.[28] Over Crowe's offering we read that his poem was 'intended to have been spoken ... but suppres'd'; and it is hardly surprising. The piece is outspokenly pacifist, and recognisable as a product of the same tradition of rhetoric as Wordsworth's poem of the same year, *Salisbury Plain*. Crowe is quick to attack time-serving Court poets:

> too oft
> The poet bending low to lawless power
> Hath paid unseemly reverence, yea and brought
> Streams clearest of th'Arnian fount to wash
> Bloodstain'd ambition.

If war involved only those who wished to make it, the situation might be different; but, stressing the divide between statesmen and the 'people', a theme in which we recognise a tradition of rhetoric linking the conservative 'Country Party' poet Langhorne, Wordsworth (in both *The Old Cumberland Beggar* and in *Salisbury Plain*) and Joseph Fawcett, Crowe asserts that it is the innocent who invariably suffer:

> But Alas!
> That undistinguishing and deathful storm
> Beats heaviest on th'exposed innocent,
> And they who stir its fury, while it raves
> Stand at a safe distance, send their madness forth
> Unto the mortal ministers that wait
> To do their bidding. Ah! who then regards
> The widow's tears, the friendless Orphan's cries,
> And famine, and the ghastly train of woes
> That follow at the dogged heels of war.

By contrast, the other pieces in this collection share a bellicose, patriotic fervour evidently far more to the taste of the College authorities.

Crowe, then, remained true to his 'ultra-Whig' principles, and suffered – presumably with philosophical good grace – suppression. The poem for which he is best known, *Lewesdon Hill*, has an equally interesting history. Crowe used the view from Lewesdon Hill to map out his dissident Whig political beliefs; he names his Whig heroes, and he insists on the need for all the traditionally Old Whig virtues that support and maintain an ordered society. To a late eighteenth-century readership it was unmistakably a dissident Whig manifesto, as were so many of the books already on the shelves at Racedown; Milton's prose works, selections from Algernon Sidney, John Toland, Oldham, Chillingworth and Gordon, and an account of Stowe Gardens designed to celebrate the Old Whig principles of William Pitt the elder.[29] This was not how the poem came to be known to all its readers in the early nineteenth century, however. In

1816 *Lewesdon Hill* was printed in Vicesimus Knox's *Elegant Extracts*, and Knox's text continued to appear in various editions and anthologies until it arrived in the footnotes of present-day literary criticism as a *landscape* poem of great significance for Wordsworth. What had actually happened, however, was that Knox had produced a version shorn of its key political passages. In 1795, Wordsworth had the unexpurgated text of 1788.

In his Advertisement to the poem Crowe explains that his 'choice of subject ... may seem perhaps to confine him to topics of more rural and local description'; he is insistent, however, that his subject lies beyond these 'narrow limits', and is more 'general and important', and that the connection between these more general and important subjects and the landscape will at every stage be apparent.

The view from Lewesdon is one of plenitude and variety, and the comparison between the beauty of the view in spring, and the false colours of fashion is quickly introduced:

> So gorgeously hath Nature dressed thee up
> Against the birth of May; and, vested so,
> Thou dost appear more gracefully array'd
> Than Fashion's worshippers; whose gaudy shews,
> Fantastical as are a sick man's dreams,
> From vanity to costly vanity
> Change ofter than the moon. (32–8)

In retiring from the 'false complexions' (51) of the world of fashion, we may appreciate also that Crowe is lifting himself above a too literal view of the countryside itself:

> Above the noise and stir of yonder fields
> Uplifted, on this height I feel the mind
> Expand itself in wider liberty. (68–70)

The sensibility expressed arises from precisely that tension between an iconographic use of nature and the realities it reveals (the 'stir of yonder fields') which led Wordsworth on from his early attempts at verse – specifically *An Evening Walk* – towards the more sophisticated response to nature apparent in the poetry he was to write from 1795 onwards. Crowe follows the above passage with a denial of the charge that 'retirement' is necessarily escapism:

> But conscience, which still censures on our acts,
> That awful voice within us, and the sense

> Of an hereafter, wake and rouse us up
> From such unshaped retirement; which were else
> A blest condition on this earthy stage. (76–80)

The fact remains, however, that the 'life of toil' to which he refers is
not an encounter with the toil going on amidst the beauty of the
scene he regards. As is so often the case with eighteenth-century
hilltop and pastoral poetry, no labourers are described until we meet
the inevitable good shepherd, 'Rechasing, lest his tender ewes
should coath / In the dank pasturage' (121–2). After relatively plain
language, Crowe's description of the shepherd brings with it a series
of obscure dialect words requiring a footnote. Potential agrarian
reality is thus masked by picturesque effect; dissident Whig ideology
was not equipped to question rural depravation.

The analogic view of the natural world tends to see man as
essentially harmful, tainting the natural goodness and richness of the
location. In *Lewesdon Hill* we find that the true guardian of the sheep
is not the shepherd, but the river which rises on the hill. The river
remains pure from its source to the point – not so very far away –
where it drops into the sea.

Looking critically at the social conditions of the labourers who
sustained the rural prospect was simply not Crowe's concern; he
sought to paint a picture of a world naturally good, displaying both
variety (thus social variety or inequality was not in itself bad), and
the means whereby a naturally ordered society could contain and
succour all its various parts. In the manner of a true eighteenth-
century landscape enthusiast, he encouraged man to follow nature as
a means of discovering God's will for ordering society.

In order to make the necessary connection between his image of
the pure, unselfish spirit of the stream which gives life to the whole
valley, and human society, Crowe invokes a child who died at an
early age; again a foretaste of Wordsworth's own use of childhood
and innocence:

> They also can discourse
> Wisely, to prove that what must be must be,
> And shew how thoughts are jogg'd out of the brain
> By a mechanical impulse; pushing on
> The minds of us, poor unaccountables,
> To fatal resolution. (156–61)

For Wordsworth reading *Lewesdon Hill* at Racedown, Crowe's use of
the child to mark the importance of the affections and the feelings as
against a mechanistic, determinist concept of reason, would have
constituted a timely reassurance that the political beliefs to which he
was committed need not be dependent on Hartley's associationism
or Godwinian rationalism; a more deeply rooted tradition of
religious sensibility was involved.

The kind of determinism Crowe describes rules out the quality of
freedom most prized by his Commonwealthman mentors: 'of this be
sure; / Where Freedom is not, there no virtue is' (168–9). What this
view allows for is hardship in life as well as joy. In *The Excursion*
Wordsworth repeatedly claims that suffering may bring spiritual
rewards. Having learnt that freedom was not a quality to be won
through legislation and materialist political activity, he turned to the
more conservative Old Whig concept that true liberty constituted
freedom of conscience. In Crowe's words:

> But that the mind is free,
> The Mind herself, best judge of her own state,
> Is feelingly convinced; nor to be moved
> By subtle words, that may perplex the head,
> But ne'er persuade the heart. (184–8)

The stress for Crow is on 'feelingly convinced', a theory of liberty
that could ride out the stormy seas of France's failure to achieve
freedom by political means.

We are reminded here of the need to study carefully the way
eighteenth-century poets used figures in their landscapes. In an
eighteenth-century political context, needless suffering as it occurred
on a day-to-day basis in the countryside was traditionally represented
by a small and largely unrepresentative set of circumstances, even
where the poetry set out to be critical of the nation's political
leadership. The myth of pastoral felicity made any comprehensive
indictment of rural poverty virtually impossible for the pastoral poet
to contemplate.

In *Lewesdon Hill* Crowe clearly intended to suggest that 'natural'
disasters may conceivably be for the greater good in that they incite
compassion for others, and serve to put man – otherwise inclined to
ape God (especially when he goes to war) – in his place. Crowe gives
an account of the wreck of the *Halswell* which had taken place two

years before off Seacombe, a point on the Dorset coast to the south-east of Lewesdon. This is presented as an integral part of the lesson his undisturbed view of the countryside is teaching him; adversity is an unavoidable part of the human condition, which while it afflicts, will also heal. The road leading inland from the coast looks like 'a path of pleasure, drawn by art / Through park or flowery garden for delight', whereas in fact its beauty originates in its submission to the controlling hand of nature, as it seeks to find its way inland 'By soft gradations', making life as easy as possible for 'way-worn feet' (221–50).

Nature is here keeping the suffering she inflicts through the hilly landscape to a minimum; and both the 'natural' course of the road and the 'natural' disaster of the *Halswell* are shown as a necessary part of life, while war is not:

> And blest are they,
> Who in life's toilsome journey may make pause
> After a march of glory: yet not such
> As rise in causeless war, troubling the world
> By their mad quarrel, and in fields of blood
> Hail'd victors, thence renown'd, and call'd on earth
> Kings, heroes, demi-gods, but in high Heaven
> Thieves, ruffians, murderers; these find no repose:
> Thee rather, patriot Conqueror, to thee
> Belongs such rest; who in the western world,
> Thine own deliver'd country, for thyself
> Hast planted an immortal grove; and there
> Upon the glorious mount of Liberty
> Reposing, sit'st beneath the palmy shade. (250–63)

Crowe's reference to George Washington, the 'patriot Conqueror' of the western world, retiring after the American War to Mount Vernon, his estate, was deemed politically acceptable by Vicesimus Knox. What followed, however, had to go, for it moved the poem well out of the orbit of polite landscape description. The poem goes on to praise Pasquale Paoli, 'Patriot Prince, / Hero, Philosopher', the defender of Corsica against the French. The castle building and imperial ambitions of the French are described with scorn, and the theme is expanded in a lengthy footnote (264–319). Paoli's name occurs regularly as an idol of Commonwealthman and Old Whig writers and publicists in the eighteenth century. In consequence his story had come to have dubious political associations for a conservative Whig like Knox, despite his laudable campaign against French despotism.[30]

There follows a curious section describing the coast to the west of Chesil Beach, and the cat-and-mouse games of smugglers and excise men. The emphasis throughout the poem, as we are seeing, is on what is 'natural' and what is not. Paoli is a 'virtuous' man; France's behaviour is 'unnatural' and 'arrogant'. Using the sporting metaphor of fox and hounds, Crowe now enters into the spirit of smuggling as a game sanctioned – as was hunting – by nature. It may well have been a sport from which he benefited while in Dorset; if this was so, Knox evidently had not had the same luck, and the passage was also cut.

Knox was to be happier with the description of Eggardon Hill, which lies to the east of Lewesdon (358–80); but this was followed by a glowing panegyric of Thomas Hollis, whose estate lay to the north of Eggardon at Corscombe. Knox's version of the poem dispenses with Hollis and his Commonwealthman ideals, and moves on to the sentimental tale of a young country girl who stoops to folly. She comes to a bad end, breaking her parents' hearts in the process. These lines were not in the 1788 version; they were written at a later date by Crowe and were added to his own 1804 edition of the poem.

Of Hollis, Crowe wrote:

> Fain would I view thee, Corscombe, fain would hail
> The ground where Hollis lies; his choice retreat,
> Where, from the busy world withdrawn, he lived
> To generous Virtue and the holy love
> Of Liberty, a dedicated spirit:
> And left his ashes there; still honouring
> Thy fields, with title given of patriot names,
> But more with his untitled sepulchre.
> That envious ridge conceals thee from my sight. (381–9)

Almost certainly in need of explanation for Wordsworth here would have been the reference to Hollis as having 'honoured' his fields 'with title given of patriot names'. In fact there can be few better examples of the way political conviction was stamped on the face of the landscape in eighteenth-century England, not excepting the numerous well-documented landscape gardens of the period. Hollis quite simply named portions of his estate, fields, farms and woods, after prominent political figures, delegating the useless areas to villains, and the fruitful parts to heroes. The names used for fields included New England, Adams, Russell, and John Toland; farms were named after Milton, Sidney, Russell (again), Harrington and Neville. Wordsworth now knew that he was living only a few miles away from a landscape transformed into a record of Commonwealth-man political history.[31]

Over against Hollis's estate, Crowe sets 'The noble Digby's mansion' at Sherborne, using a resumé of its history to attack the greed and superstition of kings and their favourites, effectively an attack upon the whole ethos of Court life which Hollis rejected, tainted by implication with Roman Catholicism. Raleigh, a great man of Hollis's stamp, owed his destruction to his preparedness to involve himself in the world of political chicanery which Hollis shunned. The theme of temporal transience is emphasised as Crowe's eye then moves north and west to where Glastonbury Tor is blotted from view by inclement weather as soon as seen. This commonplace moralising on the insubstantiality of material things tempted Knox back to the original text.

The final lines of *Lewesdon Hill* must have struck Wordsworth as especially apt to his own case. The poet descends from the hill, where his vision has been clear, where the shades of Washington, Paoli and Hollis have been invoked as types of the perfect patriot statesman; he descends to 'join the worldly croud', knowing that his finer feelings will pass away 'Even as this goodly prospect from my view' will fade. Wordsworth may be thought of in his Racedown days as struggling back up the hill from his 'earthy-rooted cares' as he reflected on a dissident Whig view of the troubles that beset him and his country.

For Wordsworth pastoral poetry lay at the heart of a literary crisis where the formal representation of 'labour' was concerned. Changing economic and social circumstances challenged a static paternalistic concept of a unifying order discernible within the variety of the world. As Crowe in particular has illustrated, the evolution of a dissident or disaffected position in relation to the political Establishment during the eighteenth century did not amount to an outright rejection of faith in paternalism. The politics of pastoral at their most radical remained atavistic, and unresponsive to a distinct, self-consciously 'working' class.

We have also to recognise that it was not Wordsworth's inheritance of a pastoral tradition in poetry alone that could teach him to mistrust the contemporary political establishment. Pastoralism could embody an angry reactionary political position, and frequently did. Fully to understand Wordsworth, we must recognise evidence in his work of the continuation of a specifically dissident Whig strand of pastoral, 'republican' zeal which owed its vigour primarily to the survival of a Commonwealthman political tradition throughout the century. In eighteenth-century literature, the distinction between these two positions is frequently blurred, usually because the writers themselves were prepared to countenance ambiguities that critics subsequently often failed to appreciate. To understand later developments in the shadow of the French Revolution, however, it becomes very necessary to take it into account. It was to the Commonwealthman tradition that Akenside, Beattie and Crowe inclined, and it was to that same tradition that Wordsworth gravitated, developing a firm belief in the emphasis laid by men like Molesworth and Molyneux on the need for a spirit of disinterested moral obligation where the vocation of political service was concerned.

2
An Evening Walk: the pastoral tradition in early Wordsworth

The scenes which he describes have been viewed with a Poet's eye and are pourtrayed with a Poet's pencil ... Their faults are such as a young Poet was most likely to fall into and least likely to discover.
                    (Dorothy Wordsworth to Jane Pollard, 16 February 1793)

In many respects *An Evening Walk* is a typical late eighteenth-century landscape poem, a sentimental exercise in the pastoral genre showing very little of the political awareness to be found, for example, in *Lewesdon Hill*. But there are clear indications as the poem progresses that Wordsworth had difficulties in following a traditonal pastoral poetic formula. In the following discussion of *An Evening Walk* the intention is twofold. Firstly, to establish how the traditional pastoral mode is present in the poem, both through landscape description and the depiction of figures in the landscape; and secondly, there will be a consideration of how the difficulties encountered began to shape Wordsworth's later, more mature poetry along lines which nevertheless preserved a fundamental continuity with the eighteenth-century political implications of pastoral.

If we compare the opening lines of *An Evening Walk* with a stanza from James Beattie's *The Minstrel* (1771–74), a poem Wordsworth held in permanent high regard, the derivative way in which the younger poet describes landscape becomes evident. This is how Beattie's Edwin encounters natural objects:

> Thither he hied, enamoured of the scene.
> For rocks on rocks piled, as by magic spell,
> Here scorched with lightening, there with ivy green,
> Fenced from north and east this savage dell.
> Southward a mountain rose with easy swell,
> Whose long long groves eternal murmur made:
> And toward the western sun a streamlet fell,
> Where, through the cliffs, the eye, remote, surveyed
> Blue hills, and glittering waves, and skies in gold arrayed.[1]

Wordsworth, himself the wandering minstrel, begins:

> Far from my dearest friend, 'tis mine to rove
> Thro' bare grey dell, high wood, and pastoral cove;
> His wizard course where hoary Derwent takes
> Thro' crags, and forest glooms, and opening lakes,
> Staying his silent waves, to hear the roar
> That stuns the tremulous cliffs of high Lodore;
> Where silver rocks the savage prospect chear
> Of giant yews that frown on Rydal's mere;
> Where peace to Grasmere's lonely island leads,
> To willowy hedgerows, and to emerald meads;
> Leads to her bridge, rude church, and cottag'd grounds,
> Her rocky sheepwalks, and her woodland bounds;
> Where, bosom'd deep, the shy Winander peeps
> 'Mid clustering isles, and holly sprinkl'd steeps;
> Where twilight glens endear my Esthwaite's shore,
> And memory of departed pleasures, more. (EW, 28–30:1–16)[2]

The well-trained, discriminating eye of the poet identifies contrasts and variety in the scene which combine to give an overall impression of harmony and contentment. It becomes apparent, however, that we witness a gradual taming of the wild, unpeopled 'savage prospect', as progressive evidence of civilised life is introduced: 'the tremulous cliffs of high Lodore' give way to the 'rude church, and cottag'd grounds'.

What most markedly distinguishes the opening lines of *An Evening Walk* from the passage by Beattie, however, is Wordsworth's obsession with an identifiable, *real* landscape. By the end of the passage from *The Minstrel*, Beattie has placed us in a landscape of 'glittering waves, and skies in gold arrayed', recognisable to his cultured readership chiefly from their acquaintance with paintings in the style of Claude or Richard Wilson. The traditional structure for this kind of poetry was the long, tenuous sentence that created a subtle transition from a landscape actually perceived towards an introverted state of meditative reflection.[3] Wordsworth's catalogue of verifiable place names implies that he is particularly concerned to explore the relationship between what is actually seen and the emotions experienced. The reader is left with a still debatable choice to make between the 'memory of departed pleasures' and the alternative source of feeling derived from an immediate experience of the landscape.

What this suggests is that Wordsworth no longer found an important aspect of the traditional pastoral format entirely convincing. In its reality, the landscape possessed certain uncompromising qualities, and if the relationship between seeing and feeling was to be properly understood, more sophisticated treatment was required than reference to previously executed artistic models. To a contemporary reviewer, therefore, *An Evening Walk* understandably appeared to have 'a degree of obscurity' and 'harshness both in construction and the versification'.[4]

Akenside had suggested that you had only to look about you to learn from nature – God's art – the art of ordering society; in Goldsmith's *The Deserted Village* the pastoral landscape was accessible only through memory, for now 'Amidst thy bowers the tyrant's hand is seen / And Desolation saddens all thy green'.[5] This, as Richard Feingold has pointed out, is a crisis with direct consequences for the poet: 'one of the casualties of the new rural order is poetry itself, evicted from Auburn along with the men and women scattered about by the emergence of the new masters'.[6] Bearing in mind what has already been said about the opening lines of *An Evening Walk*, it is worth recalling too Raymond Williams's comment that 'What is novel in *The Deserted Village* is the sense of observation of a precise and visible social location.'[7]

When Akenside himself made 'One effort more' to revise *The Pleasures of Imagination* in 1770, it was to the redeeming power of a remembered landscape he turned, in a far less confident mood than before, to seek in nature what was by then felt to be both the lost guide of his political convictions, and the justification of his role as poet-philosopher: 'Who now her tender discipline obey, / Where dwell ye?'[8] The treatment of memory in eighteenth-century poetry was largely controlled by associationist philosophy, and it is in characteristically graduated associationist terms that Wordsworth attempts to reconcile object and idea:

> While, Memory at my side, I wander here,
> Starts at the simplest sight th'unbidden tear ...
>
> (EW, 34:43–4)

The 'unbidden tear' implies a response triggered by memory, it is not created by the actual landscape. The imaginative process, with its enforced 'degree of obscurity', leads the poet's steps towards an enclosed, secretive spot, indicative of the mind turning in upon itself, rather than confidently seeking the hilltop so characteristic of earlier poems in this genre:

> – Then Quiet led me up the huddling rill,
> Bright'ning with water-breaks the sombrous gill;
> To where, while thick above the branches close,
> In dark-brown bason its wild waves repose,
> Inverted shrubs, and moss of darkest green,
> Cling from the rocks, with pale wood-weeds between;
> Save that, atop, the subtle sunbeams shine,
> On wither'd briars that o'er the crags recline;
> Sole light admitted here, a small cascade,
> Illumes with sparkling foam the twilight shade.
>
> (EW, 36–8:71–80)[9]

The landscape of *An Evening Walk* is not depicted with the confidence employed initially by Akenside; Wordsworth's reflective, introverted mood tends at times to cast doubt on the trustworthiness of picturesque scene painting. The lack of cohesion between landscape and feeling was in part an expression of late-eighteenth-century political experience arising from the dissociation of ideological conviction and actual social conditions.

This relationship between pastoral poetry and political ideology revolves to a significant extent around the presentation of figures in the landscape. Crowe's decision not to populate the Dorsetshire landscape seen from Lewesdon as it realistically would have been was in itself a political statement, albeit achieved through negative means.[10] From *An Evening Walk* we can appreciate that Wordsworth intended from the first to include labourers as an integral part of his 'prospect', but he nevertheless instinctively sought to preserve the traditionally pastoral concept of order they – or their condition – could so easily threaten.

The first signs of life in the poem are heard and not seen:

> Th'unwearied glance of woodman's echoed stroke;
> And curling from the trees the cottage smoke. (EW, 42:107–8)

We then begin to see people, etched into the poem like figures in a Gilpin landscape, at first hardly distinguishable from the country lane in which they are discovered:

> Their pannier'd train a groupe of potters goad,
> Winding from side to side up the steep road.
>   (EW, 44:109–10)[11]

In his later poetry Wordsworth investigated the aesthetic of this kind of picturesque rendering, and often exploited the contrast between a view of humanity idealised through the demands of picturesque arrangement, and an honest, frequently a literally closer view of the individual and his or her circumstances. In doing so he revised, but arguably never sought to dislodge the underlying assumptions of the paternalistic politics of pastoral. In the second volume of *Lyrical Ballads* (1800), for example, in the fourth poem of the series *Poems on the Naming of Places*, the first fifty lines paint a transparently superficial impression of Grasmere at harvest time. The fisherman seen on the shore of the lake is at once denounced as 'An idle man, who thus could lose a day / Of the mid harvest, when the labourer's hire / Is ample.' His presence is an affront to the idealised order imposed on the scene before them, an order preserved artistically by allowing us only to hear, not see 'the busy mirth' of a band of nearby reapers. With characteristic self-irony, Wordsworth is assuming the role of the eighteenth-century picturesque artist in order to criticise certain (though by no means all) aspects of the dishonesty involved:

> Thus talking of that peasant we approach'd
> Close to the spot where with his rod and line
> He stood alone; whereat he turn'd his head
> To greet us – and we saw a man worn down
> By sickness, gaunt and lean, with sunken cheeks
> And wasted limbs, his legs so long and lean
> That for my single self I look'd at them,
> Forgetful of the body they sustain'd. –
> Too weak to labour in the harvest field,
> The man was using his best skill to gain
> A pittance from the dead unfeeling lake
> That knew not of his wants. (LB, 224:61–72)

The thrust of the political statement here still lies within an eighteenth-century framework of paternalism. The improvident laziness of the man is not, after all, his own fault, even as in Book IV of *The Prelude* where we encounter a destitute discharged soldier, his pitiful state is not of his own making. The fisherman's condition has been brought about by sickness, a form of 'natural' disaster for which no political system can be directly blamed. The suggestion is that those more fortunate than he should show pity on him; meanwhile the reapers remain out of sight, still subservient, taking a ritualised place in the mind's eye where such a man might otherwise be visualised through folk memory as happy in his toil.[12] With the discharged soldier, a more dangerous and potentially radical claim to independence is made by the alienated, inactive individual. But we have to remember that the soldier's situation has been brought about specifically by war, and so avoids the inference that there is a fundamental issue relating to destitution in rural society to be addressed. Wordsworth's charitable response appears sufficient to defuse the situation, neutralising the soldier's resentment:

> and in a voice that seemed
> To speak with a reviving interest,
> Till then unfelt, he thanked me; I returned
> The blessing of the poor unhappy man,
> And so we parted. (150:498–502)

In both cases the limitations of the protest Wordsworth is registering become clear.

This argues for a significant degree of continuity between the early and the later work, and indeed, the sense of continuity is strengthened by the fact that the figures who appear in *An Evening Walk* are often those who feature in the subsequent poetry; *Peter Bell* (published in 1819, but written in 1798) tells the story of a 'potter' of the kind encountered early on in *An Evening Walk*. Before *Peter Bell* was published, however, the image of a 'pannier'd train' of potters was used to describe the band of gypsies that featured in the second version of the *Salisbury Plain* poem (1795–99), from which 'The Female Vagrant' of *Lyrical Ballads* was extracted. Wordsworth's preparedness to countenance and even eulogise the gypsies' anti-social way of life signifies the influence of Godwin's theories of property and ownership, a reflection in turn of political idealism which, as Gary Kelly has shown, owed much to Commonwealthman ideology.[13] The gypsies' 'semblance' to the potters he had seen in the Lake District indicates that he sought a picturesque resolution to their otherwise disturbingly degrading condition, holding them in this respect as much at arms length in *Salisbury Plain* as he had done in *An Evening Walk*:

> My heart is touched to think that men like these,
> The rude earth's tenants, were my first relief:
> How kindly did they paint their vagrant ease!
> And their long holiday that feared not grief,
> For all belonged to all, and each was chief ...
>
> Semblance, with straw and pannier'd ass, they made
> Of potters wandering on from door to door ...
> (Gill, 143–4:505–9, 514–15)

Again, not least because the female vagrant's situation is the result of losing her husband in the American War, the limit of protest is established.

In *Peter Bell* Wordsworth side-stepped a potentially embarrassing political concern for the condition within society of a group or class of people by focussing on just one of their number. The close-up reveals an individual far from at one with his natural environment, a point Wordsworth reinforces with descriptive language intended to outrage the connoisseur of pastoral imagery and poetic diction:

> He trudged along through copse and brake
> He trudged along o'er hill and dale;
> Nor for the moon cared he a tittle,
> And for the stars he cared as little,
> And for the murmuring river Swale. (PW II, 344:331–5)

Peter's alienation is chiefly apparent to us through the workings of his fanciful, superstitious mind; consequently, when he hears 'A murmur, pent within the earth / In the dead earth beneath the road ... A muffled noise – a rumbling sound', he believes it must presage an earthquake sent to swallow him up for his sins. The true explanation follows: ''Twas by a troup of miners made, / Plying with gunpowder their trade, / Some twenty fathoms underground' (PW II, 371:834–6, 838–40).

The explanation suggests that certain features in the landscape held a continuing fascination for the poet as well as certain types of figures. The first time Wordsworth referred to a phenomenon very similar to the one described in *Peter Bell* had been in *An Evening Walk*, where in keeping with the tenets of picturesque description, he had attempted – again by distancing it – to incorporate it into an harmonious pastoral image:

> From lonesome chapel at the mountain's feet,
> Three humble bells their rustic chime repeat;
> Sounds from the waterside the hammer'd boat,
> And blasted quarry thunders heard remote ...
>
>   (EW, 46:121–4)

'The quarry-man, far heard! that blasts the rock' later earned a mention in Book VIII of the 1805 *Prelude*. The passage in which this line occurs begins with the question, 'Why should I speak of tillers of the soil?' It is sixteen years since working men, the miners, quarrymen, shepherds, and 'The fishermen in pairs, the one to row, / And one to drop the net' had first appeared in *An Evening Walk*. They are evidence of a human world of labour in amongst the pastoral landscape of nature. The Book VIII passage (292–94:498–541) suggests that where labouring figures were concerned, Wordsworth remained uncertain as to their precise 'poetic' function. He does, however, go on to criticise his early writing to the extent that he had conceived of 'human life' as a series of 'fictions' to be 'beautified' by 'Nature and her objects'. But his recognition of the deceptions inherent in a picturesque style led him to seek through poems like *Peter Bell, Poems on the Naming of Places*, and also *Resolution and Independence*, an alternative means by which he might retrieve the underlying paternalistic politics of pastoral, and not explode them as myth.

In *An Evening Walk* Wordsworth attempted to resolve the contentious issues embedded in the pastoral mode by appealing to the aesthetic of universal order in variety which Akenside had followed. Figures seen in the act of labour are expected to show evidence of satisfaction mingled with toil, and the maintenance of a reasonable standard of living. Labour, though indisputably tiring, should not be associated in England with a condition of slavery; its crowning reward at the end of an exhausting day was independence, the much vaunted birthright of the Free-Born Briton.[14]

His presentation of quarrymen sought to achieve this idealised end in a fairly obvious way. The 'quarry's moving trains' of men and horses remain in the distance, diminishing in consequence more than just their physical size:

> Some, hardly heard their chissel's clinking sound,
> Toil, small as pigmies, in the gulph profound;
> Some, dim between th'aereal cliffs descry'd,

O'erwalk the viewless plank from side to side;
These by the pale-blue rocks that ceaseless ring
Glad from their airy baskets hang and sing. (EW, 48:145–50)

It is a technique as precarious in its means of playing off economic truth against pastoral illusion, as was the actual occupation of the quarryman, making his way along 'the viewless plank'.

The aesthetic principle employed here had been enunciated by Alexander Pope in his *Essay on Criticism* (1711), and if we take the not altogether unreasonable liberty of seeing Pope's reference to 'Figures' of speech as equally applicable to the appearance of human figures, the aesthetic dictum and its political consequences make a useful gloss for the passage quoted above from *An Evening Walk*:

I know there are, to whose presumptuous Thoughts
These *Freer Beauties*, ev'n in *Them*, seem Faults:
Some Figures *monstrous* and *mis-shape'd* appear,
Consider'd *singly*, or beheld too *near*,
Which, but proportion'd to their *Light*, or *Place*,
Due Distance *reconciles* to Form and Grace.[15]

A figure of a very different order who appears in *An Evening Walk* and in much eighteenth-century poetry of the genre to which *An Evening Walk* belongs, is the vagrant. Arguably the response to vagrancy was easier to control in terms of its political application than in the case of the labouring poor. One who is not working has no immediate right – other than through the charitable impulses of more fortunate individuals – to be anything but destitute, and though Wordsworth's representation of vagrancy in this poem is not without innovation, what it primarily shows is that earlier eighteenth-century attitudes persisted in his mind.

The vagrant's circumstances still offered a golden opportunity for critical political tub-thumping, however, based on demands for the restoration of values felt to have been embedded since time immemorial in constitutional traditions which formed the basis of modern government. What contemporary duplicity and corruption had done was to threaten these time-honoured qualities of virtue. On the other hand, the vagrant persona was part of an established literary tradition, and need not imply the recognition of a new political situation which demystified the myth of an Ancient Constitution, and the social and political structure it sought to perpetuate.

Some idea of the traditional representation of vagrancy that Wordsworth had to work from may be gained from Knox's *Elegant Extracts*. *The Beggar's Petition*, for example, is a tale of unmerited destitution, made worse by the refusal of the privileged to do their charitable duty. Criticism of privilege is surreptitiously achieved by the fact that it is a 'pamper'd menial' who refuses aid, not the Great Man himself:

> Yon house, erected on the rising ground,
> With tempting aspect drew me from my road:
> For Plenty there a residence hath found,
> And Grandeur a magnificent abode.
>
> Hard is the fate of the infirm and poor!
> Here, as I crav'd a morsel of their bread,
> A pamper'd menial drove me from the door
> To seek a shelter in a humbler shed.

The old man tells his story, and its similarity to the events described at the beginning of the female vagrant's story of *Salisbury Plain* (1793) can hardly be coincidental:

> A little farm was my paternal lot;
> Then like the lark I sprightly hail'd the morn;
> But, ah! oppression forced me from my cot;
> My cattle died, and blighted was my corn.
>
> My daughter, once the comfort of my age,
> Lur'd by a villian from her native home,
> Is cast abandon'd on the world's wide stage,
> And doomed in scanty poverty to roam.

In *Salisbury Plain* we read:

> At last by cruel chance and wilful wrong
> My father's substance fell into decay.
> Oppression trampled on his tresses grey:
> His little range of water was denied;
> Even to the bed where his old body lay
> His all was siezed; and weeping side by side
> Turned out on the cold winds, alone we wandered wide.
>
> (Gill, 29:255–61)

Though the daughter's lover in *Salisbury Plain* is not a rogue, his honesty finds no reward in employment and he is forced in desperation to enlist in the army.

The political thrust of *The Beggar's Petition* is to revive a failing paternalism. Criticism is aimed at the *nouveau riche* landowner, and is unflinching despite the poet's lack of nerve when it comes to showing us one in person; the poem's politics are in no sense therefore radical. We all, like the old man, must yearn for a return to our 'paternal lot'. And this in turn will reconcile the contemporary landscape to the landscape of memory, where labour will be healthily, reassuringly evident in people like the old man, as it is assumed to be in the case of the labourers in *An Evening Walk*. Wordsworth certainly believed that the solution to this problem lay in the reanimation of the social conscience of the rich. *Descriptive Sketches* and *Salisbury Plain* were to indicate that he associated support for the American colonists in the 1770s and the political aims of the French Revolution in its early years with that belief. But the politics of *The Beggar's Petition* had nothing in common with republicanism in France as it evolved after 1792, nor with Painite radicalism in England. In *An Evening Walk* the picturesque effect of the pastoral landscape is threatened by the presence of a female vagrant figure, and there the cause of vagrancy was directly connected with Britain's decision to go to war in North America.

The plight of vagrant women was a recurring theme in late Augustan poetry, and the central character of one poem in particular, the anonymous *A Winter Piece* reproduced in *Elegant Extracts*, has been cited as the progenitor of a type that reappears throughout Wordsworth's work:

> It was a winter's evening, and fast came down the snow,
> And keenly o'er the wide heath the bitter wind did blow;
> When a damsell all forlorn, quite bewilder'd in her way,
> Press'd her baby to her bosom, and sadly thus did say:
>
> 'Oh! cruel was my father, that shut his door on me,
> And cruel was my mother, that such a sight could see;
> And cruel is the wintry wind, that chills my heart with cold;
> But crueller than all, the lad that left my love for gold ...'
>
> Then down she sunk despairing upon the drifted snow,
> And, wrung with killing anguish, lamented loud her woe:
> She kiss'd her babe's pale lips, and laid it by her side;
> Then cast her eyes to heaven, then bowed her head, and died.

Jonathan Wordsworth has described this poem as illustrating 'the grotesque lower reaches of the tradition in which [Wordsworth] was

working'.[16] The entire female vagrant sequence of *An Evening Walk*
consists of sixty lines, and while there is much that scarcely rises
above the level of *A Winter Piece*, there is undeniable merit in
Wordsworth's ability to sustain the melodramatic effect.

The sequence begins with the description of a swan and her
cygnets, an image from nature of domestic felicity threatened by the
vagrant's presence:

> Fair Swan! by all a mother's joys caress'd,
> Haply some wretch has eye'd, and call'd thee bless'd;
> Who faint, and beat by summer's breathless ray,
> Hath dragg'd her babes along this weary way;
> While arrowy fire extorting feverish groans,
> Shot stinging through her stark o'er-labour'd bones.
>
> (EW, 60:241–6)

The Claudian, pastoral idyll is challenged in these lines, not least by
the genuinely original touch of referring to the anger of the dying
woman, an observation which would certainly have startled a well-
bred reader of *Elegant Extracts*: '... as she turns her neck the kiss to
seek, / Breaks off the dreadful kiss with angry shriek' (EW, 64:287–8).

Wordsworth also appears to be making an attempt to introduce an
element of realism into his observation of the woman; a reaction
against the poetic commonplaces of late Augustan sentimentalising.
The poet of *A Winter Piece*, for example, chained down as he or she
was by conventional rhyme, metre and rhetoric, could never have
managed to observe in the vagrant a woman who so realistically
'shakes her numb arm that slumbers with its weight' (EW, 60:251).

Perhaps most interestingly, Wordsworth was prepared to look
beyond immediate domestic circumstances for an explanation of the
woman's fate. In this we can be sure that he was following the model
set by John Langhorne in *The Country Justice* (1774–77). In *Elegant
Extracts* Knox published a short anonymous piece entitled *Apology for
Vagrants*; it is in fact lines 147–67 of *The Country Justice*, Part One:

> Perhaps on some inhospitable shore
> The houseless wretch a widow'd parent bore;
> Who, then no more by golden prospects led,
> Of the poor Indian begg'd a leafy bed.
> Cold on Canadian Hills, or Minden's Plain,
> Perhaps that Parent mourn'd her soldier slain;
> Bent o'er her babe, her eye dissolv'd in dew,

> The big drops mingling with the milk he drew,
> Gave the sad presage of his future years,
> The child of misery, baptiz'd in tears![17]

Wordsworth refashioned Langhorne's series of images to depict a woman reduced to vagrancy through the loss of her husband in the American War. Quoting Langhorne initially, he switched the reference from the Seven Years War ('Canadian Hills, or Minden's Plain') to 'Bunker's charnal hill' in an *erratum* to the first edition of the poem. The vagrant:

> eyes through tears the mountain's shadeless height;
> And bids her soldier come her woes to share,
> Asleep on Bunker's charnal hill afar;
> For hope's deserted well why wistful look?
> Chok'd is the pathway, and the pitcher broke. (EW, 62:252–6)

By comparison with the author of *A Winter Piece*, Wordsworth was clearly prepared openly to politicise his observation of vagrancy in accordance with eighteenth-century radical Whig ideology of the kind adhered to by Crowe. It should be pointed out that Langhorne's Country Party politics were not in accordance with this. To imply that British soldiers in the colonies were engaged in anything other than a totally justified war would have been anathema to him. Associating hardship and misery at home with the task of repressing rebellious British subjects (the implications of Wordsworth's lines) would have been out of the question. Elsewhere in *The Country Justice*, Langhorne scornfully attacked the colonists, though he did see corrupted patriotism at home as ultimately to blame. He made the point through a sarcastic pun on the word 'place', with its political meaning of 'office' in mind: 'Oh Patriots, ever Patriots out of place'.[18] Knox, using his privilege as editor once more, presumably felt some misgivings about Langhorne's sentiments, no doubt on the basis that any serious note of political dissent might be bad for business, regardless of its origin. He therefore decided to isolate the morally improving passage he had chosen by attempting to render it 'anonymous'.

The climax of the female vagrant section of the poem inevitably modifies our memory of the pastoral world described before her appearance; and our return to the traditional language of pastoral serenity after her death serves only to destabilise that ideal of serenity. To illustrate this properly a long quotation is required, beginning at the point where the stricken woman, though her children are dead, persists in her attempt to shelter them:

> ... vainly fears
> Thy flooded cheek to wet them with its tears;
> Soon shall the light'ning hold before thy head
> His torch, and shew them slumbering in their bed,
> No tears can chill them, and no bosom warms,
> Thy breast their death-bed, coffin'd in thine arms.
>
> Sweet are the sounds that mingle from afar,
> Heard by calm lakes as peeps the folding star,
> Where the duck dabbles 'mid the rustling sedge,
> And feeding pike starts from the water's edge,
> Or the swan stirs the reeds, his neck and bill
> Wetting, that drip upon the water still;
> And heron, as resounds the trodden shore,
> Shoots upward, darting his long neck before.
> While, by the scene compos'd, the breast subsides,
> Nought wakens or disturbs its tranquil tides;
> Nought but the char that for the may-fly leaps,
> And breaks the mirror of the circling deeps;
> Or clock, that blind against the Wanderer born,
> Drops at his feet, and stills his droning horn.
> – The whistling swain that plods his ringing way
> Where the slow waggon winds along the bay;
> The sugh of swallow flocks that twittering sweep,
> The solumn curfew swinging long and deep;
> The talking boat that moves with pensive sound,
> Or drops his anchor down with plunge profound;
> Of boys that bathe remote the faint uproar,
> And restless piper wearying out the shore;
> These all to swell the village murmers blend,
> That soften'd from the water-head descend.
> While in sweet cadence rising small and still
> The far-off minstrels of the haunted hill,
> As the last bleating of the fold expires,
> Tune in the mountain dells their water lyres.
>
> (EW, 66–8:295–328)

What is particularly interesting about this passage is the way in which Wordsworth – perhaps subconsciously – has left the presence of the dying woman hovering over the formal tranquility of the latter section by including the ambiguous lines, 'While, by the scene compos'd, the breast subsides, / Nought wakens or disturbs its tranquil tides.' The breast in question is obviously meant to belong to the poet; but there is also a telling echo from line 300, 'Thy breast their death-bed, coffin'd in thine arms'. The mother's death is not specifically alluded to, and we are left with the impression that she is still painfully dying when we read, 'Sweet are the sounds that mingle from afar . . .' The effect of the 'whistling swain', and his ingenuously callous indifference to the melodrama which has just taken place in the same landscape is potentially something new in the genre.

In the final lines of *An Evening Walk* Wordsworth appears to have in mind John Brown's poem, *Night* (EW, 80:433–4). Thomas West had incorporated it into his *Guide to the Lakes* (1778) which Wordsworth had read by this time. When he came to write his own *Guide* (first published in 1810), he too quoted it in full (O&S II, 193). Brown was associated with the dissident Whig circle of writers that included Mason and Brooke in the late 1740s. The political philosophy implicit in his popular critique of Shaftesbury, *Essays on the Characteristics of the Earl of Shaftesbury* (1751), won him the approval and friendship of Thomas Hollis.[19]

Brown's *Night* reveals a brief but significantly subversive response to the tradition of pastoral contentment, with its description of the slumbering peasants as 'oppress'd with toil'.[20] There is nothing, however, in *An Evening Walk* to suggest that this is the lot of Wordsworth's shepherds and quarrymen.

In 1788, Wordsworth was not yet ready to pursue the challenge that a political statement about rural poverty would inevitably hold for a poet writing in accordance with the conventions of pastoral verse. In his dramas, Brown, like William Mason, Thomson and Brooke could be forthright and bombastic enough. But the transition from the primitive world of *Caractacus* (Mason, 1759) or *Athelstane* (Brown, 1756) to the realisation of a Virgillian landscape in eighteenth-century England, threatened a confrontation between ideology and reality that blunted the pursuance of political logic.

Coming to terms with the proposition that it was an aesthetic 'fiction' to perceive late-eighteenth-century rural England in terms of a placid Claudian pastoral landscape lies at the heart of much late Augustan poetry, not least that of Langhorne. Donald Davie has illustrated how in Part II of *The Country Justice*, the sentiment of

Gray's *Elegy* is undercut by quoting it in the ironic context of the inhumanity of the countryside's modern overlords who owe allegiance not to the welfare of any native rural community, but to 'Brightelmstone' and Margate:

> Foregone the social, hospitable Days,
> When wide Vales echoed with their Owner's Praise,
> Of all that *ancient Consequence* bereft,
> What has the *modern Man of Fashion* left?
>   Does He, perchance, to rural Scenes repair,
> And 'waste his Sweetness' on the essenc'd Air?
> Ah! gently lave the feeble Frame he brings,
> Ye scouring Seas! and ye sulpherous Springs![21]

The ironic use made of Gray by Langhorne was not beyond the powers of the author of *The Beggar's Petition*. Where for Gray, the sunset 'leaves the world to darkness and to me', for the beggar, his experiences 'left the world to wretchedness and me'. The effect on the pastoral poetic mode of the realities of rural life, here clearly evident as an established part of the pastoral metaphor in poems Wordsworth would have been familiar with from his youth, is the worm in the bud of *An Evening Walk*. Poets were seeking out not only the vagrant but the cause of vagrancy; the consequence of which was a study of the process by which otherwise industrious persons (or their wives and children) were reduced to a dependence on charity. The implications, as Raymond Williams has argued, were potentially embarrassing for a poet with Country Party prejudices like Langhorne: 'It is as if a humane man could not bring himself to see the real origins of the misery of his time, in the class to which he was directly linked. He must either idealise their past, or explain the present by their absence and the irruption of new men.'[22]

It was an increasing awareness of contradictions between actual observation and traditional modes of feeling that forced Wordsworth to look critically at his immediate predecessors and in due course attempt to offer a revised version of pastoral. Gray, it seems, had become a prime target for criticism, and it is worth noting that it was again Gray who was singled out as an example of inadequacy in the 1800 Preface to *Lyrical Ballads*.

The social and political changes of the period were such that radical alternatives to the established solutions for the visible breakdown of rural communities were immanent. The ideological framework of paternalism – charity, patriotism, education, a disinterestedness which only periodic retirement from the demands of public life could bring – was in danger of becoming an anachronism. The pastoral vision of 'Order in Variety'[23] could no longer be counted on to reconcile poets to the fact of destitution within its republic of virtue. Images of labour and vagrancy were tending to converge. The female vagrant of *An Evening Walk* could not be spirited out of the landscape by 'The far-off minstrels of the haunted hill', or conveniently 'lost in the deepen'd darkness' of the encroaching evening (EW, 68:326 and 72:370). The 'darkness' of Gray served now only to emphasise the beggar's 'wretchedness'. Wordsworth was at this time personally embittered by Sir James Lowther's abuse of his privileged position with respect to money owed by him to the Wordsworth family, and his experiences in France were to have the effect of enabling him to see these personal frustrations in the more comprehensive context of a corrupt political system. In his next poem, *Descriptive Sketches*, he therefore came to challenge more directly the poetical conventions he had inherited, though still with the instinct of one who sought the restoration of an ideal commonwealth of virtue, rather than to usher in a radically conceived new order.

3
Descriptive Sketches (1792–93): poetic and personal crises

At the same time we must own, that this poem is on the whole less interesting than the subject led us to expect; owing in part, we believe ... to a certain laboured and artificial cast of expression, which often involves the poet's meaning in obscurity.

(*Analytical Review*, XV (March 1793), pp. 294–6)

When Wordsworth left England for France in the late autumn of 1791, he might have been forgiven for feeling that life had not dealt altogether fairly with him. His mother and father were both dead by the time he was thirteen, and Hawkshead Grammar School had become more of a home to him than Penrith, where his relationship with his guardian, Christopher Crackanthorpe Cookson, had never been easy. His dependence on Cookson was made particularly hard to bear by the knowledge that had Sir James Lowther (Lord Lonsdale from 1784) paid the considerable sum owing to his father when he died in his service, a modest independence would have been assured. Since his early teens, therefore, Wordsworth had had no reason to love the aristocracy, and arrived in France with a considerable chip on his shoulder in that respect. Cookson saw Cambridge as a means of settling his nephew into a career in holy orders, a prospect repugnant to Wordsworth. His status at St John's College as a sizar served to underline his impecunious background compared to the majority of his fellow students. Yet life at Cambridge did at least remove him from the immediate ambience of Penrith, and it seems he made the most of what opportunities there were to study where his interests lay, and to travel. In 1790 he spent fourteen weeks of the long vacation touring France and Switzerland – mostly on foot – with Robert Jones, a fellow student.

The second visit to France was planned in very different circumstances. Wordsworth pursuaded his guardian to let him use the short period of time available between gaining his degree and qualifying for ordination to go once more to France, this time with a view to studying the language. This, he suggested, would make it possible for him to offer himself as a travelling 'tutor'. The idea that Wordsworth, embittered by Lowther's use of his privileged position to avoid paying his debts, might become the travelling companion of a young aristocrat on his grand tour is unconvincing. A return to France was in fact a means of escaping his fate, at least for a while.

There is little evidence to show that at this time Wordsworth was taking any real notice of the political issues and events of the day. There is ample evidence from the letters he wrote to see him as obsessed with his personal misfortunes and aware of a political perspective only in so far as it related to his personal state.[1] In a letter written to Dorothy while walking through France in 1790, we can see how for him the French Revolution was a subject to be set within an aesthetic, picturesque frame, not a political one:

But I must remind you that we crossed [France] at the time when the whole nation was mad with joy, in consequence of the revolution. It was a most interesting period to be in France, and we had many delightful scenes where the interest of the picture was owing solely to this cause. (EY, p. 36)

His experiences in France in 1792 inevitably increased his political awareness, but arguably a politicised Wordsworth still viewed the French Revolution and the shortcomings of his own country's Government in terms of a highly personalised discontent. The unhealthily radical tone of his views at this time may be deduced from the fate of a letter he wrote to his brother Richard from Orléans in December 1791. Ten lines or so were presumably worrying enough to merit being torn away and destroyed. What remains shows a realisation that it was not just Lowther who stood in the way of a reformed society, but conceivably the whole class of men whom Lowther represented:

I find almost all the people of any opulen(ce are) aristocrates and all the others democrates. I had imagined that there were some people of wealth and circumstance favorers of the revolution, but here there is not one to be found. (EY, p. 70)

Faced with a nation in open revolt against long-standing and self-evident political injustices, Wordsworth's own assumptions and received notions of political liberty were directly challenged, and clearly he attempted to revise and clarify his position. The hold that traditional English concepts of liberty and society had on his mind was not to be easily dislodged, however. Subsequently his claims to have known what a republic of virtue was like from personal experience revealed the tenacity of such concepts. Heather Glen, for example, has drawn attention to the disparity between the Tintern Abbey of Wordsworth's poem, set in an unpeopled landscape fit for meditation, and the notorious haunt for vagrants and gypsies it had by then become. She also draws attention to his description in *The Prelude* of Cambridge as a type of equalitarian republic and the Cambridge riddled with class distinction where the poet had in fact occupied a position of the lowest degree.[2] The extent to which Wordsworth was able to clear his mind of traditional political assumptions, and fully accept what the French meant in 1792 by republicanism will be examined in the chapters which follow.

Both 'Tintern Abbey' and *The Prelude* reproduce Wordsworth's frame of mind after a time of often painful reflection on a period when there had been extreme pressure to reform society through radical political action. Of the poems already alluded to, the *Salisbury Plain* verses most clearly indicate that in the mid 1790s he saw rural society as anything but a model of pastoral republicanism. *Descriptive Sketches* is the poem actually written at the time of Wordsworth's initiation into the contemporary world of Revolution politics. As its title implies, it was intended as a traditional picturesque poem based on his memories of 1790.[3] The treatment it received in the *Analytical Review* for March 1793 suggests that something had gone wrong. This is hardly to be wondered at when we remember that even while writing of his memories of France in the first flush of revolution, a time when he felt what was happening to be very much a matter for the French and only incidentally of concern to himself, he was in fact being cross-questioned by Royalists at Orléans, proselytised by a revolutionary soldier, and falling in love with Annette Vallon, a Roman Catholic. Everything about his personal life in 1792 was running counter to the contemplative frame of mind he wished to assume in order to sustain the poetic structure of feeling for his new project.

The pressures of the moment, personal and political, resulted in *Descriptive Sketches* becoming a poem as much about the acquisition and maintenance of liberty as about the beauties of nature that he had earlier attempted to report in letters written during the tour of

1790. Though a 'minor' poem, therefore, *Descriptive Sketches* is to be considered in every way as crucial a text for understanding the poet's state of mind in the early 1790s as the *Letter to Llandaff* and *Salisbury Plain*. A study of these texts reveals much that is of value when assessing Wordsworth's subsequent development.

An Evening Walk clearly betrayed tensions in the relationship between aesthetic conventions in landscape description, and the less than picturesque realities of the countryside. Wordsworth's inherited task as a poet of such things was to resolve or at least minimise the contradictions. His eventual course of action in this respect was to approach the aesthetic issue not as an offshoot of radical political thinking in France or England in 1792, but to draw on his gradual familiarisation with the English Commonwealthman, Old Whig political tradition. This is not to argue that Wordsworth became in any strict sense a latter-day Commonwealthman, rather that he contextualised the issues in terms of the mid-eighteenth-century debates on liberty, property and power where Commonwealthman ideology was a powerful and influential source of rhetoric.

In France in 1792, Wordsworth was exposed to a wide range of specifically French political opinion, encompassing the Royalist views of *emigrés* in Orléans; sentimental, Rousseauistic republicanism; and the uncompromising populism of the Jacobins. But despite French Anglo-phobia in the latter half of the century, the interest taken in the writings of seventeenth-century English republicans remained undiminished. Milton, Sidney and Harrington, and indeed a number of poets associated with the Commonwealthman tradition, notably James Thomson, were seen as critical of the existing Establishment, and not representative of it. *Descriptive Sketches* tends to endorse this fact in its concluding passages, where Wordsworth's response to the French Revolution at first hand directs us back to the didacticism of the 1730s and the rhetoric employed by James Thomson in *Liberty* (1735–36) and *Britannia* (1727).

The most important consequence for Wordsworth of his experiences in France in 1792 was not the acquisition of specific, contemporary radical political views; it was the development of a more general sense of vocation to take a practical, politically active role in affairs. Again, it is in *Descriptive Sketches* that we can find evidence to suggest that through his conversations with Beaupuy, through contact with James Watt, and possibly through conversations with Thomas Foxlowe, an Englishman living at Orléans, he came to see the atheistical populism of the Jacobins as a threat to the Revolution.[4] He then began to nurture a vision of himself as fulfilling the role of a statesman whose prototype was to be found in the classical republican eulogies of Cicero and Cincinatus. With his fellow English republican enthusiasts in Paris, Wordsworth liked to believe that it was the more moderate Brissot and his adherents who would establish in France a Republic of Virtue based on that classical model.

One important consequence of this was the inevitable undermining of the persona in which Wordsworth undertook to write *Descriptive Sketches*, that of a dejected wanderer seeking anonymity in his retirement to a world of nature inhabited by a simple, Rousseauesque peasantry:

> For him lost flowers their idle sweets exhale;
> He tastes the meanest note that swells the gale;
> For him sod-seats the cottage door adorn,
> And peeps the far-off spire, his evening bourn!
>
> (DS, 40:19–22)[5]

But the active champion of liberty he aspired to become had little or no relevance in the world of revolutionary political reality centring then on Paris, especially after the Revolution of August 1792, when the Brissotin or 'Girondin' faction was comprehensively defeated by Robespierre. Incapable of breaking free from the political assumptions that governed both his personal quest for a purpose in life and the mode in which he sought to express himself in verse, he was faced with two tasks. In the short term he had somehow to attempt to accommodate the theme of political liberty within the poetic structure of *Descriptive Sketches*. France only served to emphasise what the Lake District had already signified; rural depravation made a mockery of the pastoral idyll as a symbol of liberty.[6] In the longer term, he was left to justify his apparent defection from the task of decisive political involvement. This latter problem lies at the heart of the constant juxtaposition of active and passive principles that inform much of the later poetry. A resolution of sorts was more swiftly achieved for the problem of *Descriptive Sketches*, one which reveals the way Wordsworth's political sense remained tethered to certain fundamental tenets of a paternalistically conceived classical republic of 'virtue', and alienated by the belief that political justice might be achieved through purely secular political processes.

Lines 45–79 of *Descriptive Sketches* are concerned exclusively with a meditation upon the import of what had happened since the walking tour as a result of the Revolution. The description of the Grande Chartreuse comes not as a picturesque memory from 1790, but uncompromisingly from the contemporary world of 1792, after the dissolution of the monasteries. The wanderer of 1790 is a figure fixed irrevocably in the past; if we are to know of the glory of Chartreuse, it will be through the poet's memory of it, and it would seem that the poet himself, and not just the Chartreuse, can only exist now in memory; both tell of 'parting Genius' (DS, 46:72). The poet is inseparable from the world for which he writes; without it he dies.

> Ev'n now I sigh at hoary Chartreuse' doom
> Weeping beneath his chill of mountain gloom.
> Where now is fled that Power whose frown severe
> Tam'd 'sober Reason' till she crouched in fear?
> That breath'd a death-like peace these woods around,
> Broke only by th'unvaried torrent's sound,
> Or prayer-bell by the dull cicada drown'd.
> The cloister startles at the gleam of arms,
> And blasphemy the shuddering fane alarms;
> Nod the cloud-piercing pines their troubled heads,
> Spires, rocks, and lawns, a browner night o'erspreads.
>
> (DS, 42–4:53–63)

This passage implies that in 1792 Wordsworth was less impressed with Beaupuy's revolutionary philosophy than *The Prelude* of 1805 suggests. The 'Power' which departs with the desecration of Chartreuse is a sombre, even forbidding force, and the poet – with a background hardly likely to make him a champion of Roman Catholicism – understandably retains definite misgivings about it. But the alternative, a 'browner night' of 'blasphemy', is far worse, and the fate of the monastery must be laid at the door of the Revolution. This is no defence of the Royalist cause, however. What the poet wishes to preserve is the pastoral republicanism of the opening paragraphs of his poem, presided over by 'Nature's GOD' (DS, 38:3). Revolutionary enthusiasm seeks to liberate peasants

living in a state of slavery, but it equally threatens their Claudian
environment, of which the Grande Chartreuse was a part:

> Strong terror checks the female peasant's sighs,
> And start th'astonish'd shades at female eyes.
> The thundering tube the aged angler hears,
> And swell the groaning torrent with his tears.
> From Bruno's forest screams the frighted jay,
> And slow th'insulted eagle wheels away.
> The cross with hideous laughter Demons mock,
> By angels planted in the aereal rock.
> The 'parting Genius' sighs with hollow breath
> Along the mystic streams of Life and Death,
> Swelling the outcry dull, that long resounds
> Portentous, thro' her old woods' trackless bounds,
> Deepening her echoing torrents' awful peal
> And bidding paler shades her form conceal,
> Vallombre, 'mid her falling fanes, deplores,
> For ever broke, the sabbath of her bow'rs. (DS, 44–6:64–79)

To break the sabbath is to destroy the rhythm of rural life, a
momentous loss given the unobtrusive but crucial role played by the
'far-off spire' (DS, 40:22) in the landscape of the idyllic rural
community described earlier in the poem; a place where the poet also
belongs. The revolutionaries, even before they were revealed to
Wordsworth in their most vicious guise in Paris in October (after
this version of the poem was completed), had about them already a
demonic propensity, defying the crosses set 'By angels' on the
heights above the monastery.

It had become common enough, as Thomas Edwards has
suggested, for the late eighteenth-century poet to see himself as
dispossessed and isolated in the natural world. Edwards describes
'the depressing picture of a rural landscape crowded with lugubrious
figures . . . busily writing poems called "A Hymn on Solitude", "Ode
to Evening", or "The Pleasures of Melancholy".'[7] In Wordsworth's
case the poetically realised situation of crisis was peculiarly relevant
to his own personal situation. He was finding himself unable to
engage with the present through the immediate past in any respect,
and most certainly not through poetry. In his description of Lake
Como we see a satisfactorily Claudian description giving way to lines
which betray insecurity and doubt. Initially Beattie's *Minstrel* is once
more the model:

>   – Thy lake, mid smoking woods, that blue and grey
> Gleams, streak'd or dappled, hid from morning's ray
> Slow-travelling down the western hills, to fold
> Its green-tinged margin in a blaze of gold ... (DS, 52:138–41)

But the picturesque image is far from innocent:

>   – Thy fragrant gales and lute-resounding streams,
> Breathe o'er the failing soul voloptuous dreams;
> While Slavery, forcing the sunk mind to dwell
> On joys that might disgrace the captive's cell,
> Her shameless timbrel shakes along thy marge,
> And winds between thy isles the vocal barge.
>   Yet, arts are thine that rock th'unsleeping heart,
> And smiles to solitude and Want impart. (DS, 52–4:156–63)

Despite its ambivalence, this passage does appear to reflect a sense that the practice of picturesque pastoral scene painting cannot now be undertaken without a serious danger of dishonesty. Wordsworth is allowing himself to be lulled into 'voluptuous dreams' not so much by the beauty of nature itself, as by the deceiving technique of *perception* which operates on nature through the medium of memory. The 'joys' of line 159 stand to be *disgraced by* a realisation that there is 'Slavery' (158), and while the self-indulgent poet practises his art, captives languish in cells elsewhere. All the trappings of the Claudian idyll, the 'timbrel' and the 'vocal barge', become powers of deception, and the 'arts' of line 162 therefore impart smiles to 'solitude and Want' not only in the sense that they teach good-natured patience to sufferers, but also in a sinisterly dishonest way, cloaking the real horror beneath and thus avoiding a confrontation with the realities of existence. Wordsworth is here beginning to indicate that poetry as he understands the art and uses it cannot grapple with the most pressing issues of the time; it is in that sense that it has become 'shameless' (160).

As a young man no longer able to identify with the past, and with future prospects back in England anything but inviting, it would not be surprising to find that Wordsworth opted to forsake his old world of poetry for a new one of direct, radical political action. To some extent this is what he endeavoured to do; perhaps, for a short while, he believed he had. But *Descriptive Sketches* betrays his hesitancy. He did not after all – as he might well have done – completely abandon the poem. What he wrote there in a mood of disillusionment signifies a mind searching for a solution to present ills through stoic forbearance as much as through political action. Wrongs would be righted when the spirit of eighteenth-century 'republicanism' – from a past he could believe in without shame – once more predominated; the revolution created by Robespierre and the Sans Culottes did not inspire the degree of confidence in him that is sometimes assumed. *Descriptive Sketches* therefore confirms in part a continuity between an attitude of mind present in 1790 that was to become dominant by the time the 1805 *Prelude* was complete, and work going forward on *The Excursion*:

> Hope, strength, and courage, social suffering brings,
> Freshening the waste of sand with shades and springs.
>
> (DS, 58:197–8)

In Book X of*The Prelude* the stoic note is once more sounded:

> Then was the truth received into my heart
> That under heaviest sorrow earth can bring,
> Griefs bitterest of ourselves or of our kind,
> If from the affliction somewhere do not grow
> Honour which could not else have been – a faith,
> An elevation, and a sanctity –
> If new strength be not given, or old restored,
> The blame is ours, not Nature's. (382:422–9)

In *The Excursion* the exaltation of the meditative spirit over transient temporal 'shows of Being' is confirmed:

> That what we feel of sorrow and despair
> From ruin and from change, and all the grief
> That passing shows of Being leave behind,
> Appeared an idle dream, that could maintain,
> Nowhere, dominion o'er the enlightened spirit
> Whose meditative sympathies repose
> Upon the beast of faith ...
>
> (PW V, 39:949–55)

The 'power of strong controul' Wordsworth evokes in *Descriptive Sketches* (72:352) as destined to bring liberty to the oppressed retains for him a spiritual and inspirational quality. Heroes of the past who have fought for liberty, Sir Philip Sidney, William Tell and General Wolfe, are described as owing their fortitude in suffering to more than humanly conceived rights. It was this spiritual quality that

Wordsworth sought in defiance of the radicalism then emerging around him in France, which, in destroying the Grande Chartreuse had sought to destroy a monument to man's spirituality.

The ultimate goal of the walking tour of 1790 was to visit Switzerland, where 'Nature, ever just' had imbued the peasantry with 'Joys only given to uncorrupted hearts' (DS, 86:490–1).[8] If a vestigial attachment to English Commonwealthman ideology effectively dampened Wordsworth's initial enthusiasm for the radical implications of the French Revolution, once clear of France he was able to introduce sentiments much closer to the heart of French revolutionary thinking. Lines 356–621 indicate an enthusiasm for Rousseau that finds expression in characteristically eighteenth-century poetic rhetoric:

> Once Man entirely free, alone and wild,
> Was bless'd as free – for he was Nature's child.
> He, all superior but his God disdain'd,
> Walk'd none restraining, and by none restrain'd,
> Confess'd no law but what his reason taught,
> Did all he wish'd, and wish'd but what he ought.
> As man in his primaeval dower array'd
> The image of his glorious sire display'd,
> Ev'n so, by vestal Nature guarded, here
> The traces of Primaeval man appear. (DS, 88–90:520–9)

The extent to which Wordsworth's evident enthusiasm for Rousseau is indicative of wholehearted support on his part for French Revolutionary politics is questionable. Mary Moorman claims that in this section of *Descriptive Sketches* in particular, we may see how Wordsworth's 'whole outlook on man had undergone a change'.[9] In fact it may be argued that it was Rousseau as he had been appropriated by the dissident Whig faction in England whom Wordsworth understood and was prepared to applaud.

Rousseau first became accessible to an English public in 1751, when William Bowyer published a translation of the *Discours sur les sciences et les arts*. Eight years later the *London Chronicle*, the *Monthly Review*, the *Critical Review*, the *London Magazine* and Burke's *Annual Register* all turned their attention to the English translation of Rousseau's *Lettre à d'Alembert surs les spectacles*. Though never winning unqualified praise, Rousseau's attack on d'Alembert's argument for a theatre in Geneva struck a familiar note when he compared 'two opposed sets of social values – the one corrupt, effeminate, and enslaved; the other simple, manly and free'.[10] English readers identified with a rhetoric in keeping with their own Whig ideology of freedom: 'English commentators recognised [in] the author of the *Lettre* ... an advocate of a strenuous public and private morality, the champion of simple manners, and the inheritor of an ancient republican tradition cherished as the nurse of virtue.'[11] Looking ahead to the appearance of *La Nouvelle Heloïse* in 1761, Edward Duffy suggests that the *Lettre* 'prepared the way for the novel. For it is this sternly moral work ... which influenced decisively the way in which the British public received and understood *La Nouvelle Heloïse*.'

Criticism of Rousseau's 'caprice and affectation of peculiarity' began to gather momentum in the 1760s, but so too did the tendency to use the man as a symbol for liberty and freedom of thought then being hounded out of Europe by tyrannical, un-enlightened governments. His eventual arrival in England in 1766 brought about a reappraisal of him by the English public: 'that which replaced admiration was a gloomy portrait of at best a madman to be pitied, at worst a scoundrel to be execrated'.[12]

After his death in 1778, however, there was a marked tendency on the part of English commentators to resurrect Rousseau the 'moral writer of true genius', as James Beattie called him. Not even the revelations contained in *The Confessions* deterred critics from asserting that Rousseau was a victim of 'civil and ecclesiastical tyranny', and that he had shown true 'zeal for virtue and the rights of his fellow creatures'.[13]

Wordsworth, as a young stranger in France in 1792, used the anglicised Rousseau to project himself out of a confused, revolutionary France, into an imagined idyll of Swiss liberty. Just as his Rousseau is the adopted figurehead praised by Beattie, and later invoked by Thomas Gales in the Sheffield *Patriot*,[14] so his Switzerland is emphatically not the country of the 1790 tour, but a Revolution-Whig substitute where the customs and manners of his own Lakeland community provide a far more potent inspiration for his imagination. In every respect we are being referred back to the indigenous political tradition that underpinned Wordsworth's early education.

The dislocation between a real and imagined landscape of

Switzerland becomes evident here as it had done in the case of
Lake Como. The image of a Swiss peasantry 'Unstain'd by
envy, discontent and pride' (DS, 94:583) could not withstand
Wordsworth's growing lack of confidence in a sentimentalised
rhetoric of liberty. At the end of the Rousseauesque account of
Switzerland we have a passage of similar syntactical difficulty to that
which followed the Claudian prospect of Lake Como. It may be that
tyranny elsewhere in Europe diminishes the significance of Swiss
liberty, or it may be that on close inspection, Switzerland itself is
found wanting, with 'No fond hand left to staunch th'unclosing
vein':

> But, ah! th'unwilling mind may more than trace
> The general sorrows of the human race:
> The churlish gales, the unremitting blow
> Cold from necessity's continual snow,
> To us the gentle groups of bliss deny
> That on the noon-day bank of leisure lie.
> Yet more; the tyrant Genius, still at strife
> With all the tender Charities of life,
> When close and closer they begin to strain,
> No fond hand left to staunch th'unclosing vein,
> Tearing their bleeding ties leaves Age to groan
> On his wet bed, abandon'd and alone. (DS, 96–8:602–13)

Through a curious and important linking of themes, Wordsworth
follows what in the end has become a pessimistic view of Swiss
liberty with an account of the shrine at Einsiedeln, and more
particularly of the pilgrims visiting it in the hope of miraculous
cures. Wordsworth was hardly likely to see anything but a means of
promoting secular tyranny in the blind superstition encouraged by
Papist religion, but Catholicism had also the aura of a long-standing
tradition of profound spirituality. Such ambiguities were present in
his treatment of the Grande Chartreuse earlier in the poem, and were
to become a particularly important ingredient of the Loire Valley
passages in Book X of *The Prelude*. Coming as it does here – forming
a bridge between a faltering portrayal of Swiss liberty and the
Thomsonian coda to the original version of his poem – Wordsworth's
lament for the Swiss shrine also takes on the quality of a deeply felt
personal lament for a dream of picturesque liberty apparently no
longer tenable in the light of rational perception:

> – From viewless lamps a ghastly dimness falls,
> And ebbs uncertain on the troubled walls,
> Dim dreadful faces thro' the gloom appear,
> Abortive Joy, and Hope that works in fear,
> While strives a secret Power to hush the croud,
> Pain's wild rebellious burst proclaims her rights aloud.
>   Oh give not me that eye of hard disdain
> That views undimm'd Einsiedeln's wretched fane.
> Mid muttering prayers all sounds of torment meet,
> Dire clap of hands, distracted chase of feet,
> While loud and dull ascends the weeping cry,
> Surely in other thoughts contempt may die.
> If the sad grave of human ignorance bear
> One flower of hope – O pass and leave it there.
> – The tall Sun, tip-toe on an Alpine spire,
> Flings o'er the desert blood-red streams of fire.
> At such an hour there are who love to stray,
> And meet the gladdening pilgrims on their way.
> – Now with joy's tearful kiss each other greet,
> No longer naked be your way-worn feet,
> For ye have reach'd at last the happy shore,
> Where the charm'd worm of pain shall gnaw no more.
> How gayly murmer and how sweetly taste
> The fountains rear'd for you amid the waste!
> Yes I will see you when ye first behold
> Those turrets tipp'd by hope with morning gold,
> And watch, while on your brows the cross ye make,
> Round your pale eyes a wint'ry lustre wake.
> – Without one hope her written griefs to blot,
> Save in the land where all things are forgot,
> My heart, alive to transports long unknown,
> Half wishes your delusions were its own. (DS, 100–2:648–79)

His Protestant response to Einsiedeln is instinctively scornful and dismissive; what he sees is a superstitious performance of grotesque, Gothic charlatanism, where simple people are misled and betrayed into a false hope, 'Abortive Joy, and Hope that works in Fear'. And yet, while this is so, he is also now aware that the leaders of the French Revolution view his own religious beliefs (let alone those of the Vallon family) in a similarly dismissive light. The eventual softening of his attitude toward Einsiedeln which develops in the second half of the passage, is the consequence of his wish that the revolutionaries would show an enlightened respect for the spiritual qualities of life. Consequently, as he reluctantly identifies with the pilgrims coming to the shrine, bearing their mental and bodily afflictions, he entertains the unnerving possibility that his own faith is about to be proved groundless:

> My heart, alive to transports long unknown,
> Half wishes its delusions were your own.

The word 'delusion' drops like a millstone into a passage which reveals, by way of analogy, Wordsworth's personal attempt to ward off an atheistical alternative to religious convictions firmly attached to the picturesque tradition of perception. The poet is tortured and confused, praying to be delivered from 'that eye of hard disdain' with which events in France seemed to threaten him.

In the end, the vacuum in the poem is filled, not by Painite, atheistical political radicalism, but by an evocation of 'Nature's GOD' in the language of the traditional libertarian rhetoric of eighteenth-century Revolution Whig ideology.

The major theoretical task of defining liberty anew in the wake of the Revolution of 1688 encouraged the evolution of a distinct poetic genre. Such poetry reiterated the conviction that patriotic Britons had welcomed the spirit of Liberty home to Albion when they rebelled against the tyranny of James II, and confirmed the fact that the new, constitutionally established King, William III, had ambitions which coincided in every respect with those of his willing, free and virtuous subjects. James Thomson was probably the most influential early Georgian poet who combined Revolution Whig rhetoric with stern and gloomy warnings that the ideals of 1688 were already being eroded.

Thomson was among the most widely read and revered poets of the mid-eighteenth century, and his popularity spread quickly to France and Spain where it endured well on into the nineteenth century. In the American colonies, *Liberty* rapidly became a seminal political text in the early years of the struggle with the British Government, as did *Britannia*; and though *The Seasons* is not so consistently political, it too was well known.[15] There is the familiar story of Coleridge's discovery of a dog-eared copy of *The Seasons* in a wayside inn, with his comment, 'That is fame ...'; for poets of Coleridge's and Wordsworth's generation, James Thomson's place as a great poet seemed as assured as that of Milton.[16] Wordsworth's knowledge of Thomson, if only from Knox, would have been comprehensive by the time he left Hawkshead.[17] Equally certain is the fact that Thomson would have been recommended to him as much for the 'beauties' of his political principles as for his powers as a descriptive poet of nature. According to Blackburne, Thomas Hollis 'respected the memory of Thomson, as a friend to liberty, and a venerator of Milton'.[18]

Wordsworth, for all his political naivety in 1792, knew well enough that the events of July and August in Paris presaged changes that were revolutionary when compared to the Rousseauistic creed of Beaupuy, and the 'republican' tradition perpetuated by English Commonwealthmen and American Colonists, no matter how verbosely or defiantly such traditions and their heroes might be eulogised. This is made clear enough by his lingering, painful unwillingness to reject the old faith enshrined at Einsiedeln, and his premonition of the arrival of a 'power 'till then unheard' in Europe with which the poem closes (DS, 114:765). He was still, like Watt, Cooper, and their compatriots in Paris, encased within eighteenth-century traditions of perception and expression. Where the English republicans in Paris had ingenuously paraded a bust of Algernon Sidney before the public as a sign of their common purpose with the French Revolution, Wordsworth wrote:

> Tho' Liberty shall soon indignant raise
> Red on his hills his beacon's comet blaze;
> Bid from on high his lonely cannon sound,
> And on ten thousand hearths his shout rebound;
> His larum-bell from village-tow'r to tow'r
> Swing on th'astounded ear its dull undying roar:
> Yet, yet rejoice, tho' Pride's perverted ire
> Rouze hell's own aid, and wrap thy hills in fire.
> Lo! from th'innocuous flames, a lovely birth!
> With its own Virtues springs another earth:
> Nature, as in her prime, her virgin reign
> Begins, and Love and Truth compose her train ...
>   Oh give, great God, to Freedom's waves to ride
> Sublime o'er Conquest, Avarice, and Pride,
> To break, the vales where Death and Famine scow'rs,
> And dark Oppression builds her thick-ribb'd tow'rs ...
>   (DS, 114–16:774–85, 792–5)

The vision and its rhetoric remain – for all its Gothic ornamentation – essentially that which Thomson had made commonplace some

fifty years before; firstly, through his account of how a free people
are reduced to a state of subjection through 'luxury ... erasing from
the mind ... The noblest sentiment of Liberty':

> While nought save narrow selfishness succeeds,
> And low design, the sneaking passions all
> Let loose, and reigning in the rankled breast.
> Induced at last, by scarce perceived degrees,
> Sapping the very frame of government
> And life, a total dissolution comes;
> Sloth, ignorance, dejection, flattery, fear,
> Oppression raging o'er the waste he makes;
> The human being almost quite extinct;
> And the whole state in broad corruption sinks.
> Oh, shun that gulf: that gaping ruin shun!
> And countless ages roll it far away
> From you, ye heaven-beloved! May liberty,
> The light of life! The sun of humankind!
> Whence heroes, bards, and patriots borrow flame,
> Even where the keen depressive north descends,
> Still spread, exalt, and actuate your powers!
> While slavish southern climates beam in vain.

Then by his pragmatic conviction that violence is justified where it is
the only means of throwing off oppression:

> Then the good easy man, who reason rules,
> Who, while unhurt, knew nor offence nor harm,
> Roused by bold insult, and injurious rage,
> With sharp and sudden check the astonished sons
> Of Violence confounds.[19]

The poet himself, we should note, plays a key role in bringing about
this liberation, 'Straight with her hand, / Celestial red, she touched
my darkened eyes.'[20]

Wordsworth was, of course, bound for Paris to seek an active role
in bringing the regenerated world into being. He too had his
personal vision:

> Yes, as I roam'd where Loiret's waters glide
> Thro' rustling aspins heard from side to side,
> When from october clouds a milder light
> Fell, where the blue flood rippled into white,
> Methought from every cot the watchful bird
> Crowed with ear-piercing power 'till then unheard.
>
> (DS, 112:760–5)

Thomson's consistent reference to cleansing by water is dominant also in Wordsworth's imagery; the latter's specific reference to the Loiret, 'where the blue flood rippled into white' refers us back to *Liberty* Part V and Thomson's more generalised statement: 'I see the fountains purg'd! Whence life derives / A clear or turbid flow'.[21] With the rhetoric of the previous passages by Thomson in mind, it is helpful to remember that Wordsworth's early attempts at poetry owed much to the style and concepts of liberty it sustained. In 1784–85 he composed the following lines as a school exercise:

> When Superstition left the golden light
> And fled indignant to the shades of night;
> When pure Religion rear'd the peaceful breast
> And lull'd the warring passions into rest,
> Drove far away the savage thoughts that role
> In the dark mansion of the bigot's soul,
> Enlivening Hope display'd her chearful ray,
> And beam'd on Britain's sons a brighter day.
>
> (PW I, 259–60:29–36)

An overriding anxiety for Wordsworth in the later lines of *Descriptive Sketches* is the moral issue of revolution begetting violence, and losing in the process its claim to 'virtue'. The optimistic logic of Thomsonian, Old Whig ideology was to foresee the coming of an era of universal peace; but the imminent second deluge being prophesied by Wordsworth showed every sign of cleansing the imperfect world through extreme violence, and could not be considered, as we have already seen, without 'a fainter pang of moral grief'. An attempt is made to confront the problem through attention to the lessons taught by nature. The destructive force of an Alpine avalanche, an act of nature and therefore in some mysterious way a sanctified act of destructive power, is described by way of analogy. In the mountainous home of the Swiss we discover the blind, seemingly indifferent destructive power of nature; in France we are about to witness the equally natural, irresistible force of Virtue unleashed upon society when 'despot courts their blaze of gems display' while 'Even by the secret cottage far away / The lily of domestic joy decay' (DS, 110:721–3). Thomson once more supplies the precedent, this time in *The Seasons*.

Alpine avalanches in *Winter* come as a climax to his observations on the way man perverts 'open freedom' with the 'lust of cruelty',[22]

and they would seem to denote indiscriminate retribution meted out
by the power of nature:

> Among those hilly regions, where, embraced
> In peaceful vales, the happy Grisons dwell,
> Oft, rushing sudden from the loaded cliffs,
> Mountains of snow their gathering terrors roll.
> From steep to steep, loud thundering, down they come,
> A wintry waste in dire commotion all;
> And herds, and flocks, and travellers, and swains,
> And sometimes whole brigades of marching troups,
> Or hamlets sleeping in the dead of night,
> Are deep beneath the smothering ruin whelmed.[23]

The corresponding passage in *Descriptive Sketches* betrays an
equally baffled mind confronted with the majesty and power of two
mighty glaciers, at once awesomely beautiful, yet savagely destructive:

> Six thousand years amid his lonely bounds
> The voice of ruin, day and night, resounds.
> Where Horror-led his sea of ice assails,
> Havoc and Chaos blast a thousand vales,
> In waves, like two enormous serpents, wind
> And drag their length of deluge train behind.
> (DS, 106:692–7)

Though acquiescence seems well-nigh impossible, the lesson of
nature here is clearly stated as one intended to resign the mind to the
necessarily destructive aspect of regeneration when it first breaks
upon the social world.

Descriptive Sketches, therefore, mediates a sense of crisis at a
personal, political and aesthetic level. The style of the poem and the
poet himself are threatened by the coming changes. Though the
poem becomes strident in its millenarian prophesy of tyranny
vanquished, the victory of liberty in 1792 is understandably less
confidently envisaged. Akenside and Goldsmith were of course
equally insecure in their vision of a redeemed society, but Thomson
himself once more provides the precedent for the tone of doubt. The
'clear torrent' of Liberty, he writes, is muddied at the last:

> As thick to view these varied wonders rose,
> Shook all my soul with transport, unassured
> The Vision broke; and on my waking eye
> Rushed the still ruins of dejected Rome.[24]

Wordsworth tells us how 'Freedom's waves' (DS, 116:792) will 'brood the Nations o'er with Nile-like wings':

> And grant that every sceptred child of clay,
> Who cries, presumptuous, 'here their tides shall stay,'
> Swept in their anger from th'affrighted shore,
> With his creatures sink – to rise no more.

But he then concludes:

> Tonight, my friend, within this humble cot
> Be the dead load of mortal ills forgot,
> Renewing, when the rosy summits glow
> At morn, our various journey, sad and slow.
>
> (DS, 118:805–13)

The 'various journey' was not renewed; that is the last line of the first version of *Descriptive Sketches*. History itself seems to have overtaken and overwhelmed the viability of his faith both in nature, and in the picturesque style of poetry used to express that faith.

Wordsworth remained, as France entered upon Year One of its New Republic, still loath to relinquish his eighteenth-century habits of thought and expression in favour of modern political radicalism; the alternative appeared an increasingly unyielding, soulless world of violence and atheism. His self-imposed mission as he trudged towards Paris in the October of 1792 was to save the Revolution he believed he understood from the one then taking over which he could not. Inevitable changes in his attitude were taking place, but from the first those changes directed him towards an attempt to salvage and reinstate a purged form of eighteenth-century republicanism.

4
The *Letter to Llandaff*:
a crisis of political allegiance

That the constitution of this country is so perfect as neither to require or admit of any improvement, is a proposition to which I never did, or ever can assent; but I think it far too excellent to be amended by peasants and mechanics.

(Richard Watson, Appendix to his sermon of 1785, published 1793)[1]

On 8 August 1792, a declaration from the Jacobin Club pronounced that 'it is madness to trust further in the Assembly. The people must be told that the Assembly cannot save them and that only a general insurrection can.'[2] The following night the insurrection began; it heralded the Revolution of 10 August and the deposition – and ultimately the execution – of Louis XVI. The erstwhile radical wing of the Legislative Assembly led by Brissot and his supporters, a loose coalition rather than a coherent 'Girondin' party, found themselves manoeuvred into the role of potential counter-revolutionaries.[3] The September Massacres, a purge to consolidate 10 August, began on the second of the month, and the bloodletting in Paris spread to other places, including Orléans. Wordsworth was in Orléans on 3 September when the French Republic was proclaimed, and Annette Vallon was due to give birth to their child within a couple of months. He set out for Paris on foot at the end of October.

Wordsworth's contacts in the capital were with Brissotin politicians, and this is the time when it is most likely that he encountered Brissot himself (Reed, p. 137). There was a considerable contingent of English radicals in Paris at this time besides Watt and Cooper, but there is no evidence to show that Wordsworth became anything like a regular member of their group. His friendship with James Watt, however, makes it likely that he met several of them, including Felix Vaughan, the radical barrister who in the spring of that year had helped draft the regulations for the London Corresponding Society.

With the rise to power of Robespierre, the English radicals were becoming far less optimistic about the course of the Revolution.

Watt was publicly denounced by the Jacobin leader for his open criticism of the September Massacres, and accused of being a spy in the service of William Pitt. He eventually found it prudent to leave Paris and go into hiding.[4] The rights and wrongs of republicanism were not in question. The desirability of the kind of republic the Jacobins were introducing at the expense of 'Girondin' influence most certainly was. The picture emerges, then, of Wordsworth aligning himself in Paris with a republican cause already half lost; his desire would have been to restore the Revolution to what he believed was its proper course, but by early December 1792 he was back in London, presumably the result of his precarious financial and political position. On 15 December Annette gave birth to their child, christened Anne-Caroline at Orléans in his absence.

In London, Wordsworth took up residence with his elder brother Richard, who now lived in chambers at Staple Inn and acted as the family's lawyer and financial advisor. With Wordsworth clearly determined to pursue a political career in the cause of radicalism in addition to his poetry, they were an ill-matched pair; the fact that Richard was doggedly working at the Lowther case presumably provided the basis of some common ground.

An Evening Walk and *Descriptive Sketches* were published by Joseph Johnson in January 1793. There was also a plan to write a novel based on the French Romance of two star-crossed lovers, Vaudracour and Julia, while work continued on what by now was a long-standing poetic project with the female vagrant motif at its centre. By September 1793 this bore fruit in the first version of *Salisbury Plain* (Reed, 138 and 25). But political pamphleteering came first, and Wordsworth set about attacking the apostasy of Richard Watson, the Bishop of Llandaff, whose sermon, *The Wisdom And Goodness Of God In Having Made Both Rich and Poor* was reprinted with an Appendix shortly after the execution of Louis XVI had taken place on 21 January 1793. It was the Appendix that particularly enraged Wordsworth. Watson withdrew his approval of the Revolution unconditionally (formerly he had even been prepared to countenance a 'Republic'), and praised the very political and legal system that was still enabling Lowther to withhold the young poet's inheritance. In Wordsworth's eyes reactionary political views like these encouraged an aggressive extremism in France that threatened to consume the whole revolutionary movement.

Wordsworth's open letter to Llandaff was never completed. Johnson, despite his radical sympathies, presumably saw enough of it to know that he would not be prepared to publish it, although we cannot be sure even of this. The steadily increasing repression of political radicalism in England that was to reach a climax in the London Treason Trials of autumn 1794, was already beginning to drive men like Johnson onto the defensive.

No letters between Wordsworth and his sister for this period have survived, but in Dorothy's letter to Jane Pollard, dated 16 February 1792, she probably reflects her brother's views on their fate since the death of their parents:

We have been endeared to each other by early misfortune. We in the same moment lost a father, a mother, a home, we have been equally deprived of our patrimony by the cruel Hand of lordly Tyranny. (EY, p. 88)

No doubt Wordsworth's letters to his sister were in part rehearsing arguments to be used in the open letter to Llandaff, where his personal grievance against Lowther clearly contributed to the passion with which he pursued his broader attack on immoral forms of privilege: 'I allude to titles, to stars, ribands, and garters, and other badges of fictitious superiority' (44:480–1).[5]

Uncharitable though it may seem to lay such stress on the contribution of Wordsworth's personal financial crisis to the formation of his political convictions, we should remember that at this time he was still only beginning to come to terms with the broader issues informing the contemporary political debate. Neither the relatively liberal tendencies of the régime at Hawkshead under William Taylor, nor the tradition of political dissent he would have encountered at Cambridge were sufficient to prepare him for the political ferment he encountered in Paris in the autumn of 1792. While there was clearly a preparedness on the part of many English radicals to condone the violence that Robespierre argued had become indispensable if the Revolution were to succeed, it should not be forgotten that the Revolution of 1688, and subsequently the American War, continued to influence the thinking of many of the most radical reformers. Nicholas Roe has suggested that Wordsworth at this time was prepared to argue for the necessity of the September Massacres, yet the authorities to which he turned when composing the *Letter* – Sidney, Harrington, Milton, William Pitt the elder,

Rousseau, Paine – indicate by the very eclecticism of his choice a continuing ideological confusion. This is to question the adequacy of Paul Hamilton's description of the radical politics which inform both the *Letter* and *Salisbury Plain* as 'straightforward'.[6]

Ultimately there emerges in the *Letter* a tone of habitually moral, even religious outrage that suggests the continuing control of an eighteenth-century political attitude grounded in the pro-colonial rhetoric of the 1770s rather than the populism of the 1790s; it is this that undermined Wordsworth's attempts to incorporate arguments from *Rights of Man* as he set about his task of attempting to emulate Paine's attack on Edmund Burke.

Wordsworth had left Paris when the fate of the Revolution seemed to be in the balance; the necessity of violence, he believed, was due in no small measure to the way in which the political Establishment of his own country persisted in its aggressive policy towards all signs of change. But to shrug off the execution of the King in the face of Watson's fulsome protests was not necessarily a complete abandonment of pre-revolutionary political beliefs; the Commonwealthman texts he had encountered in Paris, and continued to study and set alongside Painite writings in England, had grappled with the same issues over the execution of Charles I. The *Letter* is not, therefore, a radical departure from the politics of *Descriptive Sketches*.

Wordsworth knew full well, of course, that he was confronting a potentially revolutionised response to all the social and political ill of which he was aware. The precise point at which the new radicalism left his own convictions behind remained obscure, and his doubts as to the quality and function of his own protest repeatedly confused his attempts to give utterance to his views. The fact that neither the *Letter* nor *Descriptive Sketches* were properly completed reveals a fundamentally common problem for both projects, a problem that Hamilton identifies also for *The Prelude*: 'A revolutionary re-evaluation of human nature, originating in poetic enthusiasm, becomes incoherent when it tries to justify itself theoretically.'[7]

Both the *Letter* and *Descriptive Sketches* pose as a central issue the fact that violence appears to be an inevitable corollary to the search for revolutionary solutions to political and social ills. The problem is tackled imaginatively in *Descriptive Sketches* using nature as a tutor in the way previous eighteenth-century poets had done; in the *Letter* an attempt at rational political logic is made:

I must add also that the coercive power is of necessity so strong in all the old governments that a people could not but at first make an abuse of that liberty which a legitimate republic supposes. The animal just released from its stall will exhaust the overflow of its spirits in a round of wanton vagaries, but it will soon return to itself and enjoy its freedom in moderate and regular delight. (38:275–80)

This is obviously an attempt to set the September Massacres and the execution of the King in a reassuring perspective, but the link with *Descriptive Sketches* reveals also the fact that Wordsworth's own crisis of political allegiance did not arise from having subsequently to abandon completely a political position taken up at the time of the *Letter*; the crisis had its roots further back. The seeds of alienation from the French Revolution were sown while he was in France, lamenting the fate of the Grande Chartreuse and reflecting on Einsiedeln; in London he was similarly to find himself in two minds regarding the direction taken by contemporary political radicalism. Watson's 'Appendix' expressed the reactionary position taken up by his own Government; blandly asserting 'the fixed, impartial, deliberate voice of Law, enacted by the general suffrage of free people', and this palpably false assumption alienated him also. The *Letter* shows us Wordsworth still bewildered by the relationship between traditional and contemporary radicalised forms of political protest, in part a debate between religion and an atheistic faith in reason.[8]

Three recurring themes passionately discussed in the *Letter*, violence in revolutionary situations, the dilemma of a nation that finds 'the general welfare' reflected in the 'will of society' opposed by its monarchy and privileged classes (45:518–19; 46:572), and the need for universal education to combat such circumstances (34:114–19), remained central to Wordsworth's subsequent attacks on his own Government; this was a campaign he only began to set aside after completing *The Excursion* in 1814.

The necessity of violence is only grudgingly allowed, and Wordsworth is at pains to indicate his regret at what seems to be the radical political logic of the day:

Alas! the obstinacy and perversion of men is such that she [Liberty] is too often obliged to borrow the very aims of despotism to overthrow him, and in order to reign in peace must establish herself by violence. (33:101–4)

The second theme, the impotence of the 'general will' over against that of an unrepresentative Government, presents him with no such misgivings; the situation is clear:

> The fact is that the King *and* lords *and* commons, by what is termed the omnipotence of parliament, have constitutionally the right of enacting whatever laws they please, in defiance of the petitions or remonstrances of the nation. (47:596–9)

The resolution of both problems will, however, be swift and sure given the recognition of the importance of his third theme, one that had been central to the political writings of Molesworth and his circle:

> It is the province of education to rectify the erroneous notions which a habit of oppression, and even of resistance, may have created ... it belongs to her to create a race of men who, truly free, will look upon their fathers as only enfranchised. (34:114–19)

Wordworth persisted in essentially the same criticism of the Government over subsequent years, his confidence growing as his own education and sense of political conviction gradually developed. In 1805, with the persecutors of Hardy, Thelwall and other members of the London Corresponding Society in mind, he wrote in *The Prelude*:

> Our shepherds (this say merely) at that time
> Thirsted to make the guardian crook of law
> A tool of murder. They who ruled the state,
> Though with such awful proof before their eyes
> That he who would sow death, reaps death, or worse,
> And can reap nothing better, childlike longed
> To imitate – not wise enough to avoid ...
> As vermin working out of reach, they leagued
> Their strength perfidiously to undermine
> Justice, and make an end of liberty. (X, 364:645–51, 654–6)

In 1793 he argued that where 'Political virtues are developed at the expense of moral ones', disaster, even in a state of justified rebellion, will threaten to engulf the nation. In 1809 in his pamphlet *The Convention of Cintra*, he still accused the British Government of being blind to the 'subtle – ethereal – mighty – and incalculable' power of 'moral energy' which must underpin its policies if it is to act rightly (O&S I, 34:110–11; 309:3600–10).

In Book IV of *The Excursion* 'the impious rule' of his own day is described as constraining 'the good / To acts which they abhor' (PW V, 118:298 and 299–300); and he reflects both on the weakness of 'Girondist' republicans and ineffectual English radicals who failed to realise the spiritual, 'ethereal' (118:316) strength of the principles they sought to uphold:

> For by superior energies; more strict
> Affiance in each other; faith more firm
> In their unhallowed principles; the bad
> Have fairly earned a victory o'er the weak,
> The vacillating, inconsistent good. (PW V, 118:305–9)

From *Descriptive Sketches* on, the fact that, as he says in the *Letter*, 'the principles of liberty and the march of revolutions' stand in 'apparent contradiction' haunts him (34:105–6). The solution, as it emerges in his later work, is already implicit in the *Letter*. War will always give rein to passions which mark the most debased side of human nature, 'jealousy', 'severity', 'disquietude' and 'vexation', just as they may be expected to 'contract [in the sense of diminish] the benign exertion of the best affections of the human heart'. In short, the political gains an ascendancy over the moral (34:105–11). Emphasis on the moral and spiritual foundations of republicanism, as well as the need for 'education', is an inheritance from Old Whig, Commonwealthman rhetoric of the American War period, a marker in the *Letter* as it continued to be in *The Convention of Cintra*: 'under every government of modern time till the foundation of the American republic', he wrote in the *Letter*, 'mankind have appeared incapable of discerning their true interests' (37:250–3).

As the solution is a moral one, it must therefore depend ultimately for its success not on radical legislation, but on the 'sweet emotions of compassion' (34:111), a conviction which, once stated in the *Letter*, acts as a thread on which he attempts to string his various gleanings of political theory, many of them culled from Harrington and Sidney. We are brought back eventually, as we were with *Descriptive Sketches*, to the rhetoric of Thomson. The *Letter* exhibits close affinities with the earlier poet's conception of the 'moral gravitation' of Liberty. In Book V of *Liberty*, the spirit of Liberty explains that she cannot perform her political function within the commonwealth unless it be accompanied by powerful spiritual conviction:

> Without this,
> This awful pant, shook from sublimer powers
> Than those of self, this heaven-infused delight,
> This moral gravitation, rushing prone
> To press the public good, my system soon,
> Traverse, to several selfish centres drawn,
> Will reel to ruin – while for ever shut
> Stand the bright portals of desponding fame.[9]

Such is the danger facing the French at a time of intense revolutionary convulsion. 'The animal just released from its stall' must be allowed time to 'exhaust the overflow of its spirits' in the faith that liberty is a *spiritually* sanctified cause. Repression from without may extinguish that spirit, even as such natural virtue has been extinguished in societies under corrupted monarchical systems:

Reflecting on the degraded state of the mass of mankind, a philosopher will lament that oppression is not odious to them, that the iron, while it eats the soul, is not felt to enter into it. 'Tout homme né dans l'esclavage naît pour l'esclavage: rien n'est plus certain: les esclaves perdent tout dans leurs fers, jusqu'au désir d'en sortir; ils aiment leur servitude, comme les compagnons d'Ulysse aimaient leur abrutissement.' (36:199–205)

The pivotal word in this passage is 'felt'; and with an assertion of the importance of 'feeling' comes a quotation from Rousseau's *Du Contrat social*. Paine condemned the *Contrat* on the grounds that the 'loveliness of sentiment in favour of Liberty' it expressed was not backed up by a practical revolutionary political programme.

In *Rights of Man*, of course, Paine had himself appealed in vividly emotional terms to his readers' feelings; but beneath that lay a belief in 'natural rights' grounded in rationalism and common sense. The idea of an ethereal spirit of moral good capable of acting on individuals within society to reform it, suggested to Paine the wiles of priestcraft and religion. The friction that developed between Paine and his fellow radicals over the former's determination to debunk traditional allegiances to Anglo-Saxon precedents and seventeenth-century traditions of dissent suggests also that Wordsworth's posture in the *Letter* as Painite must be viewed with caution. While this is not to accept the reading of Wordsworth offered by James Chandler which sees him as always having been a Burkean, it does reveal the insecurity of Wordsworth's political radicalism at the point when he has often been depicted as unconditionally radical in his views.[10]

Wordsworth was sincere enough in his description of Burke in the *Letter* as an 'infatuated moralist' (36:180); but what it seems he ultimately intended was to recall a recalcitrant Government to a sense of its proper responsibilities rather than to overthrow it completely. This was certainly how the argument was couched in one of his more 'modern' eighteenth-century sources for the *Letter*.

John Almon was a publisher who had always been concerned to keep alive the Revolution Whig canon of literature, and this included a proposed new edition of Molesworth's *Account of Denmark* in 1768. His politics, described by J. G. A. Pocock as 'neo-Harringtonian', were influenced by a close association with Thomas Hollis at the time when Hollis was putting much faith in the elder Pitt as the leader of the moral revival he yearned for in British politics.[11] By the time Almon published his *Anecdotes of the Life of the Right Honourable William Pitt* in 1792, he had written a biography of Wilkes, been tried and acquitted, along with Miller and Woodfall, for publishing Junius, and was a friend and associate of Wordsworth's publisher, Joseph Johnson.[12] The account which Almon gives in the *Anecdotes* of Pitt's speech to the House of Commons on 9 January 1770, has been cited as one likely model for Wordsworth's defence of the revolutionary 'animal' excesses of the French:

He owned his natural partiality to America, and was inclined to make allowance even for those excesses. That they ought to be treated with tenderness; for in his sense they were ebullitions of liberty, which broke out upon the skin, and were a sign, if not of perfect health, at least of vigorous constitution, and must not be driven in too suddenly, lest they should strike to the heart.[13]

Where Wordsworth appears closest to the original Revolution Whig theorists, Harrington and Sidney, is on the subject of the 'unnatural situation' of a king: 'The office of a king is a trial to which human virtue is not equal' (33:81; 41:388–9):

Sensible that at the moment of election an interest distinct from that of the general body is created, an enlightened legislator will endeavour by every possible method to diminish the operation of such interest. The first and most natural mode that presents itself is that of shortening the regular duration of this trust ... But this is not enough ... a sensible republican will think it essential that the office of legislator be not entrusted to the same man for a succession of years. He will also be induced to this wise restraint by the grand principle of identification: he will be more sure of the virtue of the legislator by knowing that in the capacity of private citizen tomorrow he must either smart under the oppression or bless the justice of the law which he has enacted today. (37:233–8, 241–7)

The similarity of these arguments to those found in Almon's account of Pitt's speech quoted above have been noted by Owen and Smyser (O&S I, 57–8), but Fink went much further, arguing that it 'might well have been written by Harrington himself', concerned as it is with the limitations for high office, and the principle of rotation.[14]

Wordsworth's identification of the central function of the 'Legislator' was of particular significance for Fink:

At the beginning of the passage in which are concentrated Wordsworth's principle ideas about the proper constitution of a state, we find the declaration that 'the great evils which desolate states proceed from the governors having an interest distinct from that of the governed.' There follows the proposal for an assembly of representatives or, as the poet specifically calls them, legislators ... Thus, not only is a Harringtonian principle enunciated, but a Harringtonian means for implementing it.

The parallel extends further. Wordsworth's assembly of representatives, like Harrington's senate and its Venetian prototype, has a combination of legislative and executive functions ... the parallel is close, and the amalgamating of both legislative and executive functions which characterises both writers would make it difficult to prove that it is not exact.[15]

He further pointed out how different the theory is from 'Burkean traditionalism', arguing for it as 'a permanent and unchanging element in Wordworth's political thinking ... one which is recurrent in his works, early and late'.[16]

From the earliest pages of Harrington's *Oceana* we are warned against the dangers of excess 'passion', and in the *Letter* Wordsworth continues the traditional debate on the operation of the passions in human nature that had dominated much eighteenth-century political philosophy, and from which Paine (as for example in his loss of patience with Rousseau) was attempting to break.[17] Where the 'liberty of a commonwealth' is to be maintained, Harrington wrote, 'passion in the contemplation of a man is needed', but it must be kept under strict control, 'the absence whereof would betray her unto the lusts of tyrants'.[18] 'The passion of pity', Wordsworth wrote, 'is one of which, above all others, a Christian teacher should be cautious of cherishing the abuse: when under the influence of reason, it is regulated by the disproportion of the pain suffered to the guilt incurred' (32–3:74–8). Wordsworth is aware of how the French stand to be accused; their behaviour in executing the King reveals them as having lost their finer feelings, the passion of pity. For Paine this had become a ludicrously finicky concern in the face of inhuman tyranny; Wordsworth continued to struggle for a redefinition of radicalism in recognisably eighteenth-century terms. The new republicans are men of passion, but passion redirected, and they remain capable of sorrow and pity:

It is from the passion thus directed that the men of whom I have just spoken are afflicted by the catastrophe of the fallen monarch. They are sorry that the prejudice and weakness of mankind have made it necessary to force an individual into an unnatural situation, which requires more than human talents and human virtues, and at the same time precludes him from attaining even a moderate knowledge of common life and from feeling a particular share in the interests of mankind. But, above all, these men lament that any combination of circumstances should have rendered it necessary or advisable to veil for a moment the status of the laws, and that by such emergency the cause of twenty-five millions of people, I may say of the whole human race, should have been so materially injured. Any other sorrow for the death of Louis is irrational and weak. (33:78–90)

We have here an interesting foreshadowing of a characteristic Wordsworthian approach to his later poetic subject matter. Time and again he presented himself as a man misled in his application of sentiment and attitude towards pity: 'Simon Lee', *Poems on the Naming of Places, Resolution and Independence*, and the discharged soldier from Book IV of *The Prelude* are all examples of this.

Equally apparent from the passage quoted above from the *Letter* is the persistence of the principle often quoted by way of Sidney that 'liberty cannot be preserved, if the manners of the people are corrupted'. Trenchard and Gordon used this as a rallying cry against Walpole and the 'Robinocracy', quoting Harrington an Walter Moyle as authorities, and it can be no coincidence that Wordsworth too uses Walpole when accusing Watson of discreetly ignoring the 'avowed ministerial maxims of Sir Robert Walpole' in his attempt to justify a system of government which had a well-established record for the worst kind of corruption (46:587–9).[19] Wordsworth's inclination is at all times to argue from a standpoint of orthodoxy, and this in the end is what makes the *Letter* so different in its approach from *Rights of Man*. Where Wordsworth is most aggressive, and does indeed appear to be disregarding the need for precedent, is in his direct attacks on the aristocracy, and here the personal note is seldom far off: 'I am happy to find you have passed through life without having your fleece torn from your back in the thorny labyrinth of litigation' (47:605–7).

It is interesting to note, however, that when he seeks in the latter part of the *Letter* to emulate Paine's famous onslaught on Burke, 'I am contending for the rights of the *living*, and against their being willed away, and controlled and contracted for, by the manuscript assumed authority of the dead', he reverts implicitly to an organic concept of libertarian ideology, a legitimising process which is only to be expected of him when we remember how he has shown himself to be seeking out and using the founding fathers of English constitutional history. Paine, reflecting on the view that the political structure of society is foreordained for future generations by 'Those who have quitted the world', is uncompromising:

what rule or principle can be laid down, that of two non-entities, the one out of existence, and the other not in, and who never can meet in this world, the one should control the other to the end of time?[20]

Wordsworth begins with, presumably, *Rights of Man* open by his side:

Mr. Burke rouzed the indignation of all ranks of men, when by a refinement in cruelty superior to that which in the east yokes the living to the dead he strove to persuade us that we and our posterity to the end of time were riveted to a constitution by the indissoluble compact of a dead parchment, and were bound to cherish a corse at the bosom, when reason might call aloud that it should be entombed. (48:629–35)

Watson, he argues, is presenting an even more 'dangerous and insidious' version of this doctrine; but as soon as he begins to expand this claim we can detect a belief on Wordsworth's part that 'the stream of public vigilance' (recalling the imagery of *Descriptive Sketches*) does indeed flow from the past. Where Paine claims that our reason should tell us no such stream exists, Wordsworth believes Watson guilty of attempting to dam it, which 'would by its stagnation consign it to barrenness and by its putrefaction infect it with death' (48:645–8).

Zera Fink's determination to make a strong case for seeing Wordsworth as a latter-day seventeenth-century English republican was by no means wholly successful. Like critics before and since, his assumption was that the *Letter* was ideologically coherent, and this it clearly is not. Before long the critical fashion swung in the opposite direction, and Mary Moorman's biography of Wordsworth published in the late 1950s argued for the *Letter* as an impressive statement of contemporary radical political theory, contextualised by the politics of Paine and the French Jacobins. This reading persists, and may be found unquestioningly reiterated in Jonathan Wordsworth's *The Borders of Vision*; the *Letter*, he writes, 'depends on Thomas Paine'.[21] This in fact is to confirm the late-nineteenth- and early-twentieth-century picture of Wordsworth, where he is portrayed as a convert to Jacobinism who subsequently came to know better.

Latterly the traditional arguments of the *Letter*, and its eighteenth-century Whiggish rhetoric which suggests an English rather than a French context for its political beliefs, have once more been the subject for comment. John Turner, in stark contrast to Moorman's praise of the *Letter*'s 'eloquence', describes it as 'chiefly remarkable for its poverty of argument and its ostentation of rhetoric'. For much of the time, he argues, it uses 'the traditional dissenters' images in which Wordsworth apprehends that mystification of truth which is the peculiar triumph of the ruling classes in denying man his rightful future'.[22]

Like so much of Wordsworth's greatest poetry, the *Letter* records an evolving state of mind, not the summation of a fixed position. Fink would after all appear to be closest to the truth when he emphasised the influence of Revolution Whig political theory on Wordsworth's political manifesto. A helpful contribution to this debate has come from Jonathan Arac, who has discussed the way in which the poet's entire output was born of a struggle to reach a conclusion forever untenable.[23] The need to conceive of the poem on the page as in some way a final statement is especially inappropriate to Wordsworth's manner of composition. What the *Letter* reveals, in conjunction with *Descriptive Sketches*, is the considerable extent to which his attempt to find a political and aesthetic identity was informed by eighteenth-century radical Whig thinking of the American War period and before, and the extent to which this qualified his adoption of latter-day, Painite radicalism.

It is therefore by no means surprising to find that when Wordsworth moved from the composition of the *Letter* to the composition of a poem, he modelled it in the first instance on James Beattie's *The Minstrel*. The picturesque account of the Scottish landscape rendered by Beattie in Spenserian stanzaic form, and his soleful, freedom-loving hero, Edwin, belonged to the cultural tradition of other Whig poets like Thomson, Akenside (before he changed sides in the 1760s), Chatterton and Crowe, and was thus more genuinely suited than *Rights of Man* to inspire Wordsworth's attempt to continue his reflections on man and society. The new poem, *Salisbury Plain*, became a project to which he returned many times, revising and rewriting while at the same time he approached his creative maturity through other poems cast in a variety of different verse forms.

5
Poetry of alienated radicalism

Three years a wanderer round my native coast
My eyes have watched yon sun declining tend
Down the land where hope to me was lost;
And now across this waste my steps I bend:
Oh! tell me whither, for no earthly friend
Have I, no house in prospect but the tomb.
(*Salisbury Plain*, Gill, 34:388–93)

At Hawkshead School Wordsworth had come to know the Calvert family. Raisley Calvert was the steward of the Duke of Norfolk's properties at Greystoke, and on his death in 1791 he was able to leave his two sons, William and Raisley, comfortably off. The elder son, William, was in London in 1793, and he suggested to Wordsworth that together they make a tour of the West of England. There was nothing to keep Wordsworth in the capital; his two published poems had been as yet indifferently received, and what hopes he might have had of an active role in the political world had not materialised. The two men left London towards the end of June, spending most of July on the Isle of Wight. Britain had declared war on France in February, and on 28 July the Convention (which had come into being in September of the previous year) passed a decree of outlawry on eighteen of the leading Brissotin deputies.

The two men left the island in early August intending to cross Salisbury Plain and make their way by a circuitous route into North Wales. Wordsworth then planned to travel to Manchester and make contact once more with James Watt, and from thence he meant to visit Dorothy who would by then be with her mother's relations at Halifax.

In a letter to Jane Pollard written early in July, Dorothy made what turned out to be a prophetic comparison of her brother with Edwin, the Minstrel of James Beattie's poem (EY, pp. 100–1). Somewhere near Salisbury Wordsworth and Calvert parted company,

and the former did indeed find himself wandering alone in a barren
landscape in a state of distraction very like Edwin:

> and Edwin raised his eyes
> In tears, for grief lay heavy at his heart.
> 'And is it thus a courtly life,' he cries,
> 'That man to man acts a betrayers part?
> And dares he thus the gifts of Heaven pervert,
> Each social instinct, and sublime desire?[1]

These two or three evidently traumatic days on Salisbury Plain
triggered Wordsworth's poetic faculties, and as he made his way on
to Robert Jones's house in Wales, he began to compose *Salisbury
Plain* (Reed, pp. 315–16).

Much of the spring and early summer of 1794 was spent with
Dorothy in the Lake District. William Calvert had loaned Wordsworth
his Keswick house, Windy Brow, and when Dorothy left in June to
visit her cousins at Rampside on the Furness coast, her brother
stayed on at Keswick to nurse Raisley Calvert who was becoming
seriously consumptive. Calvert died on 9 January 1795, bequeathing
Wordsworth a legacy of £900.

There are four versions of the Salisbury Plain material. The first
belongs to the time of Wordsworth's tour with William Calvert, and
was completed at Windy Brow in the spring of 1794. Its origins
certainly go back before the solitary walk across the Plain, but it was
that experience which enabled Wordsworth to bring to completion a
'vagrant' poem he had been contemplating since at least 1791, itself
no doubt a development from the vagrant passage of *An Evening
Walk* (Reed, p. 333 and 5–7).

Within a year, however, he was beginning to revise and extend the
poem, a process which produced by 20 November 1795 a new poem
virtually ready for the press, *Adventures on Salisbury Plain*; but
despite the flurry of activity that seems to have surrounded this new
manuscript, no poem appeared in print, and Wordsworth continued
spasmodically to revise it through to 1799. In the meantime, the
original incident, the story of a female vagrant, was printed as a self-
contained poem in *Lyrical Ballads* (Gill, pp. 7–9). After 1799,
though he continued to tamper with *The Female Vagrant* of *Lyrical
Ballads* for later editions, no work took place on the *Salisbury Plain*
text until 1841, when after further changes it was published in
1842 under the revised title of *Guilt and Sorrow; or Incidents upon*

Salisbury Plain in *Poems, Chiefly of Early and Late Years* (Gill, pp. 13–14).

The period of Wordsworth's life that may be considered as constituting his literary apprenticeship from 1787 to 1797 came to be dominated in its latter stages by two ambitious projects, both profoundly political. In addition to the *Salisbury Plain* poem, he began in 1796 to write a tragedy, *The Borderers*. The latter has been described by Marilyn Butler as 'a stylized account of the French Revolution' where 'the denouement for each of the principles is pure moral fable'.[2] Where *Salisbury Plain* is concerned, Wordsworth chose to address issues that had become real to him as a consequence of the French Revolution through setting the action of the poem in the period of the American War of Independence. The technical discipline he chose was the Spenserian stanza form adopted by Beattie in *The Minstrel*. The evidence therefore begins to suggest that Wordsworth was to a significant extent formulating his response to the French Revolution in the light of earlier debates and issues. James Beattie, the poet with whom he was closely identifying, was a moral philosopher of the Scottish Common Sense School, a movement deeply influenced through Hutcheson, Thomas Blackwell, Hollis and others by the writings of Molesworth, Toland, Moyle, Molyneux and their contemporaries.[3]

With Beattie as his model, Wordsworth found it possible to express his sense of political disaffection and betrayal without committing himself to aspects of contemporary political radicalism that had failed to gain his confidence. The female vagrant motif sets *Salisbury Plain* within a traditional poetic genre at a time when radical political thinking was prepared to challenge every aspect of tradition. For Wordsworth, feeling was not to be overshadowed by reason and common sense, and the vagrant was salvaged as a type of eternal victim, against whose plight transient radical political enthusiasms might be judged, and through whom more fundamental remedies might ultimately be sought.

The *Letter to Llandaff* alone indicates Wordsworth's knowledge by now of the eighteenth-century Revolution Whig tradition that informed so much radical political rhetoric in England in the 1790s. The London Corresponding Society and the Society for Constitutional Information had been nurtured on Commonwealthman texts which Hollis had worked to maintain in print, and which he had shipped off to the colonies by the boat-load. John Thelwall, one of those imprisoned for treason in 1794, and with no reason to expect anything but the worst during the protracted period spent waiting for his trial to begin, produced at this time a series of sonnets to liberty in which he extolled the Revolution Whig, Commonwealth-man heroes Algernon Sidney, Hampden and Russell.

A seminal document for those who regarded themselves as heirs to the Revolution Whig tradition of incorruptibility was Robert Molesworth's Preface for the 1721 edition of his translation of Francis Hotoman's *Franco-Gallia* (originally written in 1574). Of *Franco-Gallia* itself, Molesworth explained its relevance 'for the perusal of Englishmen ... especially at this Time' by quoting Bayle, who claimed that Hotoman proved beyond doubt that 'the Kings [of France] came to the Crown by the Choice and Suffrages of the Nobility and People; insomuch, that as in former Times the Power and Authority of *Electing* their Kings belonged to the *Estates of the Kingdom*, so likewise did the Right of *Deposing* their *Princes* from their Government'. Molesworth's intention was to argue that, having established this order of things through the Revolution of 1688, Whig leaders of the Junto like Portland and Sunderland were cynically prepared to jettison those principles in the interests of retaining their personal positions of power.[4]

This was the context in which Thomson, Henry Brooke, John Brown and William Mason, writers with Old Whig sympathies if not patrons, conceived of their poetry, novels and verse dramas. Despite their approximately classical format, their works were true to the spirit of Molesworth's Preface, often using the device of presenting ancient 'Gothic' history as metaphor and precedent for analysing contemporary corruption. Mason's *Caractacus* (1759), for example, depicts British Liberty rudely downtrodden by Roman military might, aided by apostate, corruptible Britons. In his political writings, Molesworth had similarly confronted an alien and complacent classical model of society with a vigorous, native Gothic sensibility immediately relevant to the country's political needs. Hotoman was to be placed alongside Cicero on the well-informed Englishman's shelves.

Beattie's *Minstrel* is a poem which continues in the traditional rhetoric used by Thomson, Brooke, Mason and Akenside. The continuity that Wordsworth thus sought to re-establish, relied on

the survival of a mutually interdependent aesthetic of nature
imagery and eighteenth-century libertarian rhetoric; he needed to
confirm the interrelationship between the two, while at the same
time taking account of the changes that had undeniably taken place
in society.

The pastoral world was evident in eighteenth-century poetry as
much by its absence as by its presence; as much by its association
with a lost Golden Age as with the attempt to describe its
perpetuation. The location of Salisbury Plain, therefore, provided a
telling – if hardly original – metaphor for Wordsworth's conviction
that 'foul Error's monster race' stalked the land, filling 'Th'Oppressor's
dungeon' with hapless victims. As with the latter section of
Descriptive Sketches, the language here is strongly reminiscent of
Thomson, though we can also see that he wished to reproduce a
degree of Spenserian diction:

> No shade was there, no means of pleasant green,
> No brook to wet his lips or soothe his ear,
> Huge piles of corn-stack here and there were seen
> But thence no smoke upwreathed his sight to cheer;
> And see the homeward shepherd dim appear
> Far off – he stops his feeble voice to strain;
> No sound replies but winds that whistling near
> Sweep the thin grass and passing, wildly plain;
> Or desert lark that pours on high a wasted strain.
>
> (Gill, 22:46–54)

Wordsworth here describes the loss of pastoral felicity that had
occupied a central, reconciling role in *An Evening Walk*, and that had
originally been intended to operate in the same way in *Descriptive
Sketches*.

There are two glimpses of the lost pastoral world in the 1793–94
version of *Salisbury Plain*, the first comes with the beginning of the
female vagrant's narration at stanza 26:

> 'By Derwent's side my father's cottage stood,'
> The mourner thus her artless story told.
> 'A little flock and what the finny flood
> Supplied, to him were more than mines of gold.
>
> (Gill, 28:226–9)

The second comes immediately after her narration is over:

> But now from a hill summit down they look
> Where through a narrow valley's pleasant scene
> A wreath of vapour tracked a winding brook
> Babbling through groves and lawns and meads of green.
>
> (Gill, 34:406–9)

The two wanderers look down from the heights of the Plain and see, in effect, the ideal Virgillian world of pastoral from which they and their generations have been driven. Given Wordsworth's choice of the 1770s rather than the 1790s as the narrative context of the poem, it is worth mentioning that accounts of colonial society depicted as Virgillian pastoral were not uncommon, and they rarely came without confirming the assumption that such bliss was contained within an essentially patriarchal political system.[5]

In *Salisbury Plain*, the use of Gothic literary form signifies the need to register a cultural and political loss reflected also in much Augustan classical poetry. It is the unnatural war with the colonies, waged by a government motivated by greed, that is responsible for reducing a demi-Paradise to a blasted heath; and this in turn has reduced the woman to her present state. Her husband, unable to earn enough to support her and their children, joins the army, and she and the children travel with him:

> How changed at once! for Labor's cheerful hum
> Silence and Fear, and Misery's weeping train.
> But soon with proud parade the noisy drum
> Beat round to sweep the streets of want and pain.
> My husband's arms now only served to strain
> Me and his children hungering in his view.
> He could not beg: my prayers and tears were vain;
> To join those miserable men he flew.
> We reached the western world a poor devoted crew.
>
> (Gill, 31:298–306)

Within a short time, her husband, fighting for an army 'That lap, their very nourishment, their brother's blood', is killed, and the children die of fever; 'despairing, desolate', she returns to England (Gill, 31:315 and 323).

In writing this first version of the poem, Wordsworth in many ways abandons the Painite and French models for revolution, though in one not particularly remarkable respect he concurs with Painite thinking, his championship of reason over superstition:

> High o'er the towers of Pride undaunted rear
> Resistless in your might the Herculean mace
> Of Reason ...
>
> (Gill, 38:543-5)

There is nothing in the poem, however, that could not have been written a decade or so before; indeed, as we have already seen, the rhetoric takes us back to Thomson's *Liberty*, and confirms how closely the young poet had read Thomson, Brooke, Akenside and Beattie.[6]

While it is clear that Wordsworth was no lover of his country's Government, his reasons for opposition stem from his beliefs that an earlier, purer social order (associated aesthetically with pastoral imagery) had been corrupted and destroyed by an increasingly materialistic establishment; indeed the present Government is so corrupt that it has failed to recognise the just cause that inspired the French to overthrow their rulers, they can only seek to destroy brutally all attempts to reform and revive the ailing constitution of England:

> Insensate they who think, at Wisdom's porch
> That Exile, Terror, Bonds, and Force may stand:
> That truth with human blood can feed her torch,
> And Justice balance with her gory hand
> Scales whose dire weights of human heads demand
> A Nero's arm. Must Law with iron scourge
> Still torture crimes that grew a monstrous band
> Formed by his care, and still his victims urge,
> With voice that breathes despair, to death's tremendous verge?
>
> (Gill, 37:514-22)

In 1805 Wordsworth attempted – with hindsight – to define his position at this time in a passage written for Book X of *The Prelude* which is wholly consistent with the way he actually seems to have felt in 1794. Commenting first on France under the Jacobins, he wrote:

> I read her doom,
> Vexed inly somewhat, it is true, and sore,
> But not dismayed, nor taking to the shame
> Of a false prophet. But rouzed up, I stuck
> More firmly to *old tenets*, and, to prove
> Their temper, strained them more; and thus, in heat
> Of contest, did opinions every day
> Grow into consequence, till round my mind
> They clung as if they were the life of it. (402:796-804)

The language of *Salisbury Plain* suggests that in 1794 Wordsworth's 'radical republicanism' was already to a significant degree an expression of the 'old tenets' (my italics above) of eighteenth-century political disaffection.[7]

The second version of *Salisbury Plain* introduced more characters, and the semblance of a plot. Wordsworth, influenced by Godwinian philosophy, was increasingly concerned to explore the way relationships between his protagonists might help reveal the truths he sought to impart.[8] The lone, anonymous traveller of the first version of the poem who encounters the vagrant woman is identified in the later text as a sailor, equally a victim of his country's war-like policies, 'Death's worst aspect daily he survey'd / Death's minister ...' (Gill, 125:83–4). Having done two years' voluntary (and presumably peaceful) service, he returns home only to be pressganged 'to rouze the battle's fire' (Gill, 128:81). He is refused any pay when finally discharged, and sets out to return home to his wife and children destitute; he already considers himself to have been turned into something akin to a murderer by the State. In desperation he robs a man, and in the process kills him (Gill, 125:98–9).

The true guilt lies at the door of 'the slaves of Office' who 'spurn'd / The unfriended claimant' when he returned from the wars (Gill, 125:91–2); but this particular victim of the State enjoys no easing of his personal sense of remorse in consequence. The sailor meets a decrepit soldier, another of society's cast-offs despite his patriotic service. The soldier is looking for his daughter, and after the two have parted the sailor then meets the female vagrant. Her story is told as before, but now she acts as the comforter of the sailor. The pair of them encounter a gypsy family, and the sailor intervenes with words of humanitarian wisdom to stop the father beating his child. This is followed by the discovery of a dying woman, who turns out to be the soldier's daughter, and who also turns out to be the sailor's wife. The story of the murder committed by the sailor is told once more by the dying woman, and the sailor determines now to face 'Justice' and gives himself up to the authorities. The brutal retribution suffered by the murderer is a mockery of true justice, and provides Wordsworth with an opportunity to dramatise the attack on society with which he had closed the poem of 1793–94:

> They left him hung on high in iron case,
> And dissolute men, unthinking and untaught,

> Planted their festive booths beneath his face;
> And to that spot, which idle thousands sought,
> Women and children were by fathers brought;
> (Gill, 153:820–4)

The changes show Wordsworth emphasising the individuality of his characters, and thus their alienation from any kind of existing social or political context – radical or otherwise. Their only hope for survival lies in their inherent virtues of love and sympathy. Nothing can supply them with these, they must come from them in isolation or not at all. Even the inhabitants of the tiny settlement in the pastoral valley agree that the sailor must give himself up to the law.

From the reconciliation that is achieved for the gypsy family, and the spontaneous charity of those living in the valley in the 'rustic Inn', we are encouraged to believe that society may yet regain a corporate sense of the love and charity which is not yet quite extinguished in the sailor's soul (Gill, 150:677–84).

The dissident political tradition to which this poetry belongs is made increasingly clear by Wordsworth's revisions, as we would expect after his introduction to many of those in Godwin's circle, and to the Pinney family and friends. The defeat of England in the American War provided a lasting lesson for all who would seek to ignore morally inviolable principles in pursuit of power and wealth, and who imagined that brute force could overwhelm the contrary power of virtue. Yet the temptation to challenge 'God and Nature'[9] is apparently irresistible to wicked men, and thus virtue would seem to exist in this world only in conjunction with suffering. The sailor is caught in a ghastly paradox; the sense of spiritual calm he wins from his virtuous exertions on behalf of the victimised gypsy child is achieved at the price of his own inconsolable guilt. The paradox of suffering within the pastoral beauty of *An Evening Walk*, and the paradox of liberty accompanied by violence exposed in *Descriptive Sketches* and the *Letter to Llandaff*, is pessimistically reaffirmed (Gill, 149:665–6). The radical philosophy of Paine which sought to sweep away all social ills through the application of rational political principles is denied as a policy as morally damaging as that of contemporary reactionary politicians.

Salisbury Plain is a resolutely anti-war poem in line with the beliefs (though not the style) of Crowe, and of Joseph Fawcett's *The Art Of War* (1795), and it reflects Godwin's similarly pacifist convictions.

In 1785, John Almon published *An Asylum for Fugitive Pieces in Prose and Verse*, where both the sentiment and the style adopted by Wordsworth were readily to hand:

> And can Britannia's sons, possess'd
> With frenzy, stab a brother's breast?
> With unbecoming stupor gaze,
> Nor grieve while kindred cities blaze?
> Their hands in bloody carnage steep,
> While widows mourn and orphans weep?[10]

The war of 1793 is the immediate source of Wordsworth's anger, but in the poem it is the American War that the poet chooses to focus on as politically relevant to the argument. The plight of the vagrant, at the point where the whole family faces starvation, looks as though it may be alleviated through war. The lesson, clearly intended to be applied to the current 'proud parade' (Gill, 31:300) in favour of war with France, is that no solution or salvation of any kind may be expected from any such abstract, politically conceived commitment. The vagrant's comment emphasises the inhumanity of a mistaken quest for military glory: 'Oh dreadful price of being! to resign / All that is dear in being' (Gill, 31:307–8). 'All that is dear in being' is that individual quality of sympathy, the ability to respond spontaneously to another's need, a 'common kindness' where the impulse remains as mysterious as the unbidden tear experienced by the poet of *An Evening Walk*. Here, in a way far removed from Paine's secular rationalism, with its scepticism of Rousseau and its implicit rejection of the sense of religious power Wordsworth had known at the Grande Chartreuse and Einsiedeln, is the basis of the poet's continuing attack on the contemporary policies of war and Empire.[11]

The suffering of the female vagrant in *Salisbury Plain*, and in the later versions of the soldier, the sailor, and the sailor's wife, all imply redemption achieved through the quality of compassion these individuals may inspire in others – the same lesson, in other words, to be learnt by the reader of 'Simon Lee' in *Lyrical Ballads*. The power of nature in the picturesque form of *An Evening Walk* had been driven out, though not quite extinguished; it had not yet acquired for Wordsworth a more resilient pantheistic power. The promise of redemption in *Salisbury Plain* therefore comes unaided by anything but the instinctive response of one desolated human being for another. The forgetting of self through a natural impulse of compassion towards another sufferer diminishes 'the terrors of the night', and offers a prospect of redemption mirrored in the pastoral prospect of 'a narrow valley's pleasant scene' that immediately follows (Gill, 34:401).

What is still lacking in the poetry is the insight of the kind recorded in the Simplon Pass passage of *The Prelude*, where nature is broken down only to be reassembled as a vision of a unified creation, subsuming pain and suffering born by individuals by uniting things in a sense of one great purpose.[12]

In 1793–94, before the West Country period, all the existing aesthetic props had been knocked away, as *An Evening Walk* and *Descriptive Sketches* had threatened they might be, and Wordsworth's appeal is to the very emptiness of a situation which serves to illustrate one remaining dramatic truth, that, in Langhorne's words, he still 'felt as man, and dropp'd a human Tear'.[13] From here there is only one way open to him, and that is back to the essentially paternalistic traditions and habits of thought that preserve the value of feeling; back in part to the context within which Langhorne had criticised society in 1775, lamenting the loss of a Country Party paternalism. The following stanza does indeed echo the moralising of *The Country Justice*:

> The proud man might relent and weep to find
> That now, in this wild waste, so keen a pang
> Could pierce a heart to life's best ends inclined.
>
> (Gill, 126:109–11)

At the turn of the previous century dissident Commonwealthman and conservative Country Party adherents had had much in common, and J. G. A. Pocock has argued that 'the pamphlets and politicians who made use of the Country ideology were adopting the posture of a radical right; but their terminology and ideas were extensively borrowed by the radical left when one began to appear in George III's reign'.[14] Langhorne's theme of a disordered and dying pastoralism was certainly a precedent for Wordsworth's poem:

> Has the fair Vale, where Rest, conceal'd in Flowers,
> The Breeze, that, balmy Fragrance to infuse,
> Bathes its soft Wing in Aromatic Dews,
> The Stream, to soothe thine Ear, to cool thy Breast,

> That mildly murmers from its crystal Rest; —
> Have these less Charms to win, less Power to please,
> Than Haunts of Rapine, Harbours of Disease?[15]

Wordsworth's line, 'No brook to wet his lips or soothe his ear' (Gill, 22:47) set against Langhorne's 'The Stream, to soothe thine Ear, to cool thy Breast', suggests the possibility of a copy of *The Country Justice* in the library of Robert Jones, where he began to write the poem down, and almost certainly one at Windy Brow. Further to this, Wordsworth's appeal through the female vagrant and the sailor solely to the strength of character possessed by his victims, is in keeping with Langhorne's use of his vagrant, and the 'pitying Robber' who finds her, to bring home the moral of his poem.[16]

In *Romantics, Rebels and Reactionaries*, Marilyn Butler discusses at some length the eighteenth-century cultural context of Wordsworth's work. 'His juvenilia', she writes, 'are associated with naturalness and often also with a culture earlier than that of the present day.'[17] The tradition he embraced and subsequently continued to praise in the 'Essay, Supplementary to the Preface' of 1815 is that of 'the nature-poet and Spenserian James Thomson', over against that of Dryden, Pope and Johnson.[18] What may now be added to this observation is the important fact that a crucial political divide is implicit between the two eighteenth-century traditions thus defined. On the one hand, the Old Whig or Commonwealthman tradition of dissent, increasingly documented and stressed now by historians but still largely ignored in literary studies of the eighteenth century; and on the other, an Augustan tradition essentially supportive of the status quo. Butler is inclined to take Wordsworth's commitment to an eighteenth-century model as an indication of his fundamentally conservative, 'reactionary' position, and to identify the radicalism detected in his work by contemporaries most markedly in *Lyrical Ballads*, as the result primarily if not exclusively of this theory of language, and its dangerously democratic implications when encountered in the late 1790s:

If Wordsworth's contributions to the *Lyrical Ballads* had appeared a decade earlier – and there is nothing in them that could not have been written in 1788 – they would hardly have attracted attention, except for their merits. As it was, literary excellence was an additional offence. It made Wordsworth more readable, and therefore more dangerous.[19]

Butler is here revealing only a part of the truth; she fails to take account of the specifically dissident strain of political thought that had gradually been appropriating the concept of 'Gothic' as a term of political, constitutional significance even while Shakespeare, Spenser and indigenous 'primitive' balladry were being explored as literary evidence of an alternative cultural and political model to the one established in Augustan England by the classicism of Dryden, Pope and Johnson.

The association of Wordsworth's frame of mind by the time *Lyrical Ballads* were published in 1798 with Painite radicalism (the connection made in Francis Jeffrey's account of the *Ballads* in the *Edinburgh Review*) is one that lingers on. In conceding Wordsworth's extreme application of neo-classical ideas to language as that which exposed its 'subversive potential', Butler argues against the case for a 'Jacobin' Wordsworth, and depicts him as a fundamentally reactionary poet.[20]

The coping stone of this theory rests with Butler's reading of *The Borderers*. Critical readings of this work have varied immensely in their interpretations of its politics. Butler's argument that it is a Burkean, counter-revolutioary piece in defence of the *ancien régime* has recently been questioned by John Turner, who suggests that its sense of alienation from contemporary radical political theory (specifically that of William Godwin) does not entail an acceptance of political conservatism. In his recent study of Godwin, Peter Marshall follows Mary Jacobus's view that Godwin's influence over Wordsworth was 'never as thorough-going as has sometimes been claimed'. More recently still, Nicholas Roe has challenged this view, but Marshall's reading of *The Borderers* should still be taken into consideration, it is 'not so much an exposure of Godwinism, but of the misuse of reason and the dangers of pride'.[21] The moral of the play, Turner argues, remains embedded in a dissident response to the contemporary situation, but it is an increasingly individualised, moralistic and indeed religious brand of dissident thought.

On the eve of compiling *Lyrical Ballads*, Wordsworth remained disenchanted with the politics of *Reflections on the French Revolution*, and the motives and consequences of Pitt's war-time politics, at home and abroad. The anger expressed in the *Letter to Llandaff* and in the first two versions of *Salisbury Plain* (represented of course in *Lyrical Ballads* by 'The Female Vagrant') was unabated. It is perhaps something akin to a Freudian slip that has led Marilyn Butler to refer to *Salisbury Plain* throughout her discussion as *Guilt and Sorrow*, which she dates 1791–94. As the final version of *Salisbury Plain* (revised in 1841 and published for the first time under that title in 1842), *Guilt and Sorrow* is without doubt a 'reactionary' version of both earlier dissident texts.

The Borderers was written after Wordsworth had begun to establish a number of influential contacts with men whose political education owed much to the Old Whig and Commonwealthman traditions. These were people for whom the rhetoric of honourable 'retirement' in the face of corruption, materialism and greed at the expense of the Commonwealth still rang true. The Commonwealthman piety of Hollis's paternalistic morality continued to have an influence, along with the dissident Whig pacifism evident in Crowe's poetry; William Frend, George Dyer, Francis Wrangham, James Losh and the Pinney family were all friends in need when Wordsworth arrived in London in February 1795. The offer of Racedown Lodge by Pinney as a place of work and – in keeping with the political climate in which he now moved – of 'retirement', included as we have seen a working library of Old Whig texts. In October Wordsworth sent William Mathews his own copy of *Cato's Letters* by Trenchard and Gordon, Old Whig publicists of the early eighteenth century.

It is difficult to imagine a play which presents *ancien régime* politics in a Burkean light emerging from this context. The representative of an earlier, morally incorruptible political world is Baron Herbert. At the time of the play, Herbert has been bereft of all his possessions and reduced to vagrancy. In Herbert we can recognise the Revolution Whig ideal of the great statesman, a wise, generous Harringtonian legislator; a figure every bit as alienated from the reactionary political world of the 1790s as were the radicals of that period. Herbert's imminent danger from the disenchanted, politically cynical Rivers is a fable of the impending fate of the Old Whig cause, forged in the years of opposition politics which fought William III's proposals for a standing army, urged religious toleration, the relative liberalisation of education, more frequent parliaments, and stricter control over the tenure of high office.[22]

It should be emphasised, however, that unlike the *Salisbury Plain* poems, *The Borderers* contains virtually no specific political referents to tie it in with the contemporary political debate. The action is set in the reign of Henry III, and whatever contemporary political comment the play is deemed to have must be arrived at primarily by what the reader actively seeks to find. In this respect it suggests a retreat on Wordsworth's part from tackling the problem of his own political position head on. When he came to do so once more, in, for example *The Old Cumberland Beggar* of 1797–98, and in other poems designed for *Lyrical Ballads*, the political position he adopted was reaffirmed in a way which reveals a new mastery of the means by which he could accommodate the dilemmas of the poet–statesman he yearned to become. Two dominant themes to emerge in this respect were political tenets central to the Commonwealthman and Old Whig traditions, 'retirement' and 'education', and these now form the basis of a reading of *Lyrical Ballads*.

6

The West Country years: 'wise passiveness'

I cannot at this moment read a tale
Of two brave Vessels matched in deadly fight
And fighting to the death, but I am pleased
More than a wise Man ought to be; I wish,
I burn, I struggle, and in soul am there.

(Home at Grasmere, HG, 96–8:929–33)

Superficially, it has always appeared that at the point when the politicking stopped, the finest poetry of Wordsworth's career began to be written. The poetry selected for discussion in the following chapters illustrates that what Wordsworth wrote during the time he spent in Dorset and Somerset, and thereafter, does not signify a setting aside of things that had concerned him before; rather he evolved new strategies to engage with fundamentally the same issues – public and private – which had dominated his thoughts since his second visit to France in 1792. In the poems he wrote for *Lyrical Ballads* (1798–1800), for example, there are a number of recurring themes which tend to link all the poems regardless of other perfectly proper groupings which have been made.[1]

Particularly significant in this respect is the tendency to contrast a life of 'action' with one of 'passive' reflection, the latter assuming a state of retirement from worldly affairs. A specifically political reading of the poetry need not follow from this, but with the influence of a dissident Whig political tradition clearly evident in his thinking, and given also that 1795 marked his own 'retirement' from the political mêlée in London, Wordsworth's interest in active and passive principles of behaviour, and the wisdom and morality to be learned from studying them, begin to suggest a political sub-text for the poetry which, though it will never provide a complete reading of any one poem, can in a number of cases significantly add to existing readings.

By August 1795, Wordsworth was in Bristol en route for

Racedown Lodge; he had been verging on a state of nervous
exhaustion for some time, and by November it was clear that he was
indeed suffering from a nervous breakdown:

Money worries, career dilemma, family hostility, quarantine from Dorothy,
problematic political commitment, city life, an abandoned lover, an
illegitimate child: one need but list Wordsworth's circumstances during the
period in order to appreciate his anxiety.[2]

The political situation seemed daily to be worsening. The passing of
the Seditious Meetings Act and Treasonable Practices Act in
October had been followed by a series of riots in Bristol, while the
relative security he gained at Racedown was accompanied by an
isolation which gave him time to brood on both affairs of state and
on more personal matters. Recovery was a long process, and the
sedentary life of Racedown that helped bring on the crisis, no doubt
played its part in effecting a cure.

   The Wordsworths were to live at Racedown from September
1795 to July 1797, when they moved to Alfoxden House, Somerset.
This brought them within easy walking distance of Coleridge who
was living at Nether Stowey. When the arrangement to live at
Alfoxden ended in June 1798, plans were already in the making for a
trip to Germany. After a series of local tours based on Bristol which
included visits to Tintern Abbey and Liswyn, Wordsworth, Dorothy
and Coleridge left the West Country for London at the end of
August. In September, Cottle published *Lyrical Ballads*, a collection
of poems that in itself scarcely bears witness to the intense creative
activity that had gone on during the previous three years, and on 16
September Wordsworth, Dorothy, Coleridge and a young man
called John Chester sailed for Hamburg. The Wordsworths returned
without Coleridge and Chester in May of the following year, and it
was seven months later on 20 December that they took up residence
at what we now know as Dove Cottage, Grasmere. They were to
remain there until May 1808.

   It is by no means overstating the case to say that the foundations
of Wordsworth's major creative work were laid between the time of
his arrival in Dorset and his leaving Alfoxden, a period of just over
two and a half years. He wrote much and planned even more, in his
mind as well as on paper, clearly coming to believe that in the course
of these years he had achieved a profound insight into his own

emotional and intellectual being and its relationship to society. In *The Pedlar* of 1798 he used the implicitly pantheistic phrase, 'one life', to express the visionary experience of these years, 'one life ... O'er all that moves, and all that seemeth still'.[3] Virtually everything that Wordsworth was to write of significance after he left Alfoxden, if not drawing directly on notes or lines actually written at this time, was to draw on his memory of a redemptive experience of intense creativity; the later work attempted to memorialise that experience, to analyse experiences before and after it in the light of that vision, and was most urgently intended to reconcile him to the subsequent loss of that vision.

Although research still continues in the attempt to date the poetry of this period, we do have an increasingly clear picture of the way Wordsworth began to write and plan ahead. His work on *Salisbury Plain* continued through to the autumn of 1796, by which time he became chiefly concerned with *The Borderers*. He had aready begun *The Ruined Cottage*, yet another variation on the female vagrant theme originating in a fragment entitled *Incipient Madness*. Before leaving Racedown he had completed *The Borderers*, *The Ruined Cottage*, and another poem, *The Old Cumberland Beggar*.[4] During the winter months of 1797–98, the idea of a volume of contrasting 'Lyrical Ballads' was discussed with Coleridge, while the Coleridgean concept of a philosophical poem in epic proportions began to take shape around *The Ruined Cottage*. This was to be called *The Recluse*, and Wordsworth never lost his conviction that completing this 'great work' was the major task of his life.

By late spring of 1798, Wordsworth had written many of the Lyrical Ballads, some of which had been composed as early as the previous autumn.[5] He had written his account of the meeting with the discharged soldier, and was working on other passages also destined for *The Prelude*, though he did not begin to assemble this poem until some months later in Germany. For the present, they were fragments intended eventually to take their place in the grand design. By no means all the *Prelude* material he wrote now found its way into the poem he completed in 1799. While writing *The Pedlar* in the spring of 1798, he was also working on other passages that were eventually incorporated into the only part of *The Recluse* he fully completed and published, *The Excursion*. During April and May he wrote *Peter Bell*. *The Excursion*, then, was growing contemporaneously with *Lyrical Ballads* and *The Prelude*; it is still too often thought of as a later poem.[6]

Wordsworth's energies were evidently being poured into the task of composition in a way they had never been before; it became customary among his acquaintances to depict this as a time when all political enthusiasm (which is to say radical political enthusiasm) was set aside. This required both Coleridge and Cottle, for example, to refer to the activities of a Government spy sent to watch Wordsworth's and Coleridge's movements as a farcical interlude in their lives.[7] The seriousness with which political issues continued to be discussed is more accurately reflected in Coleridge's poem of 1798, *Fears in Solitude*. While renouncing any allegiance he may have had to France, Coleridge there also castigates the moral depravity of his own nation and its successive governments in the course of the century, 'A vain, speech-mouthing, speech-reporting Guild / One Benefit-Club for mutual flattery . . .'[8] Contacts with radical political figures also continued. John Thelwall settled at Liswyn Farm in Brecknockshire, and Wordsworth, Dorothy and Coleridge visited him there in the summer of 1798.

Wordsworth's increasing awareness of the contemporary connotations of political radicalism resulted in a retreat from the enthusiasm with which he had at first declared himself to be a 'republican' and a 'democrat'. When brandished nostalgically alongside the memory of Sidney or Harrington, republican rhetoric was one thing; but for a radical Whig of the old school like Pinney, and for his protegé now also, the fruits of the new Republic in France made such ritualised professions of faith no longer so easy to sustain.[9] It was still possible, however, to salvage something of the old cause of liberty through the tradition of moral and political philosophy that formed a recurring strand in the politics of dissent adopted by families like the Pinneys, and which Coleridge had absorbed from prominent radicals like Price and Priestley. This constituted the belief that man stood in need of being educated into a fuller understanding of his latent spiritual and imaginative faculties, it meant emancipation through the exercise of reason, while insisting that human dignity and liberty lay not in reason alone, but in the spiritual self-knowledge that might be expected to follow from it.

It is an interesting reminder of the political tradition that Wordsworth was evidently still being encouraged to study, to discover that in March 1798 James Tobin sent him a copy of Henry Brooke's tragedy of 1739, *Gustavus Vasa*, to read. Tobin's father was in partnership at Bristol with John Pinney's son Azariah. Writing to thank Tobin for the gift, Wordsworth desribed the play as 'a strange composition of genius and absurdity' (EY, p. 210). In its time, *Gustavus* was considered sufficiently seditious for it to be banned from the stage; Brooke was by then already a marked man on account of his Commonwealthman politics. The play was reprinted in 1796 and 1797 as propaganda for the anti-slavery campaign of the time. Brooke was also known to the Wordsworths for his satirical novel, *The Fool of Quality*, which Dorothy reports having read and enjoyed in March 1796 (EY, p. 166).[10]

Set against the Commonwealthman tradition which Brooke represents, the political philosophy of William Godwin which Wordsworth was at this time reading was both more modern and more radical. In Hazlitt's words, 'The author of Political Justice took abstract reason for the rule of conduct and abstract good for its end.'[11] In *Political Justice* (1793) Godwin wrote that 'truth, when adequately communicated, is, so far as relates to the conviction of the understanding, irresistable'.[12] When Wordsworth settled at Racedown he was still deeply influenced by the rationalist creed that Godwin had evolved by 1793. Rationalism then began to give way (as it did with Godwin himself) to a philosophy which sought to reconcile abstract reason with more subjective, instinctive states of mind. This in fact was doing no more than reaffirm the empirical tradition of philosophy in Britain that traced its origins back to John Locke.

Locke's argument that the mind was initally a blank sheet, subsequently acquiring all its ideas through experience, was of course very pertinant to the political situation created by the Revolution of 1688. If you believed that the workings of nature, which included the evolution of society, were to be understood from the workings of the mind, then the conviction that the mind at birth brought with it no innate ideas was indeed helpful if you wished to argue that it was not unnatural to dispose of the Stuart line of kings. There was no innate right of succession; a Nation might with full justification acquire its rulers in the light of experience, and if its experience of a ruler was of a man apparently bent on absolutism and Popery, rebellion was justified.

The political implications of Locke's theories, as H. T. Dickinson has shown, were in the event too radical for many Whigs, and Dickinson's thesis significantly modifies the prominence generally given to Locke as a founding father of Whig political philosophy.[13] The Whig response to Locke was effectively to soften or humanise nature, moving the basis of the arguments justifying the Revolution from reason towards a concept of mind as a source of truths that arose naturally, spontaneously and instinctively. Imagination and feeling necessarily therefore began to be stressed, and Shaftesbury – Robert Molesworth's mentor – declared that 'common sense is the natural, instinctive and instantaneous knowledge of certain moral and philosophical truths which is shared by the great majority of mankind'.[14] The Scottish Common Sense School of philosophy, dominated by Hutcheson, and including Reid and Beattie, continued to explore the territory of feeling, making, as Shaftesbury put it, 'a formal Descent on the Territories of *the Heart*'.[15] A quasi-scientific investigation of the existence of moral truths in relation to physiological processes was subsequently supplied by David Hartley (1705–57).

Philosophy here was very clearly the handmaid of political expediency; Locke, Hutcheson, Shaftesbury and Beattie were overtly of Whig persuasion, and in turn fed a more radical Whig, Commonwealthman tendency. Hutcheson himself was within the Real Whig camp of Molesworth, Trenchard, Gordon and Moyle. Beattie was tutored at Marischal College, Aberdeen, by Thomas Blackwell, a disciple of Hutcheson. Also among Hutcheson's pupils were Joseph Priestley and Thomas Brand Hollis of the Society for Constitutional Information. Hutcheson was one of the authors Thomas Hollis had attempted to revive in new editions in the second half of the century.

Priestley's Unitarianism and radical political beliefs were also influenced by the writings of Molesworth's friend, John Toland, the freethinker now generally credited as the first to coin the term 'Pantheist'.[16] Molesworth's and Shaftesbury's generation concentrated their minds on the 'moral sense' in man, where it might be found, and how – through education – it might be activated. They were thus led, as Sidney had been before them, to investigate the operations of the passions rather than the more clinical faculty of reason. Akenside's *The Pleasures of Imagination* rendered this philosophical enquiry into Miltonic blank verse, endemically Whig in its pursuit of the spirit of social and aesthetic liberty.

Jonathan Wordsworth has taken *The Ruined Cottage*, written between April and June 1797, and *The Pedlar* (eventually added, or more accurately reconciled, to *The Ruined Cottage*), written between January and March 1798, as the two key texts of the period which illustrate Wordsworth's shift in emphasis away from his commitment to Godwinian rationalism. The final composite version of *The Ruined Cottage* and *The Pedlar* became Book I of *The Excursion*.

To describe the philosophy of the poet at this latter time, Jonathan Wordsworth quotes the reference in *The Pedlar* to the 'one life' that was perceived:

> O'er all that moves, and all that seemeth still,
> O'er all which, lost beyond the reach of thought
> And human knowledge, to the human eye
> Invisible, yet liveth to the heart ...[17]

Coleridge undoubtedly influenced this transition, though Jonathan Wordsworth argues that he did not remould the poet's belief to the extent it is sometimes suggested.[18]

There remains, therefore, an argument for continuity in Wordsworth's developing thought, a continuity in which pantheistic concepts involving the idea of 'animated matter' had a significant role to play. In 1782, in *Matter and Spirit*, Priestley wrote:

The Divine being, and his energy, are absolutely necessary to that of every other being. His power is the very *life* and *soul* of everything that exists; and, strictly speaking, *without him, we* ARE, as well as, *can* DO *nothing*.[19]

What was in one respect new for Wordsworth, was at the same time leading him back to the major sources of political opinion that influenced him in the early 1790s: 'the belief in animated matter was seriously put forward by scientists of the day – by Darwin, Priestley and Hutton, among others – and was certainly current among the Girondist and Unitarians whom Wordsworth may be presumed to have met in 1792–3.'[20] As a solution to Wordsworth's personal sense of alienation, this tradition of philosophy encouraged him in the attempt he now envisaged to marshall within one poetic statement (his 'main work', *The Recluse*, in conjunction with all his shorter pieces) an explication of liberty and freedom which, with its essentially eighteenth-century emphasis on moral philosophy and its vision of 'total harmony', would challenge both modern atheistical radicalism and the cynical policies of the existing British Government.

While acknowledging the change that takes place between *The Ruined Cottage* and *The Pedlar*, therefore, it is also important to appreciate that Wordsworth's political position remained fundamentally unaltered. In this respect he confirms Antonio Gramsci's definition of a 'traditional intellectual'; he is seeking out 'intellectual categories which were pre-existing and which, moreover, appeared as representatives of an historical continuity uninterrupted even by the most complicated and radical changes in social and political forms'.[21] Jonathan Wordsworth argues that: 'there is a consistent and continuing Wordsworth, whose values are unchanged, and whose individuality is felt as much in *The Pedlar* as in *The Ruined Cottage*.[22]

Philosophical enquiry in the eighteenth century was by no means only a Whig enterprise, and by no means wholly dissident in its intentions, nor were there consistently clear battle lines drawn up on politically defined issues or problems. The fact remains, however, that there was an exiled Whig interest influencing much of the theorising on mind, matter, and morality that went on. When Wordsworth explores the dichotomy between active and passive principles in *Lyrical Ballads*, he is building in part on the foundations already laid by the emphasis Whig philosophers had given to the virtues of 'retirement', which allowed for objective reflection on the political health of the nation.

Passive reflection is kept at arm's length in 'Simon Lee' by the paraphernalia of the narrative poem, its sing-song metre, its attention to detail; it is a poem which reproduces the narrator's interest in action: the preparation for the 'tale', Simon's efforts to chop the root of an old tree, the narrator–poet's decision to help. Reflection, 'silent thought' as the poem describes it, in contrast to the intrusive noise of the poem's metrical beat, only becomes possible after the 'doing', and the doing of the deed actually disturbs the regular metre, replacing it with a series of prosaic lines. From a condescending helper, the narrator is transformed – through the very lack of anything physical left to do – into a much wiser man who sees beyond the specific act to a more profound, general problem which is at once essentially political and human:

> – I've heard of hearts unkind, kind deeds
> With coldness still returning.
> Alas! the gratitude of men
> Has oftner left me mourning. (LB, 63:101–4)

'Simon Lee' was among the poems singled out by Francis Jeffrey in the *Edinburgh Review* for being as seditious politically as it was unacceptable aesthetically. The central figure, an old, physically decrepit huntsman, was not only patently not a sufficiently 'poetic' subject, he belonged to a class of men whose livelihood depended wholly on being serviceable to a privileged employer, and who were therefore in danger of becoming destitute at a moment's notice. If Simon himself was an unlikely recruit to Jacobinism, younger men in his position might well be expected to turn radical, given the present political climate. Wordsworth's adoption of a mock sentimental verse style to tell his tale constituted a satiric thrust at the political as well as the poetic insensitivity of contemporary magazine poetry and its readership, and Jeffrey clearly registered this as a criticism of much more than just a literary genre.

In 'Anecdote for Fathers', which immediately followed 'Simon Lee' in the 1798 edition of *Lyrical Ballads*, there is a thinly veiled reference to the dilemma of having to choose between an active political life, and one of contemplative retirement, 'wise passiveness'.[23] The poem reveals the extent to which Wordsworth's mind was engrossed with the nature of his own political life, and whether indeed he could think of himself as having one, as much as it was with the actual political issues at stake.

Discussion of this poem generally centres on its presentation of the idea that the instinctive response of the child is to be valued in itself, and that too great an emphasis on rationalisation may be harmful and destructive.[24] The philosophical point is made through differentiating between two categories of knowledge. It may come as a gift of untrammelled human instinct, as it does with the child Wordsworth catechises; or it may be that which is rationally explicable, capable of being codified and thus taught through human agency. Failure to realise that instinctive wisdom is the 'better lore' (LB, 66:58) may lead distressingly to education in little more than lying, or at least specious, devious reasoning. Wordsworth elaborated this point some years later in *The Friend*:

There is a life and spirit in Knowledge which we extract from truths scattered for the benefit of all ... a life and a spirit, which is seldom found in knowledge communicated by formal and direct precepts. (O&S II, 8:21–6)

The narrator of 'Anecdote for Fathers' asks a child where he would rather live, at Kilve or Liswyn Farm. The answer is Kilve; not, one suspects, the expected answer, for although the adult is careful to maintain a neutral tone at the time of asking, he subsequently betrays his own preference for Liswyn by his inability to 'understand' the child. More accurately, he has the sense of being contradicted, and at once attempts to justify his own preference and belittle the child's judgement:

> 'Why this is strange,' said I.
>
> 'For here are woods and green-hills warm;
> There surely must some reason be
> Why you would change sweet Liswyn Farm
> For Kilve by the green sea.' (LB. 65:40–44)

This goes so far as to imply that Kilve is to be thought of as in some way unnatural or unreal with its 'green sea'. Green is the property of the woods and hills of Liswyn. When pressed for an explanation, the child, forced to satisfy his persistent interlocutor, evidently lies, grasping at the first thing he sees to give a sufficiently tangible reason:

> 'At Kilve there was no weather-cock,
> 'And that's the reason why.' (LB, 66:55–6)

The naming of places in 'Anecdote for Fathers' has not been given sufficient attention in the past, and if we reflect on Kilve and Liswyn Farm for a moment, the poem reveals aspects of its moralising that otherwise remain hidden. Kilve is on the Somerset coast, near where the Wordsworths were then living. In other words it represents quite specifically the choice Wordsworth had then made in favour of 'retirement', relinquishing his attempt to become part of the active political world. This resolve is challenged in the poem by the poet's own preference for Liswyn Farm, where the radical London Corresponding Society member John Thelwall lived. Thelwall was by this time a man on the point of being hounded out of what had been a life of intense political activity, though, as E. P. Thompson has argued in his defence, he was far from laying down the cudgels.[25] Political activity of Thelwall's kind, however, might appear by this time to have been energy expended in vain. The choice offered to the boy was therefore charged for Wordsworth with a significance that related to the central debate of his life, and to the issues that lay at the heart of the *Salisbury Plain* poem.

For eight verses of the poem the adult insists on a reasoned, Godwinianly correct answer from the child, who has no objective explanation. He therefore grasps at the first thing he sees, the weathercock at Liswyn, and, with a topsy-turvy logic reminiscent of 'The Idiot Boy', says he prefers Kilve because it does not have one. This answer takes to itself the nature of an ironic symbol of truth, the child's response revealing an ingenuous wisdom, the specifically political implications of which are uncompromising. At Kilve there is no fickle weathercock, forever turning with the changing breeze. Unlike the politician of Liswyn, the poet of Kilve has overcome the uncertainty of purpose and direction. The child has called Wordsworth back to his right mind, and to his true location:

> Oh dearest, dearest boy! my heart
> For better lore would seldom yearn,
> Could I but teach the hundredth part
> Of what from thee I learn. (LB, 66:57–60)[26]

'Simon Lee' and 'Anecdote for Fathers' invite in different ways a reading that recognises the poet's sense of political engagement. 'The Thorn' and 'The Idiot Boy' have by comparison no such political dimensions.

'The Thorn' is one of several poems in the collection that registers Wordsworth's critical response to the popular balladry of the day, and in particular to the Gothic balladry of Gottfried Bürger;[27] it is effectively an exposition of a central dictum laid down in the Preface to *Lyrical Ballads*, that 'the feeling therein developed gives import-ance to the action and situation and not the action and situation to the feeling', a specific contradiction of the popular ballad formula (O&S I, 128:161–3). The suffering portrayed in this poem gathers strength the more illusive it becomes; as Heather Glen explains, 'the customary controlling polite speaker is questioned by voices other than his or her own'.[28] What 'The Thorn' does is to expose a wide, and ever-widening gap between what the literal-minded, super-ficially inquisitive narrator of the poem is able to produce by way of a narration, and anything like a serious engagement with the suffering state of Martha Ray.

The narrator, as active principle, overwhelms the poem, even as the adult overwhelms the child in 'Anecdote for Fathers', with endless questions. The questions in 'The Thorn' are put by a listener to the narrator's tale:

> 'Now wherefore thus, by day and night,
> 'In rain, in tempest, and in snow,
> 'Thus to the dreary mountain-top
> 'Does this poor woman go?
> 'And why sits she beside the thorn
> 'When the blue day-light's in the sky,
> 'Or when the whirlwind's on the hill,
> 'Or frosty air is keen and still,
> 'And wherefore does she cry?–
> 'Oh wherefore? wherefore? tell me why
> 'Does she repeat that doleful cry?' (LB, 72–3:78–88)

The narrator's response is to put together what amounts to a lengthy and detailed account of the woman's story which includes the assumption that she murdered her child, offset continually by the reminder that it is all hearsay, and not to be trusted. His response to the verse above is repeated throughout:

> I cannot tell; I wish I could;
> For the true reason no one knows ... (73:89–90)
>
> No more I know, I wish I did ... (75:1155)
>
> I cannot tell; but some will say ... (77:214)
>
> I cannot tell how this may be ... (78:243)

The tale partakes of Gothic fantasy, and as with 'Simon Lee' the temptation to make a tale, 'action and situation', tends to trivialise the meaning. The tragedy will emerge from reflection undertaken in a mood of wise passiveness, in retirement from the world of the narrator and his associate gossips.

Wordsworth's later note to this poem, suggesting that the narrator is a retired sea captain, should remind us, perhaps, of the passage from *Home at Grasmere* which heads this chapter. When Wordsworth wished to point up the specifically political dilemma that the dichotomy of active and passive presented, his thoughts turned – understandably in a period of great sea battles – to the navy and the insidiously romantic attraction of naval heroics; we shall encounter an important example of this later in *Benjamin the Waggoner*. The political significance of the active and passive dichotomy appears to have been completely displaced in 'The Thorn', as it seems also to be in 'The Idiot Boy'. Displaced is not, however, to say removed. Marjorie Levinson has argued for the way in which certain Lyrical Ballads 'seek to resolve formally, through certain representational strategies' a range of 'sociopolitical themes which had occupied Wordsworth and others less than a decade before and which had become, in the light of the post-revolutionary world, awkward on a number of levels'.[29] In 'Tintern Abbey', for example, Levinson claims that the poet achieves 'the displacement of ideological contradiction to a context where resolution could be imagined and implemented.'[30]

'The Idiot Boy' arguably achieves just such a resolution, offering its major protagonists, the idiot and Betty Foy his mother, as representatives of the passive and active principles respectively. Superficially, as Wordsworth himself was well aware, this poem might appear to be little more than an over-long comment on how the foolish may confound the wise. In fact 'The Idiot Boy' is a case in point of 'the displacement of ideological contradiction'; it owes its conception as much to the poet's political thinking and the way the activist streak in his character continued to haunt him, as to any more general theme or observation on human nature.

The poem tells the story of Betty Foy, who, because she panics, is responsible for a poem far in excess of the length it need have been. Wordsworth's laconic lines in 'Simon Lee' indicate with what distaste, and indeed serious concern, he viewed the long sentimental poems so favoured by contemporary publishers:

> My gentle reader, I perceive
> How patiently you've waited,
> And I'm afraid that you expect
> Some tale will be related. (LB, 62:69–72)

In the second stanza of 'The Idiot Boy' we read:

> – Why bustle thus about your door,
> What means this bustle, Betty Foy?
> Why are you in this mighty fret –

> And why on horseback have you set
> Him whom you love, your idiot boy? (LB, 86:7–11)

Betty's obsession to be 'bustling' (brilliantly conveyed in these lines) sets in motion a train of events that put her beloved idiot boy in danger, and the local doctor to considerable inconvenience; and the complications take a great many stanzas to resolve. The resulting test of the reader's stamina is itself partly the lesson this poem is designed to teach. The sick woman Betty wishes to help proves not to be seriously ill, and had Betty paused and shown a 'wise passiveness', she would no doubt have discovered this at the start. In the fragmentary 'Essay on Morals' written in Germany, 1798–99 (discussed in detail in the following chapter), Wordsworth makes the point very clearly. It is when 'we have been unworthily employed', he explains, 'that we are all activity and keenness.' Our '*good* actions' require no such justification, 'we feel internally their beneficent effect'; but we must first foster the right conditions and the right frame of mind to be able to feel 'internally', rather than react superficially as does Betty (O&S I, 104:43–9).

In like manner, the youthful, condescending narrator of 'Simon Lee' almost misses the truly significant point of his good deed towards the old huntsman because his thought is concentrated on *doing* the good deed, and his words – linked glibly to the 'doing' and not the 'thinking' – are thus small-talk (as they are initially with the narrator of *Resolution and Independence*). In 'Simon Lee' our thoughts are directed towards the social politics which have created the immediate situation of Simon's abandonment in old age by his employer, and how this might be overcome. In 'The Idiot Boy' we are left to provide for ourselves a possible connection between the sick old lady needing help, and Wordsworth seeking his proper role in relation to the ills of society when rightly diagnosed. Such wisdom is concealed within the apparently inappropriate response of Johnny to his mother's anxiety. Against Betty's ineptitude, the child's serenity effectively inverts the knowledge of the worldly wise:

> 'The cocks did crow to-whoo, to-whoo,
> 'And the sun did shine so cold.' (LB, 101:460–1)

Images of inversion and contradiction appear at key points throughout Wordsworth's poetry. *The Prelude* abounds in them: the intrusion into an idyllic moonlit landscape of the mendicant soldier in Book IV overturns the romantic dreaming that preceded it; the anti-climax of crossing the Alps heralds the remarkable Simplon Pass passage in Book VI where all nature becomes an experience of contradictions; and in Book XIII Wordsworth climbs Snowdon to see the sunrise, discovers instead the moon, and rather than standing upon a lofty mountain top, finds himself to be 'on the shore ... of a huge sea of mist / Which meek and silent rested at my feet'. Far from being taken up above the world, his mind is drawn – against every image previously given to describe the climb – downwards into the earth, 'That dark deep thoroughfare' where 'Nature lodged / The soul, the imagination of the whole' (460:40–65). Betty Foy's idiot child has this wisdom, his vision of the world is a true one, contradicting the would-be sensible mother.

In Kelvin Everest's discussion of the theme of 'retirement', undertaken with particular reference to Coleridge, he emphasises the sense of uncertainty that late-eighteenth-century poets experienced, in terms of their relationship to the reading public, a situation very different from the one enjoyed by Pope or Thomson. 'The Idiot Boy' might even seem to suggest that a wise view of the world gained through retirement from its 'bustle' might now be deemed idiocy by the majority. Everest notes Maren-Sophie Rostvig's seminal work on retirement, which locates its origins as a literary genre with ousted Royalists in the seventeenth century. The addition of ousted Whigs after 1688 to the purveyors of the retirement ideal is not mentioned, and needs to be. The increasing need for Coleridge and Wordsworth to justify assumptions which bound together retirement, passivity and wisdom, assumptions they could no longer assume were widely held, resulted in their poetry, unable to assume a public sympathy, locating the 'grounds of belief ... internally and subjectively', in 'a new emphasis on the structuring power of consciousness over reality.'[31] The 'focus on states of mind', Everest suggests, is particularly evident in *Lyrical Ballads*. There is a crisis in the relationship between private experience and public life the shock of which is mediated by poems like 'Simon Lee', 'The Thorn' and 'The Idiot Boy'.

One particularly striking expression of the tension between the active and passive principles occurs in 'The Complaint of the Forsaken Indian Woman', which was placed towards the end of the 1798 volume, becoming in 1800 the penultimate poem, 'Tintern Abbey' conculuding the collection.

'The Complaint' moves from focussing on the state of mind of 'idiocy' to that imagined to accompany imminent death. The mood of the doomed woman vacillates between submissiveness to death on the one hand, and on the other, belief that resignation had perhaps been encouraged prematurely:

> Oh how grievously I rue
> That, afterwards, a little longer,
> My friends I did not follow you. (LB 109:26–8)

Death becomes here part of a dramatic metaphor for the ultimate retirement. Indecision, the strength of instinctive human affections, the parting of mother and child, the sense of inevitable loss and failure all combine in a harrowing recreation of a situation where little if any relief is allowed. Wordsworth's lack of initiative when it came to making an active contribution in the political arena (in France or England), and his sense even at the time of writing 'The Complaint' that his powers as a poet were on the wane, would both seem to inform at a personal level his depiction of the woman left to die by her tribe.

It may at first seem strange that in the context of the *Lyrical Ballads*, a series of poems predominantly based on rural life in Dorset and Cumberland, Wordsworth should decide to include a poem inspired by the discovery that it was the custom among certain American Indians to abandon a dying member of the tribe when that tribe was emigrating. However, his reflections on the conflicting emotions of a mother in this situation, her wish to remain with her child and her equally strong attachment to the welfare of her people as a whole, a people now prepared to leave her to die, renders 'The Complaint' consistent with the major themes that inform the other poems in the collection. The subject matter provided Wordsworth with a situation with which he was clearly able to identify, not least because memories of Annette and their child were no doubt also woven into its fabric. That there is a political point of reference at the heart of the 'feeling therein developed' is given further credence by the fact that a likely model for 'The Complaint' was Thomas Day's political poem of 1775, 'The Complaint of the Dying Negro'.[32]

'Hart-Leap Well', the first poem in Volume II of the 1800 *Lyrical Ballads*, is in many respects a very different kind of poem from those so far considered. In its use of a medieval tale for subject matter, it seems initially to be something of a throwback to the Gothic balladry of Percy's *Reliques*. The poem, however, is in two contrasting parts, and therein lies its purpose. The first part, using Spenserian diction and a galloping metre, tells the story of Sir Walter, a knight who pursues a hart long after the rest of his companions have fallen exhausted by the wayside. The style of the poetry, combined with what we are told of the knight's feelings, suggest excitement, firm resolution, and all the glamour of aggressive action:

> 'Another Horse!' That shout the Vassal heard,
> And saddled his best steed, a comely Grey;
> Sir Walter mounted him; he was the third
> Which he had mounted on that glorious day. (LB, 127:5–8)

But Wordsworth himself occasionally undercuts the expected sentiment, and it is therefore important to stress that while the chase is in progress, the knight is carefully portrayed as oblivious to all but the excitement that accompanies his resolve:

> Joy sparkled in the prancing Courser's eyes;
> The horse and horseman are a happy pair;
> But, though Sir Walter like a falcon flies,
> There is a doleful silence in the air. (LB, 127:9–12)

The hunt has changed from what seemed legitimate sport to something more sinister in its implications:

> Where is the throng, the tumult of the chace?
> The bugles that so joyfully were blown?
> – This race it looks not like an earthly race;
> Sir Walter and the Hart are left alone. (LB, 128:25–8)

When Sir Walter finally catches up with the Hart, he finds it lying dead by a spring at the foot of a hill, 'it was at least / Nine roods of sheer ascent' (LB, 129:49–50). The hart has met its death by plunging down the precipice, and the knight discovers 'Three several marks with which his hoofs the beast / Had left imprinted on the verdant ground' (129:51–2).

> Sir Walter wiped his face, and cried, 'Till now
> Such sight was never seen by living eyes:
> Three leaps have born him from this lofty brow,
> Down to the very fountain where he lies. (LB, 129:53–6)

As the second part of the poem makes clear, the knight's mood of elation and sense of achievement are ill founded, as are his plans to build a 'Pleasure-house' and 'basin for that fountain in the dell' on the spot where the incident occurred. He intends to enlist the help, we should note, of 'A cunning Artist' (LB, 129:57, 62, 61).

Part II brings us to the present time, the Spenserian flourishes disappear, and Wordsworth, in the plain, dogged and sometimes repetitive manner that so annoyed some of his early critics, describes his own discovery of Hart-leap Well, and how he hears its story related by a passing shepherd. As with 'Anecdote for Fathers' and 'The Idiot Boy', there is a very simple moral immediately available from the state of the place. Eyeing what appears to be a mortally wounded pastoral landscape, the shepherd says 'I've guessed, when I've been sitting in the sun, / That it was all for that unhappy Hart.' (LB, 132:139–40)

The poet himself was evidently feeling for the beautiful hunted creature in the first part of the poem, and despite the knight's excitement, it is clear that a grossly unnatural deed has been perpetrated:

> Then home he went, and left the Hart, stone-dead,
> With breathless nostrils stretch'd above the spring.
>
> (LB, 130:77–8)

Four lines later we are given the chilling information that before long 'A cup of stone receiv'd the living well.'

But in the second part Wordsworth only provisionally accepts the shepherd's explanation. Just as there are at least two perceptions of the hunt in Part I, so there exists a superficial interpretation of its meaning, and a more profound one:

> 'Grey-headed Shepherd, thou hast spoken well;
> Small difference lies between thy creed and mine;
> This beast not unobserv'd by Nature fell,
> His death was mourn'd by sympathy divine.
>
> The Being, that is in the clouds and air,
> That is in the green leaves among the groves,
> Maintains a deep and reverential care
> For them the quiet creatures whom he loves. (LB, 133:161–8)

Wordsworth is here taking a broader view of events informed by the 'one life' philosophy, his reference to 'The Being, that is in the clouds and air, / That is in the green leaves among the groves' indicates this clearly. In consequence what is in the shepherd's eyes a story of local interest, tied to specific people at a specific time, becomes a matter of universal significance.

Obsessive activity (the unbridled 'passion' so feared by Harrington) is once more shown as untrustworthy; and in the image of the hunt, 'the tumult of the chace ... The bugles that so joyfully were blown' (128:25–6), we have certainly to allow for a private reference to the misleading influence of revolutionary enthusiasm that had laid waste Wordsworth's mind in previous years. The contrast he drew in *The Prelude* between his childhood experience of skating in the company of others:

> imitative of the chace
> And woodland pleasures, the resounding horn,
> The pack loud bellowing ... (I 52:462–4)

and as a lone figure 'retired ... from the uproar' where the 'visible motion' of the earth itself became apparent to him, a sobering, controlling influence, points to the same moral (52:476 and 486).

It was through his immediate, personal experience of political enthusiasm (comparable within the structure of the peom to the specific story about Sir Walter) that Wordsworth came to his understanding of the wider moral issues involved. Just as we need the Gothic ballad of Sir Walter (once more prompted by one of Bürger's poems) to be present for the modern Lyrical Ballad to work, so we need a sense of the poet's personal drama to appreciate the underlying moral, and what Jonathan Wordsworth has interpreted as an anticipation of 'the non-political millenium of love and knowledge'.[33]

Despite Jonathan Wordsworth's tendency to emphasis the religious vision that emerges from Wordsworth's work at the expense of political conviction, it begins to become increasingly clear just how intimately bound up with his immediate experiences of political choice and commitment the *Lyrical Ballads* poems tend to be. In a variety of ways they repeat the poet's own personal drama, albeit in a manner that displaces, or relocates the political issue. In this respect the crisis of relationship between poet and public discussed by Everest plays a central role in the formulation of the poetry, and complements Levinson's detailed account of 'Tintern

Abbey'. According to Levinson, 'Tintern Abbey' is essentially political in its conception, dealing with its subject in the manner of, say, 'Anecdote for Fathers' in so far as it creates an alternative set of circumstances through which it may address those issues.[34] The essential difference between poems like 'Anecdote for Fathers', 'Simon Lee', 'The Thorn', 'Hart-Leap Well', and 'Tintern Abbey' is that in the former group an inadequate, popular poetic formula is ironically undermined, while in 'Tintern Abbey' the landscape or prospect genre is taken and transformed into something which arguably achieves a new and perhaps unique form of poetic expression.

The extent to which the poet's experience of a deeply personal political anguish could contribute to even the apparently simplest poetry represented in *Lyrical Ballads* is evident from 'The Childless Father'. This immediately precedes 'The Old Cumberland Beggar', a poem as overtly political as 'The Childless Father' appears immersed in its world of private sorrow.

In the 1800 Preface Wordsworth cites this poem as an exemplar of the way feeling could give meaning to action and situation. The action is indeed minimal, essentially an old man gently closing the door of his cottage; here then is not even the possibility of drama that accompanies Simon Lee's efforts with the recalcitrant tree root. The 'feeling' centres on the death of the old man's daughter; as with so many of the Ballads – the 'Lucy' poems, 'The Complaint', 'We Are Seven', 'Michael' – the theme is one of acute loss:

> The bason of box-wood, just six months before,
> Had stood on the table at Timothy's door,
> A Coffin through Timothy's threshold has pass'd,
> One Child did it bear and that Child was his last.
>
> (LB, 204:109–12)

The reader's response to bereavement at a personal, private level constitutes the basis from which any reading of this poem must begin; but the use of contrasting activities once again must alert us to a social and, by implication, political dimension in the poem that remains as an unresolved counterpoint to the private, internalised statement, even as it did in the poet's life.

The old man's grief has separated him from the wild and energetic activity of the hunt, referred to here yet again. Personal tragedy imposes a passive solemnity on the father, closing the door with a 'leisurely motion', while on the hillside the chase pursues its wild, chaotic course. The hunt, coming down through the picturesque poetic conventions employed, for example, by Crowe in *Lewesdon Hill*, has for its metaphorical meaning society in full, collective career; and the old man, like Wordsworth, is forced into an alienated stance, sensing in consequence a more profound depth of feeling and meaning than anything accomplished at a collective level. He goes, in due course, to be once more a part of the 'Noise and the fray', but 'with a tear on his cheek'.

The Wordsworth of *Lyrical Ballads* is no less a political poet than the fugitive writer of *Salisbury Plain*, 'wise passiveness' has rather made possible an alternative and more mature basis from which to reflect on the issues at stake.

7
Goslar:
patriotic and domestic love

That sense of dim similitude which links
Our moral feelings with external forms.
(*The Prelude*, Part One, 17:164–5)

The expedition to Germany of 1798–99 was a failure. The party split up, Coleridge travelling on to study at Ratzeburg and Göttingen, while the Wordsworths found themselves in what promised to be the less expensive city of Goslar. Their intention had been to become sufficiently proficient in the language to undertake translations of what in England were now the fashionable works of German poets and philosophers. But they remained unable to gain the necessary entrée into Goslar society and swiftly declined, as one critic has suggested, 'into misery and homesickness.'[1] Wordsworth's dislike of 'sickly and stupid German Tragedies'[2] may well owe at least something to painful memories of the indifference bordering on ostracism meted out by Goslar bourgeois society, not to mention the unprecedentedly cold winter that imprisoned the pair of them there for some five months.

The history of Wordsworth's creative achievements during this period should be seen in the context of a set of circumstances that bear a number of important similarities to the situation following his return to England in 1792. The enforced retirement at Racedown (grudgingly born for much of the time[3]) was experienced all over again, but was arguably made even worse by virtue of its being in a foreign country. In Dorset Coleridge had appeared, and had been instrumental in beginning to recreate a social world and a sense of purpose within it for the poet. Now there was nothing but the longing to return to the north of England, and the additional injury of Coleridge's absence 'in a very different world from what we stir in', as Dorothy somewhat tartly wrote; 'he is all in high life, among Barons counts and countesses'. (EY, p. 245)

It was understandably therefore not Germany but England that dominated Wordsworth's mind at this time. He began to write and assemble autobiographical and reflective passages into the first Part of what became the two-part *Prelude* of 1798–99, to compose the 'Lucy' poems, and also to work at further possible revisions of the *Salisbury Plain* text (Reed, p. 261). Writing according to Dorothy, was undertaken in a state of considerable mental and physical discomfort (EY, p. 236). Wordsworth's sense of isolation manifested itself in the visionary intensity with which such incidents as the skating episode and stealing the boat were recalled for *The Prelude*, and with the atmosphere of melancholy that distinguishes 'A Slumber Did My Spirit Seal', 'Strange Fits of Passion I have Known', 'She dwelt among th'untrodden ways' and 'Ruth' from the earlier Lyrical Ballads.

The peculiar circumstances of Goslar did not obliterate the political debate that had informed the conception of the 1798 *Lyrical Ballads*. In many ways they were inclined to intensify it. The skating episode from *The Prelude* has already been noted in this respect, with its competing elements of the intoxicating, wild, collective hunt, and the contrasting solitary experience of profound tranquility. *The Prelude*, focussed though it was on childhood memories, was being composed as an answer to the charge he continued to level at himself of failing to respond actively to the political challenge of events some six years before. Left alone on Salisbury Plain he had agonised over his inadequacies and short-comings with respect both to his public and private life; now his failure to integrate left him once more isolated, painfully writing himself into an autobiographical justificaton of wise passivity, while still brooding over the manuscript of *Salisbury Plain*.

Before considering the poetry in this light, it is important to remember that a prose work was contemplated and begun in Goslar, the 'Essay on Morals'. In 1793 Wordsworth had attempted to state his political position in prose, and the polemic of the *Letter to Llandaff* complemented the poetic statement of *Salisbury Plain*. Now, once more composing poetry in a time of unhappiness and even despair, he decided once more to review his political position, with a wish characteristic of eighteenth-century radical Whig thinking to stress the importance of 'morality' and the 'affections'. The poet of 1799 continued to measure aesthetic practice against political conviction formulated in prose, and to seek ways of reconciling the two. The problem of reconciling an eye trained in picturesque perception with a mind overwhelmed by political injustice had begun to be apparent with the female vagrant sequence of *An Evening Walk*; it had become a central issue for *Salisbury Plain*, while in the first volume of *Lyrical Ballads* it was addressed more obliquely through the narrative technique of poems like 'Simon Lee', where the picturesque setting of 'the sweet shire of Cardigan' acquires an ironic edge once the condition of the old huntsman living there is described. In 'The Thorn' it is the narrator's superficial perception – of people and of natural objects like the thorn – that suggests a hopeless lack of understanding and sympathy between society and the poet's tragic subject, the outcast Martha Ray.

Now this same sense of a potentially tragic rift began to help shape *The Prelude*. Wordsworth was by this time aware also of a loss of creative power, and he was acutely aware – in common with many other poets of the period – of a gulf existing between poet and reader, and most vividly during this time of unexpected and uncomfortable exile, he felt the widening gap between his present state and that of his childhood in the Lake District. The pressure caused by conflicting claims on his energies in adult life continued to lie at the heart of his creative efforts: the claims of action and wise passiveness, of social life and the 'retirement' necessary for creative work, of 'Two consciousnesses – conscious of myself, / And of some other being' (*Prelude* 14:30–1). In *The Prelude* Wordsworth began to develop the view that such apparent conflicts might not be irreconcilable, but rather that they might be complementary, even as childhood was to adulthood, and with this came the notion that he was to reflect not on opposites, but on primary and secondary facets of self-knowledge.

The creative impetus that lies behind the writing of the two-part *Prelude* can only properly be appreciated when we take account of the poet's political frame of mind revealed in the 'Essay on Morals'. From his uncomfortably 'passive' state in Goslar, Wordsworth began the Essay by stating his opposition to the belief that 'the actions of men' may be the subject of a systematically contrived set of rules. It was the active principle he wished to analyse, considering what 'action' signified, and how it came about. Our actions, he argued, are the result of 'habits':

I know no book or system of moral philosophy written with sufficient power to melt into our affections [?s], to incorporate itself with the blood and vital juices of our minds, & thence to have any influence worth our notice in forming those habits of which I am speaking. (O&S I, 103:18–22)

In the Essay Wordsworth does not clearly define what he means by 'habits', but the intention behind the terminology begins to be apparent from this passage. Moral philosophy rationalised into systems, not moral philosophy itself, is inadequate. The Essay was intended to reveal a means of understanding and describing sources of action, and it initiates a quest for a moral philosophy that will lead to, or 'influence', good actions. To this end moral philosophy must in some sense be understood as organic, residing in 'the blood and vital juices of our minds', a sentiment echoing what had already been stated in 'Tintern Abbey'.[4] Implicit in this is a theoretical justification for the subject matter of *The Prelude*, impressions from nature gained in childhood which have consequently become part of the poet's consciousness. Informing this view is Wordsworth's awareness of the structures of the eighteenth-century debate on the mind and the way knowledge was acquired. In *An Evening Walk* he had observed that 'the simplest sight' may invoke 'th'unbidden tear'. This brief and unexceptional reference illustrates a concept of associationism between that which is observed to be physically present and the 'affections'; from the mid 1790s this belief gradually evolved into a far more complex and sophisticated theory of discrimination between poetic subject and object. The influence of Hartleyan associationism was crucial to this development, though Wordsworth came to consider Hartley's approach too mechanistic; to some degree still influencial was Locke's theory of related 'primary' and 'secondary' qualities in the acquisition of understanding.[5]

Seeing himself as the victim of an erroneous association of thought and action in the early 1790s, Wordsworth looked again at habits of mind, the bases of our actions, and considered what the primary source might constitute if our secondary, active response was to bear fruit of any worth. The target of the Essay is very clear. By suggesting that our actions are the results of 'habits', Wordsworth is claiming that what we do originates from a motivation not satisfactorily analysed by 'such books as Mr. Godwyn's [*sic*], Mr. Paley's, & those whole tribe of authors' engaged in that quest (O&S I, 103:3–4). Wordsworth is attacking reason when it assumes

the guise of Godwinian rationalism, as he had done in *The Borderers*.
Political sensibility, he believes, clearly cannot be dealt with
separately from the primary influence of 'the blood and vital juices of
our minds':

Can it be imagined by any man who has deeply examined his own heart that
an old habit will be forgone, or a new one formed, by a series of
propositions, which, presenting no image to the [?mind] can convey no
feeling which has any connection with the supposed archetype or fountain
of the proposition existing in human life? (O&S I, 103:23–8)

In Part Two of *The Prelude* he was to write of 'That sense of dim
similtude which links / Our moral feelings with external things'
(17:164–5), and in utilising the philosophical position proposed in
the Essay he reveals the underlying reason for his imaginative
reconstruction of early childhood years. The scheme of *The Prelude*
was to provide a poetic structure capable of reconciling archetypal
moral instincts with political initiative, Wordsworth's overwhelming
personal psychological need in the wake of the events of 1792–93.
The 'old habit' of mind is morally sound because it is seen as linked
to images absorbed by him from his early years, images associated
with 'external things'. By contrast the rationally conceived 'series of
propositions' that rose before him for the first time in 1792–93 are
revealed with growing clarity as superficial; things falsely grafted
onto an otherwise healthy mind:

I have said that these bald and naked reasonings are impotent over our
habits, they cannot form them; from the same cause they are equally
powerless in regulating our judgments concerning the value of men &
things. (O&S I, 103:33–6)

Man as a political animal is not being rejected here; such a notion
was always alien to Wordsworth's thinking. What is being recog-
nised is the secondary, or *subsequent* quality of a practical political
consciousness; it is only rightly conceived of when it is understood
to be an extension of the so-called 'old clothing' of our minds, not an
alternative frame of mind which must first strip that old clothing
away (O&S I, 103:28–30). We start, Wordsworth writes, with
'things' which eventually we must find words for. Political theorists
who believe they begin with a blank sheet, and are at liberty to
create political man without reverence for an existing moral code
already endemic to nature, take 'words' as their absolutes and

endeavour to make 'things' justify the subjective meanings of their words:

The whole secret of this juggler's trick [?s] lies (not in fitting words to things (which would be a noble employment) but) in fitting things to words. (O&S I, 103:31–3)

The purpose of *The Prelude* is in fact to give these 'things' a conceptual framework; thus the experie. ~e of seeing the solitary girl with the pitcher, or seeing the mountain peak rise above what was hitherto believed to be the horizon, the terminating point of the world of experiences, is a fitting of 'words' to 'things' (*Prelude* 48–50:394–412). In these revelatory experiences – or things – reside the fundamental moral and spiritual qualities of human life; words are their servants. They are what we measure by, not what we should seek to measure. This point was to be recast in clearer and more forthright terms in the 1800 Preface to *Lyrical Ballads* in a passage now familiar: 'the feeling therein developed gives importance to the action and situation and not the action and situation to the feeling'. This belief lay at the heart of Wordsworth's dissatisfaction with contemporary views of what constituted a poetic subject, and from it sprang his new style of writing, a way of using words – of presenting poetry – fundamentally antagonistic to the demands of an Augustan reviewer like Jeffrey.

'Words' in the Essay have become in the Preface 'action and situation', the superficial or secondary quality of composition, while 'things' relate to the more profound 'feeling therein developed', a phrase picking up Wordsworth's insistence earlier in the Preface that 'the passions of men are incorporated with the beautiful and permanent forms of nature' (O&S I, 124:85–6). In the 'Essay on Morals' we find that the degree of influence which rational argument should have on our 'conduct & actions' (O&S I, 103:11) is held to be considerably less than Godwin had claimed in *Political Justice*:

We do not *argue* in defence of our good actions, we feel internally their beneficent effect; we are satisfied with this delicious sensation; &, even when we are called upon to justify our conduct, we perform the task with languor and indifference. Not so when we have been unworthily employed; then it is that we are all activity and keenness; then it is that we repair to systems of morality for arguments in defence of ourselves; & sure enough are we to find them. (O&S I, 104:43–9)

Despite the failure of the Essay to progress beyond a few sketchy paragraphs, the part it played as an initial point of reference for the project of *The Prelude* should not be underestimated. The Essay makes it clear that Wordsworth's mind was intent still upon the issues raised by his experiences in the early 1790s. As he came to find that *The Prelude* was developing the capacity to sustain and investigate the issues in question, it is not surprising that the prose exercise was soon discarded. Defining the c... gmatic 'things' of the Essay, therefore, became a problem for the poet, where he conceives of 'eternal things' perceived through the 'delicious sensation' of childhood experience:

> Ah, not in vain ye beings of the hills,
> And ye that walk the woods and open heaths
> By moon or star-light, thus, from my first dawn
> Of childhood, did ye love to intertwine
> The passions that build up our human soul
> Not with the mean and vulgar works of man,
> But with high objects, with eternal things,
> With life and Nature, purifying thus
> The elements of feeling and of thought,
> And sanctifying by such discipline
> Both pain and fear, until we recognise
> A grandeur in the beatings of the heart. (4:130–41)

The 'mean and vulgar works of man' refer to actions emanating from the systematic political philosophies of Godwin and Paley and their like (past and present), a dangerously rationalist view over against the guidance of 'life and Nature, purifying thus / The elements of feeling and of thought'.

In Part Two the poem continues the search for the sources of our good actions, 'that still spirit', through a sensuous invocation of childhood:

> O, ye rocks and streams,
> And that still spirit of the evening air,
> Even in this joyous time I sometimes felt
> Your presence, when, with slackened step, we breathed
> Along the sides of the steep hills, or when,
> Lightened by gleams of moonlight from the sea,
> We beat with thundering hoofs the level sand. (17:133–9)

Though it may not be immediately apparent from the text, the theme of a search for political wisdom informs the contrasting active and passive experiences of the 'slackened step' and the 'thundering hoofs' remembered and described here. When the French Revolution eventually became the overt subject for Books IX and X of the extended 1805 *Prelude*, Wordsworth chose to quote verbatim from what had then become Book II, lines 138–44: 'Along the margin of the moonlight sea, / We beat with thundering hooves the level sand' (388:565–6). The reappearance of the same contrasting images in Book X is set in the context of recalling the effect that the news of Robespierre's death had had on him. The Book X passage therefore suggests that when the reminiscence was first noted in 1798–99, it was not without its deeper personal significance. The recollection is there – in the two-part *Prelude* and in later versions – because of the politically 'beneficent effect' the 'Essay on Morals' was concerned to discuss at the time when the two-part poem was first being written.

The passages from the original *Prelude* and from Book X of the 1805 poem appear even more closely allied in imagery and political import if we look at their wider contexts in the case of each text. News of the death of Robespierre is preceeded in Book X by the poet's account of his visit to the grave of William Taylor, the headmaster at Hawkshead whom Wordsworth so revered; there he describes at length the landscape, bringing together the contrasting 'smooth sands / Of Leven's ample aestuary' with the distant mountains in a vision of reconciliation and wholeness, of 'one life':

> Over the smooth sands
> Of Leven's ample aestuary lay
> My journey, and beneath a genial sun,
> With distant prospect among gleams of sky
> And clouds, and intermingled mountain-tops,
> In one inseperable glory clad – (384:474–9)

In the paragraph following the passage from Part Two quoted above, we read again of a landscape where mountains harmonise with a peaceful foreground, though instead of the 'smooth sands', we are shown the 'calm smooth lake' of Coniston (17:156); and here, as in Book X, our thoughts are directed elegaically towards death:

> And there I said,
> That beauteous sight before me, there I said
> (Then first beginning in my thoughts to mark
> That sense of dim similitude which links

Our moral feelings with external forms)
That in whatever region I should close
My mortal life I would remember you,
Fair scenes – that Dying I would think on you,
My soul would send a longing look to you,
Even as that setting sun, while all the vale
Could nowhere catch one faint memorial gleam,
Yet with the last remains of his last light
Still lingered, and a farewell lustre threw
On the dear mountain-tops where first he rose.

(17–18:161–74)

Book X perceives a crucial relationship between the political significance of Robespierre's death, and the awesome sense gained of hard-won fulfilment from a unifying, 'one life' vision derived from contemplating natural objects; and with this tutelary experience comes the enhanced memory of the person who taught the poet when he was a boy. Such sensitivity exists also in the early lines on Coniston. Though the process of reading meaning back into the 1798–99 text from the 1805 *Prelude* is important to this argument, it is only a part of the process. The 'Essay on Morals' reveals a mind already focussed on the major themes elaborated in the later books, and the two-part *Prelude* itself indicates Wordsworth becoming uncomfortably aware that his account was beginning to sound far too sophisticated as a description of how he had felt as a child; in consequence he inserted a bracketed clause, 'dimming' what was by 1799 becoming very clear to him indeed, and then added a rather awkward footnote to complete the paragraph:

'Twas then my fourteenth summer, and these words
Were uttered in a casual access
Of sentiment, a momentary trance
That far outran the habit of my mind. (18:175–8)

The whole passage (140–79) continued to give Wordsworth concern, and he omitted it from the 1805 text. It was restored in the 1850 version to Book VIII.

The *Lyrical Ballads* of 1798 revealed a profound change in Wordsworth's understanding of both poetic language and subject. From its earliest draft fragments, *The Prelude* equally distances the poetry of the West Country years from the earlier phase which culminated in *Salisbury Plain*. The Miltonic blank verse denotes the poet's continuing sense of a literary continuity with an English epic tradition rooted in seventeenth-century politics and culture, and despite the originality of what he set himself to achieve during his time at Racedown and Alfoxden, it remains important to stress the way the influence of eighteenth-century radical Whig thought resulted in a fundamental continuity in his work.

The change from the late Augustan form of *An Evening Walk* and *Descriptive Sketches* to the 'strange imaginative power'[6] of the blank verse of 1798–99 was not occasioned by a profound change of political conviction. It evolved from a series of experiments undertaken to establish a style – or styles – which would reflect the poet's sense of a need for a society radically reformed in accordance with eighteenth-century radical Whig precepts; and this had been at the root of his poetry since *An Evening Walk*.

The themes of guilt, judgement, and individual hardship remained firmly fixed; he sought, in his quest for the source of man's primary moral instincts, an explanation for the inevitable loneliness and struggle of individuals who must make their way 'with difficult steps ... against the blowing wind'. If we recall the sailor's encounter with the gibbet early in the second version of *Salisbury Plain* (Gill, 126: 112–16), we can indeed see how he was, in his now habitual manner, returning constantly in his poetry to a central theme, the interrelation of political virtue and integrity with the sources of his own imaginative powers. In Part One of the 1798–99 *Prelude* the fiction of *Salisbury Plain* is blended with autobiography in the following passage:

> We had not travelled long ere some mischance
> Disjoined me from my comrade, and, through fear
> Dismounting, down the rough and stony moor
> I led my horse, and stumbling on, at length
> Came to a bottom where in former times
> A man, the murderer of his wife, was hung
> In irons. Mouldered was the gibbet-mast;
> The bones were gone, the iron and the wood;
> Only a long green ridge of turf remained
> Whose shape was like a grave. I left the spot,
> And reascending the bare slope I saw
> A naked pool that lay beneath the hills,
> The beacon on the summit, and more near
> A girl who bore a pitcher on her head,

> And seemed with difficult steps to force her way
> Against the blowing wind. It was in truth
> An ordinary sight, but I should need
> Colours and words that are unknown to man
> To paint the visionary dreariness
> Which, while I looked all round for my lost guide,
> Did at that time invest the naked pool,
> The beacon on the lonely eminence,
> The woman and her garments vexed and tossed
> By the strong wind. (9:304–27)

The significance of the gibbet as a terrifying symbol of guilt haunting the poet, has not fundamentally changed in its transference from the Spenserian didactic narrative to the Miltonic autobiographical poem, though the means by which a resolution to the implied crisis of conscience was sought had certainly changed.

The latter nine lines of the passage from *The Prelude* are a powerful realisation of Wordsworth's state of mind when on Salisbury Plain; the 'visionary dreariness' he experiences as he seeks his 'lost guide' combined with the image of the solitary girl struggling forward against the wind, epitomise the period of his life where we must eventually locate the underlying inspiration for *The Prelude*; that is to say, *not* childhood, but the traumatic years after his return from France. The clue to that location lies in the appropriation from *Salisbury Plain* of the gibbet, encountered in 1793 after the loss of his companion (his 'guide'), William Calvert. In *Salisbury Plain* the suspended body is swung 'by the tempest sweeping by', in *The Prelude*, though the body is no longer in evidence, the girl struggles against the blowing wind. What is new in the mind of the man composing *The Prelude*, is the conviction now that he had been tutored even as a child to encounter and survive such 'dreariness'. As a memory of childhood, the experience is now one that unites it with permanent forms of nature; in other words it signifies potential reconciliation for the whole creation of God, its relevance goes far beyond the material and political world of mankind that dominates *Salisbury Plain*. Within this context it is possible, though not without a struggle, to look for a framework of order and reason that may restore a temporarily unbalanced mind.

Cross-references of this kind to *Salisbury Plain* indicate that the political issues of the early poem remain central to the composition of the later work, though as with the Lyrical Ballads already discussed, the politics have become submerged or, as Marjorie Levinson and David Simpson have argued, 'displaced' through the introduction of forms of alternative discourse.[7]

Wordsworth's initial enthusiasm for the French Revolution informs the opening lines of Part Two of *The Prelude* by way of contrasting once again active and passive principles. He is at once the ingenuous disciple of Beaupuy, keen to act in accordance with his new-found desire to root out political injustice; he is the active but essentially unenlightened philanthropist of 'Simon Lee', filled with the 'eagerness of infantine desire'; he is the sadder and wiser young man who parted from the discharged soldier on the road to Hawkshead; or again he is the poet who so drastically modified his opinion of the fisherman in *Poems on the Naming of Places*, offering there his own poem as 'a monitory voice to tame / The pride of virtue and of intellect':

> Ah, is there one who ever has been young
> And needs a monitory voice to tame
> The pride of virtue and of intellect?
> And is there one, the wisest and the best
> Of all mankind, who does not sometimes wish
> For things which cannot be, who would not give,
> If so he might, to duty and to truth
> The eagerness of infantine desire?
> A tranquilizing spirit presses now
> On my corporeal frame, so wide appears
> The vacancy between me and those days,
> Which yet have such self-presence in my heart
> That sometimes when I think of them I seem
> Two consciousnesses – conscious of myself
> And of some other being. (14:17–31)

For Wordsworth the French Revolution was assuming the character of an aberration, a series of political events distorting the true course of progress towards greater social and political justice. The *Prelude* of 1798–99 therefore excludes direct reference to the political event, and offers instead memories of childhood calculated to reaffirm the political philosophy he had initially and erroneously supposed to be informing the revolutionary upheavals of the 1790s:

> No delicate viands sapped our bodily strength:
> More than we wished we knew the blessing then

> Of vigorous hunger, for our daily meals
> Were frugal, Sabine fare. (15–16:79–82)

This is training not just in 'bodily strength', but also in spiritual and moral healthiness, and it accords with the puritanical strain so often encountered in Real Whig political philosophising. It is an attitude which persists when Wordsworth finally turned to the French Revolution as subject matter for the poem in 1804. The political context in which Book IX firmly places the virtuous qualities of 'ancient homliness, / Manners erect, and frank simplicity' (322:219–20) to be found in the 'poor district' where Wordsworth was born, is not peculiar to the latter books of the 1805 version; it was there from the first in the 1798–99 *Prelude*, along with the 'Sabine fare', and the cautionary gibbet brought forward from *Salisbury Plain*.

The influence of eighteenth-century political philosophy is equally important in the following passage from Part Two, and operates again as an implicit critique of later radical political initiatives:

> Thus day by day my sympathies increased,
> And thus the common range of visible things
> Grew dear to me: already I began
> To love the sun, a boy I loved the sun
> Not as I since have loved him – as a pledge
> And surety of my earthly life, a light
> Which while I view I feel I am alive –
> But for this cause, that I had seen him lay
> His beauty on the morning hills, had seen
> The western mountains touch his setting orb
> In many a thoughtless hour, when from excess
> Of happiness my blood appeared to flow
> With its own pleasure, and I breathed with joy.
> And from like feeelings, humble though intense,
> To patriotic and domestic love
> Analogous, the moon to me was dear:
> For I would dream away my purposes
> Standing to look upon her, while she hung
> Midway between the hills as if she knew
> No other region but belonged to thee,
> Yea, appertained by a peculiar right
> To thee and thy grey huts, my native vale. (19:215–36)

The poet's 'sympathies' are initially awakened by his awareness of natural objects; there is an undiscerning, instinctive delight and love brought forth by the sun as it shines on the mountains. His later love of the sun has become a more self-conscious, less mystical experience of thanksgiving for his own continued 'earthly life, / Which while I view I feel I am alive', the thrice repeated 'I' emphasises the change.

The moon had also influenced him, operating in a more subtle, gentle way on his consciousness to inspire feelings 'To patriotic and domestic love / Analogous'. It was the moon, also, that led him to 'dream away my purposes'; yet another reference to inactivity paradoxically associated with profound revelation.

Complaints that 'patriotic and domestic love' were increasingly rare commodities in the body-politic were something of a commonplace in eighteenth-century English poetry, the two qualities generally being represented as interdependent. The 'vagrant' poems of the period drew inexhaustibly on this theme, as did more extended pieces like Langhorn's *The Country Justice*, Goldsmith's *The Deserted Village* and Crabbe's narratives. Wordsworth had shown himself well acquainted with the genre by the time of *Descriptive Sketches*, where the luxury of 'despot courts' is accompanied by the 'decay' of 'domestic joy' (DS, 108–10:720–5). In *The Prelude* he linked the experiences of his own childhood to a political sentiment in strict accord with an eighteenth-century view of social harmony and order. The characters that began to gather on Salisbury Plain in Wordsworth's mind from 1793 on were all representative of blighted domestic and patriotic love in various forms; the modern world made it difficult if not impossible for them to sustain these virtues because there was no longer a healthy contact between political life, and the moral teachings implicit in the 'sympathies' we see revealed by 'Nature's GOD' to the child in *The Prelude*.

An aesthetic lapse of judgement was synonymous in Wordsworth's mind with the harmful effects of a consciousness torn between political expediency and the permanent moral truths made manifest in 'the common range of visible things'. As the 'Essay on Morals' indicates by its incomplete state, in 1798 Wordsworth was gradually abandoning the idea that he was capable himself of constructing or maintaining a philosophical system through which he could codify his beliefs. Most importantly, he was recognising that the very act of constructing such an essay was tending to contradict the conviction that tempted him to the task. The Essay actually ends in mid-sentence with an admission that he finds he is on the point of

contradicting himself. By way of contrast, the two-part *Prelude* does
begin to suggest a model of consciousness within which the
interdependent actions of political and aesthetic judgement might be
understood to operate.

Coleridge had of course instructed Wordsworth enthusiastically in
theories of how the mind might be presumed to respond at different
levels to a variety of stimuli. This was consistent with what Basil
Willey has described as the 'widespread desire' in the eighteenth
century 'to equate the moral and the physical world'.[8] *The Prelude*
identifies a primary source of wisdom and knowledge, out of which
grows a secondary (though no less important) power which, only
when deferring to the primary wisdom, serves as a sound basis of all
political judgement and activity, the 'surety of my earthly life'.[9]
Wordsworth also had his knowledge of recent history to help him in
this formulation. The *Letter to Llandaff* alone indicates that he was
well aware of the radical, pro-colonial Whig interpretation of
constitutional history that became particularly prominent at the time
of the American War. The first principles of the British Constitution
had been perverted to a point where political practice was almost
totally dissociated from the ideals of its first cause. We find him
persisting in this view in his pamphlet *The Convention of Cintra* in
1809.[10]

The operation of a primary and a secondary power on the mind,
and the importance of the relationship between them, becomes a
crucial part of Wordsworth's explanation of the way that after 1792
he had been misled by his enthusiasm for the rationalist political
priorities he subsequently attacked in the 'Essay on Morals'. In Part
Two of *The Prelude* he wrote:

> Those incidental charms which first attached
> My heart to rural objects, day by day
> Grew weaker, and I hasten on to tell
> How Nature, intervenient till this time
> And secondary, now at length was sought
> For her own sake. But who shall parcel out
> His intellect by geometric rules,
> Split like a province into round and square?
> Who knows the individual hour in which
> His habits were first sown even as a seed?
> Who that shall point as with a wand, and say
> 'This portion of the river of my mind

> Came from yon fountain'? Thou, my friend, art one
> More deeply read in thy own thoughts, no slave
> Of that false secondary power by which
> In weakness we create distinctions, then
> Believe our puny boundaries are things
> Which we perceive, and not which we have made.
> To thee, unblinded by these outward shews,
> The unity of all has been revealed;
> And thou wilt doubt with me, less aptly skilled
> Than many are to class the cabinet
> Of their sensations, and in voluble phrase
> Run through the history and birth of each
> As of a single independent thing.
> Hard task to analyse a soul, in which
> Not only general habits and desires,
> But each most obvious and particular thought –
> Not in a mystical and idle sense,
> But in the words of reason deeply weighed –
> Hath no beginning. (19–20:237–67)

The 'sympathies' which we saw in the previous passage awakened by natural objects are the primary source of all thoughts and actions, of 'patriotic and domestic love', binding religious, moral, political and social promptings together in a single, unified motivation, 'The unity of all'. The objects themselves are secondary, they are 'outward shews', or as in the 'Point Rash Judgment' poem, deceptive 'lovely images' comparable to his picturesque perception of Lake Como in *Descriptive Sketches*. In Wordsworth's own experience, however, with the passage of time, 'Nature' in its physical manifestations was accorded a primary role in his mind; she was 'sought / For her own sake', and not allowed to impart her teachings unhindered. The passage then reverts to the familiar terminology of the 'Essay on Morals' in order to emphasise the error this misguided relationship to nature signifies: 'Who knows the individual hour in which / His habits were first sown even as a seed?' He refers again in line 263 to our 'general habits and desires'. The mind is attempting to enforce its will on nature. Nature should be allowed to seek the mind, it is not the mind's business to use nature in an attempt to satisfy its own subjective demands on knowledge. The 'geometric rules' of Godwin may give the impression that the human mind is potentially all-knowing, but in fact it will never be able to trace the 'habits' of man to their ultimate source.

Coleridge, Wordsworth concedes, would be able to argue this point far more effectively than he himself can. Of his own skill in philosophical argument, he wrote dismissively in 1800 that he had been 'Contented if he might enjoy / The things which others understand'.[11] He had already tried without much success in the 'Essay on Morals' to explain the error of measuring that which should itself be used as a measure for other things. Now, trying a different emphasis, he returned to the point, explaining that 'our puny boundaries are things / Which we perceive, and not which we have made'. The 'puny boundaries' are the political structures by which 'In weakness we create distinctions' without reference to the primary, unifying power of wisdom in nature, which 'Hath no beginning'.

He went on to develop this argument in Book X, where 'this after worship' and 'this second love' are phrases used to describe his misguided determination to take an active role in politics at a time when political ambition was still the primary motivating force in his life. he had yet to learn that the 'ritual' of public life had to emanate from God 'Who send'st thyself into this breathing world / Through Nature and through every kind of life' (380:381–400). Action was not in itself despicable, but to *act* properly (and in Book VIII l.670 he uses italics) the motive must be sound:

> of this faith
> Never forsaken, that by acting well,
> And understanding, I should learn to love
> The end of life and everything we know. (VIII 302:674–7)

Wordsworth's political position in the two-part *Prelude* remains best understood, therefore, when placed alongside the radical Whig, Commonwealthman tradition of eighteenth-century political philosophy. The need for a paternalistic 'monitory voice' (14:18) and the emphasis on 'moral feelings' (18:165) are expressed repeatedly. Equally derivative is the spiritual, at times pietistical inspiration behind the notion that when we contemplate natural objects in our search for the mysterious origins of 'The passions that build up the human soul', it is nature '*sanctifying* by such discipline' the 'human soul' that leads us towards an understanding of the truth (4: 130–41 my italics).

At the end of the two-part *Prelude*, prompted in part no doubt by a letter from Coleridge in which he outlined his view of the purpose of *The Recluse*, the implicit reference to recent political events – 'these times of fear, / This melancholy waste of hopes o'erthrown' – is clear, as also is his awareness of his position now as an apparent apostate, open to the 'sneers / On visionary minds' (26:478–9, 485–6). But with a firm gesture towards the Classicial Republican tradition which he had embraced, he faces the future with 'A more than Roman confidence':

> I yet
> Despair not of our nature, but retain
> A more than Roman confidence, a faith
> That fails not, in all sorrow my support,
> The blessing of my life, the gift is yours
> Ye mountains, thine O Nature. Thou hast fed
> My lofty speculations, and in thee
> For this uneasy heart of ours I find
> A never failing principle of joy
> And purest passion. (25:487–96)

8
The 1805 *Prelude*:
retirement and education

> May books and Nature be their early joy,
> And knowledge, rightly honored with that name –
> Knowledge not purchased with the loss of power!
> (*Prelude*, 174:447–9)

In the course of the years following the Wordsworths' return to England, *The Prelude* gradually grew into a poem of thirteen Books reflecting on the 'growth of a poet's mind' from early childhood, through university, the French Revolution, to a lengthy meditation on 'Imagination, How Impaired and Restored', followed by a 'Conclusion'. The contrast between active and passive states upon which so many of the *Lyrical Ballads* turn, releasing in those poems a deeply personal expression of uncertainty and tension, continued to inform the way the subject matter for the early *Prelude*, and now its successor, was chosen and narrated. In Book VII, for example, Wordsworth reflects upon how it was that the 'gross realities' of life in London could give him glimpses of a deeper spiritual reality 'seen and scarcely seen':

> If aught there were of real grandeur here
> 'Twas only then when gross realities,
> The incarnation of the spirits that moved
> Amid the poet's beauteous world – called forth
> With that distinctness which a contrast gives,
> Or opposition – made me recognise
> As by a glimpse, the things which I had shaped
> And yet not shaped, had seen and scarcely seen,
> Had felt, and thought of in my solitude. (252:508–16)

The 'contrast ... Or opposition' revealed, for example, within the skating episode, came to be mirrored throughout the poem. Turning once more to Book VII, 'London', he describes the 'Babel din' (234:157) of walking in the London streets:

> Meanwhile the roar continues, till at length,
> Escaped as fom an enemy, we turn
> Abruptly into some sequestered nook,
> Still as a sheltered place when winds blow loud. (236:184–7)

This is an obvious reminder of the time when, as a child, Wordsworth had left his fellow skaters and retired 'from the uproar ... / Into a silent bay' (5:170–1), and ceasing all physical motion discovered a sense of profound, mysterious motion in nature. The passive side of the equation, however presented, includes the 'monitory voice' of a wisdom which sees into the life of things.

Book III opens with the excitement and bustle that surrounded Wordsworth's arrival at Cambridge. But the contrast to this scene of intense activity is not long coming:

> Oft did I leave
> My comrades, and the crowd, buildings and groves,
> And walked along the fields, the level fields,
> With heaven's blue concave reared above my head. (96:97–100)

Although the mountains are missed, this retreat from the 'Gowns grave or gaudy, doctors, students, streets, / Lamps, gateways, flocks of churches, courts and towers –' (92:30–1) frees the mind to dwell on the 'one life', or as it is specifically described in Book III, 'the one presence, and the life / Of the great whole' (98:130–1):

> I looked for universal things, perused
> The common countenance of earth and heaven ...
>   (96:110–11)

Interwoven with the recurring juxtaposition of active and passive states – mental and physical – are two important and closely related themes: retirement and education. The history of retirement as a political ideal has already been mentioned; education has a similar pedigree, becoming very much a part of the Old Whig, Commonwealthman vocabulary in the years following the Revolution of 1688 and the Revolution Settlement. The insistence on retirement as a worthy alternative to an active role in the body-politic was obviously congenial to Wordsworth, though the evidence suggests that belief in it was never easily achieved. Enforced retirement from public life had been a *fait accompli* for Whigs like Molesworth, and later Chatham (as surely as it had been for Tories like Bolingbroke and to some degree Swift). In these circumstances there was little for it but to make a virtue out of the necessity of reflecting on the state of the nation unhindered by day-to-day responsibilities, in the constant hope of an eventual call to return to practical political action.

Conyers Middleton's popular *Life of Cicero* (1741) contributed significantly to the process of reifying the ideal of retirement, and in doing so indicated the educational as well as the personal benefits of 'a calmer scene'. Cicero, we are told, had a number of retreats, the most favoured being his 'Tusculan house':

it was about four leagues from Rome, on the top of a beautiful hill, covered with the villas of the nobility, and affording an agreeable prospect of the city, and the country around it, with plenty of water flowing through his grounds ... Its neighbourhood to Rome gave him the opportunity of a retreat at any hour, from the fatigues of the bar, or the senate, to breathe a little fresh air, and to divert himself with his friends or family.

The villa was far enough away from Rome to afford a morally reinvigorating experience of pastoral order (social and family life existing in a harmonious relationship with natural forms and 'fresh air'), yet it stood within sight of the city to which he could return at a moment's notice.

Beyond this lay two more remote alternatives, the latter of which is distinctly Gothic in character, though Middleton insists still upon the necessity of there being relatively easy access to Rome:

When a greater satiety of the city, or a longer vacation in the Forum, disposed him to seek a calmer scene, and more undisturbed retirement, he used to remove to Antium, or Astura. At Antium he placed his best collection of books, and, as it was not above thirty miles from Rome, he could have daily intelligence there of everything that passed in the city. Astura was a little island ... a place peculiarly adapted to the purposes of solitude, and a secure retreat, – covered with a thick wood, cut out into shady walks, in which he used to spend the gloomy and splenetic moments of his life.[1]

Through his account of Cicero, Middleton presented a precise analogue for the concept of political retirement so crucial to the thinking of Real Whigs, a situation where 'patriotic and domestic love' might be reinvigorated, and, in the case of Antium, where intellectual activity replaced 'a greater satiety of the city'. Middleton's own political position reflected Real Whig sympathies, and Cicero is portrayed as a quintessential Whig hero, endowed with libertarian leanings that shocked mid-eighteenth-century readers of a less radical persuasion.[2] What is clear from Middleton's account is the way in which his concept of the great statesman incorporates an aesthetic ideal; the wholesome influence on the moral sense of a pastoral setting is emphasised by a hilltop location, in keeping with the 'prospect' genre used by Crowe in *Lewesdon Hill*.

Wordsworth's use of a 'retirement' motif in his poetry registered his continuing concern with the specific political dilemmas of his life, dilemmas inextricably bound up in his mind with more abstract issues of perception and taste endemic to the pastoral, prospect tradition. The 1805 *Prelude*, no less than its two-part predecessor, revolves around the French Revolution as the formative experience of the poet's mind, and reveals that his manner of reconciling himself to his lack of political judgement then, originated in the tradition of eighteenth-century radical Whig thinking. He elided the political crisis with the contemporary aesthetic one that called into question the honesty of picturesque figurations of labour. His disillusionment with revolutionary France made it impossible for him to countenance a new, politically radical understanding of society as potentially divided between a working class, and a wholly irresponsible class which comprised the privileged possessors of capital and thus power. Personally situated midway between the labourers and hard-pressed small farmers on the one hand, and the landowning aristocracy on the other, he pursued a solution which avoided identifying completely with the claims of either group.

David Simpson has commented on the contradictions inherent between Wordsworth's instinctive political sympathies and his actual social position. Referring in part to the poem 'Gipsies' (1807), he argues that:

Wordsworth was ... in a no man's land between the bourgeois commitment to place and property and the vagrant ease imaged in the gypsies' tents. No more could he, an insecure poet, be at one with the rural owner-occupiers who were economically and spiritually 'their own upholders, to themselves / Encouragement, and energy, and will'.

As Wordsworth is unsure of his own place in this ideal economy, so too is his portrayal of it as an objective entity also unstable and inscribed with conflict.[3]

Wordsworth's knowledge of the working class and vagrancy was rooted in rural picturesque imagery; subsequent accounts were likely to remain, as Simpson argues with reference to 'Michael',[4] politically unspecific and idealised, or as Wordsworth himself can indicate, something less than sympathetic:

Now and then we meet a miserable peasant in the road or an accidental traveller. The country people here are wretchedly poor; ignorant and overwhelmed with every vice that usually attends ignorance in that class, viz – lying and picking and stealing etc etc. (EY, p. 154)

A passage like this (written while at Racedown to Mathews) might after all appear to locate Wordsworth's true sympathies with the privileged sections of society, and reveal any kind of radical gesture before or since as tokenism. It is therefore important to recognise that the assumption of class superiority expressed here was not exceptional among radicals in the 1790s.

In John Thelwall's *The Peripatetic* (1793), for example, the radical London Corresponding Society member reports encounters with labourers in the course of a journey through Kent, lamenting their demeanour in terms very similar to those Wordsworth was prepared to use in his correspondence. While Thelwall refuses to apologise for what is often the ignorance, greed and irresponsibility he discovers in the people he meets, he is in no doubt who is ultimately to blame. The ruling classes have failed utterly to shoulder the responsibility that should accompany their privileged position; but how can they be expected to educate the lower orders by example when their own education is 'carelessly resigned to pedants, sycophants and drivellers'?[5]

Education in the broadest sense of how knowledge becomes apparent, how its worth might be assessed, and then how best disseminated, had become a central issue for eighteenth-century Enlightenment minds. Advances in science in the late seventeenth and early eighteenth century stimulated what was fundamentally a very different approach to the enquiry into the workings of the mind from what had gone before, in the belief that what hitherto had been treated as a matter of impenetrable mystery might ultimately be revealed as within the grasp of the human intellect. The effect this in turn had on debates over the more precise issue of practical education, its institution and its methods, was considerable.

John Locke's *Thoughts Concerning Education* (1693) reflected the general atmosphere of renewed speculation and confidence; but with Locke we have also a reminder of how education became a specifically political issue in the course of the Glorious Revolution.

For Real Whigs, the nature of education in a free state became a major feature of their propaganda campaign against the Whigs in power. The function of education was to inculcate citizens with the sacred principles of liberty and toleration; it should therefore cease to be controlled by the Church as a means primarily of educating the clergy. Caroline Robbins has shown how this Real Whig view: 'may be traced from Milton, through Molesworth and his famous *Preface*, Stanhope's university scheme supported by Toland, the many experiments of the mid-eighteenth century in institutions run by dissenters, to the plans put forward by John Jebb before he left Cambridge in the seventies'.[6]

Foreign travel, Molesworth argued in his Preface to *An Account of Denmark* (1693), should swiftly alert the English observor to the shortcomings of a traditional university education in Europe:

the weightier Matters of true Learning, whereof one has occasion every hour; such as good Principles, Morals, the improvement of Reason, the love of Justice, the value of Liberty, the duty owing to ones Country and the Laws, are either quite omitted, or slightly passed over: Indeed they forget not to recommend frequently to them what they call the *Queen of all Virtues*, viz. *Submission* to Superiors, and an entire *blind Obedience* to Authority, without instructing them in the due measures of it, rather teaching them that 'tis without all bounds: Thus the Spirits of Men are from the beginning inured to Subjection, and deprived of the right Notion of a generous and legal Freedom.[7]

In this respect it is interesting to reflect that Wordsworth's instincts, once settled at Cambridge, had been to pursue a variety of subjects which, while unlikely to bring him academic success, were arguably of more immediate, practical interest. Molesworth lamented the teaching of Greek and Latin 'not as being the Vehicles of good Sence, but as if they had some intrinsick Virtue ... an Elegancy of *Latin* and *Greek* Style is more sought after than the matter contained in them' (Preface). In his *Essay Upon Study* John Clarke (1687–1734) had urged students to read Locke, Newton, Descartes and Hutcheson, and urged also the need for modern languages; while Edmund Law of Cartmel, a student at St John's, later fellow of Christ's College and Bishop of Carlisle, held similar views and influenced Jebb, Disney, Hartley and Francis Blackburne.[8] It is unlikely that Wordsworth had any detailed knowledge of the earlier eighteenth-century figures mentioned here, though some acquaintance with Law's views might

perhaps be assumed given his birthplace and eventual bishopric. How-
ever, his study of modern languages (Italian, French and Spanish), of
mathematics, his 'veneration for the name of Newton',[9] and his
continued reading in contemporary poetry, suggest Wordsworth's
absorption of educational theories developed in dissident Whig
circles. It should also be appreciated that, as Nicholas Roe has
recently reminded us, a lively and pervasive tradition of religious and
political dissent of which the poet was certainly aware, and which
owed its inception to the writings of Molesworth, Clarke, Law and
others, continued to flourish at Cambridge well on into the 1790s.[10]

The first book to be added to the two-part *Prelude* contained
Wordsworth's thoughts on the latter stages of his formal education,
'Residence at Cambridge'. Formal education is here shown as
tending to dilute the influence of precious formative powers on the
minds of its subjects. *The Prelude* effectively defines education in the
same way that James Burgh had done in his *Political Disquisitions*
(1725):

by education it is to be observed, we must understand not only what is
taught at schools and universities, but the impressions young people receive
from parents, and from the world, which greatly outweigh all that can be
done by masters and tutors.[11]

Burgh, with Molesworth and other Real Whig contempories, would
have had no difficulty in identifying with Wordsworth's comments
on the worst aspects of a Cambridge education:

> Forced labour, and more frequently forced hopes,
> And, worse than all, a treasonable growth
> Of indecisive judgements that impaired
> And shook the mind's simplicity ... (102:213–16)

Book III demands a greater sense of responsibility within both
university and the Church with respect to the purpose of education.
We have already seen how conscious Wordsworth was of the
dangers of what he here describes as 'The congregating temper' of
the young (110:392). Referring once more to the 'Roman confidence'
so dear to the hearts of eighteenth-century republicans, he
recommends that in place of 'forced hopes' encouraged by a
competitive system offering worldly status as its reward, the
atmosphere of study should inculcate 'a healthy sound simplicity, / A
seemly plainness – name it as you will, / Republican or pious'

(112:405–7). In common with eighteenth-century Real Whigs of earlier generations, Wordsworth deplores the abuse of privilege evident in Cambridge among academics and clergy, and insists that the main purpose of education is not being served by those entrusted to teach 'moral and scholastic discipline' (112:412). Where Wordsworth differs from the tradition of criticism he inherits is in the way he appeals to the imagination and nature as a basis for re-establishing the 'just authority' of education (112:430).

Different as this may seem to the political emphasis that informed the arguments of Molesworth, Burgh or Hutcheson, the Wordsworthian use of nature was to a significant degree made possible by the particular emphasis Real Whig writers laid on the value of sentiment and the feelings. For them it was a means of signifying the difference between themselves and those of a materialistic, corrupt frame of mind who were in power. Shaftesbury, for example, reflects this strategy when writing to Molesworth. The 'truly honest man', he explains, must cultivate his virtue 'from reflection':

> But the misfortune is, we Honest men (if I may speak thus presumptuously of my self) are a little mysterious our selves. There is a cloud over us, which is hard to be clear'd up. The rugged paths we walk through, give us a rugged pace; and the idle supine illiterate creatures of a Court-education, have a thousand advantages above us: and can easier borrow from our character than we from theirs.[12]

Shaftesbury's reference to the 'rugged paths' of the political wilderness he saw himself in, reminds us of the sensitivity that developed towards the rural environment in which retirement was likely to be set; cultivation of the finer feelings therefore came to be associated with an appreciation – and often the 'improvement' or adornment – of the landscape.

The relationship between Old Whig political principles of liberty and picturesque aesthetics is evident in Middleton's work, and also in Beattie's *The Minstrel*. Crowe's *Lewesdon Hill* emphasises not only the principles involved, but major figures identified with Old Whig 'honesty'. Given this context, it is perfectly understandable why the perception of nature should figure so prominently in Wordsworth's attempt to address the political crises of the 1790s in his poetry.

Much is made of the restorative powers of nature in Book IV, which initially concentrates on the joy of homecoming experienced at the first summer vacation. The climax of the book comes with the narration of an encounter by night with a discharged soldier. Book IV deals, as did its predecessor, with 'an inner falling off' (138:270), a loss of instinctive wisdom instilled by the natural objects that surrounded him in his youth, and by the society he believed it fostered:

> I read, without design, the opinions, thoughts
> Of those plain-living people, in a sense
> Of love and knowledge. (134:203–5)

Once more he uses the image of the hunt, 'This vague heartless chace' (140:304), to describe how 'dancing, gaity and mirth' (140:320) replaced solitary musing and serious reflection.

The discharged soldier passage (composed in 1798) has been widely discussed. Wordsworth offers it as yet another experience of solitude encountered in the aftermath of the din of social life. The narration itself contains a contrast between a first, fancifully Gothic impression of the man, 'his mouth / Shewed ghastly in the moonlight' (146:410–11), and his actual manner, 'A stately air of mild indifference' (146:444). The soldier is a victim of his country's aggressive foreign policy, and its callous disregard for him once sickness has rendered him useless. The way in which Wordsworth offers to help him, and the soldier's response, reveal the same elements of unresolved social and political tension that are present in 'Simon Lee'. Above all else, however, it is a profoundly 'educational' moment, destined to inform the habits of Wordsworth's mind more significantly than anything offered by his formal education at Cambridge.

There is an important correspondence between the character of the discharged soldier and the Cartesian dream figure of a Bedouin Arab which occurs near the beginning of Book V. Wordsworth offers the soldier a 'reproof', that:

> He would not linger in the public ways,
> But ask for timely furtherance, and help
> Such as his state required. ... (150:490–2)

And receives due admonishment:

> At this reproof,
> With the same ghastly mildness in his look,
> He said, 'My trust is in the God of Heaven,
> And in the eye of him that passes me.' (150:492–5)

The advice proffered by the poet is practical, even fastidious, revealing the degree to which he places his trust in institutionalised charity; it lacks faith in the vision of a society grounded on the achievements of individual love and self-sacrifice implicit in the soldier's words. The incident has disclosed two kinds of knowledge: the one superficial, a further expression in its way of 'The congregating temper', while the other is informed by a profound knowledge of, and optimistic belief in humanity. Our reading of the passage should also register the significance of the way Wordsworth describes himself performing a nervously active role, over against the soldier's passivity.

In the dream sequence of Book V, the Bedouin is discovered carrying two objects, a stone and a shell, both of which represent books. The stone, we are told, is '*Euclid's Elements*' (156:88), the shell 'Is something of more worth', a source of prophetic poetry 'which foretold / Destruction to the children of the earth / By deluge now at hand'. (156: 90 and 97–9) The two 'books' signify the difference between the concept of 'geometric rules' already criticised in Part Two (19:243), and now further associated with the shortcomings of the formal educational system of Cambridge, and truth perceived in imaginative terms of profound personal experience, the kind of 'education' his encounter with the soldier makes possible. The temptation to pity, and indeed patronise the soldier was rebuked at the end of Book IV; though not a repetition of his earlier insensitivity, the danger of misplaced pity is once more mentioned when the Bedouin is described:

> And I have scarcely pitied him, have felt
> A reverence for a being thus employed,
> And thought that in the blind and awful lair
> Of such a madness reason did lie couched. (158:149–52)

The meaning of the deluge, first prophecied, then realised as the dreamer witnesses its onset, has been variously interpreted. In *The Borders of Vision* Jonathan Wordsworth stresses the difference of his reading from that of Geoffrey Hartman: 'It is surely a threatened engulfment *of*, not by, imagination that causes the terror.'[13] In a more concrete sense, the prophecy relates to the onset of political events that were to overwhelm the poet's imaginative life, as a result of which he was to find himself wandering across Salisbury Plain, 'crazed / By love, and feeling, and internal thought / Protracted among endless solitudes', a potential prey indeed to 'madness' (V, 158:144–6). In this situation he was tempted to grasp at the book of Godwinian rationalism for salvation, setting aside the deeper wisdom to be found in books 'versed / In living Nature' (VI, 192:118–19) which attempt to contemplate the feelings and passions of human beings:

> ... books which lay
> Their sure foundations in the heart of man. (162:199–200)

The study of geometry in fact fascinated Wordsworth at Cambridge, and he defends it in Book VI (192:135–59). What he attacks here in Book V, given the implications for him of the prophetic dream, is the dangerous arrogance of science where it claims to contain the seeds of all knowledge. The narrative episodes of Book V, 'There was a boy ...' and the sight of the drowned man in Esthwaite, are testaments to the harrowing and perplexing tragedies of life. Wordsworth claims he was enabled to cope with these things largely because of the nature of his reading:

> for my inner eye had seen
> Such sights before among the shining streams
> Of fairyland, the forests of romance –
> Thence came a spirit hallowing what I saw
> With decoration and ideal grace,
> A dignity, a smoothness, like the words
> Of Grecian art and purest poesy. (176:475–81)

The authors of modern educational books, the product of Enlightenment arrogance, fail completely to understand the way the youthful mind benefits from beginning to discover and exercise its imaginative faculties. In 'Anecdote for Fathers' he has already satirised the modern trend; here he describes educational systems based on theories of the mind besotted by mathematically informed notions of precision as 'a pest / That might have dried me up body and soul' (162:228–9).

From 'Books' Wordsworth returns in Book VI to his Cambridge education, and the walking tour of 1790 with Robert Jones across France and into Italy. Though hardly in the normal tradition of the aristocratic Grand Tour, Wordsworth was well aware of its educational purposes:

Hence the importance of travel, whose purpose was 'to make observations upon the laws, customs, police, and manners of other countries, and to compare them with our own'. To observe Turkey and the other Asiatic states was to observe tyranny. If Rome was the standard example of a corrupted mixed government, Turkey was the exemplar of arbitrary rule ... Deprived of liberty and kept in thrall by a standing army, the people were slothful and effeminate.[14]

In his Preface to *An Account of Denmark* Molesworth had both emphasised the importance of travel, and criticised the tendency of the sons of the aristocracy to travel to France, Spain and Italy where the gracious living was inclined to 'dazzle the Eyes of most Travellers, and cast a disguise upon the Slavery of those Parts'. Throughout the century dissident Whig writers returned to the same theme. Blackburne, in his *Memoir* of Thomas Hollis, describes Hollis's two European tours as a shining example of how time spent travelling abroad could be put to good use.

Wordsworth is at pains to emphasise his continued lack of comprehension of the political realities he encountered in France in 1790, lacking the education he was not getting at Cambridge, lacking in the ability to relate the wisdom inherent in the 'spots of time' recalled for *The Prelude* to social and political life.

He concentrated instead on an experience related to the issue of the inadequacy of perception when controlled by expectations formed by picturesque aesthetics. The experience he is prepared for when crossing the Alps, and the experience he actually encounters are so different that at the time we must assume his primary response was one of having been cheated. His letter to Dorothy on the subject certainly would suggest that the account worked up for *The Prelude* is for the most part the result of hindsight.[15] Crossing the Alps revealed what for Wordsworth constituted the underlying reason for his lack of political perception. He still expected nature to conform to man-made aesthetic principles, the result of artificial discrimination and selection. Rather than a belief in the 'one life', this was tending to suggest a 'right life', discounting what to the human eye seemed out of place. Travelling down the cavernous Simplon Pass, as opposed to striding over the peaks, he was beset by a vision of nature as apparently contradictory. To resolve the conflict between what the eye had been trained to see and what it actually discovered required a recognition of a unifying power that lay beyond any work of man, political or aesthetic. Grasp the unifying aesthetic of nature, and you grasped the principles upon which human society might build a lasting unity; the mind you reflect on becomes the many-faceted mind of God, 'features / Of the same face, blossoms upon one tree' (218:568–9).

What is true of the Alps is true also of London. Experienced by a properly educated mind, even life in the city of London may ultimately leave impressions on the mind that reveal the workings of 'one mind'. In Book VII, therefore, we read:

> But though the picture weary out the eye,
> By nature an unmanageable sight,
> It is not wholly so to him who looks
> In steadiness, who hath among least things
> An under-sense of greatest, sees the parts
> As parts, but with a feeling of the whole.
> This, of all acquisitions first, awaits
> On sundry and most widely different modes
> Of education – nor with least delight
> On that through which I passed. Attention comes
> And comprehensiveness and memory,
> From early converse with the works of God
> Among all regions, chiefly where appear
> Most obviously simplicity and power.
> By influence habitual to the mind
> The mountain's outline and its steady form
> Gives a pure grandeur, and its presence shapes
> The measure and the prospect of the soul
> To majesty: such virtue have the forms
> Perennial of the ancient hills – nor less
> The changeful language of their countenances
> Gives movement to the thoughts, and multitude,
> With order and relation. (264–6:708–30)

To see 'the parts / As parts, but with a feeling for the whole' is a fundamental 'acquisition' needed to make any 'mode of education' – including time spent in the environment Wordsworth trusted least – worthwhile and fruitful. This basic acquisition, Wordsworth argues, is the result of his upbringing among the mountains. Key qualities, 'simplicity' linked to 'power', 'pure grandeur', 'virtue', 'order and relation', relate back to the way he described the Simplon Pass, to the 'simplicity' of the discharged soldier, and to the early reminiscence of stealing the boat.

We note again how Wordsworth here continues to use the term 'habit', 'By influence habitual to the mind' (266:738, 264:722) when analysing his experiences, placing this idea of education still in the context of the broader eighteenth-century debate, where Real Whigs like John Brown and Francis Hutcheson were employing the terminology to help define the source of moral and virtuous ideas:

if rational Habits and Opinions be not infused, in order to *anticipate* Absurdities: Absurdities will rise, and *anticipate* all rational habits and Opinions.[16]

Wordsworth criticises unreservedly the political and ecclesiastical rhetoric he encountered in London; here was no sound basis for a habit of mind. In this respect he continues very much in the tradition of Molesworth, Hutcheson, Burgh, Brown and Almon. Only in 1832 was the panegyric on Edmund Burke added to Book VII to allay the ironic image of the political demagogue who 'winds away his never ending horn' and 'Grows tedious even in a young man's ear' (254:539 and 543). The poet's attack on the leadership of the Church (256:544–66) should remind us that in London he had sampled a very different style of preaching, that of Joseph Fawcett, energetically apocalyptic and of a radical political persuasion that arose directly out of the Commonwealthman roots he shared with Thelwall and Godwin.[17] The early eighteenth-century Commonwealthman John Jones had argued forcibly in his *Disquisitions* (1749) for an order of service within the Church of England designed not to mystify, but to educate. It was due to the efforts of Francis Blackburne that his views became widely known in the latter part of the century:

Our ordinary people seem to want some plainer and more suitable instructions than they ordinarily have. Our Church seems to have designed for them the plainest, as we may judge by her homilies: But her homilies (which are now neither so plain, nor on some accounts so proper, as they were intended to be at first) are seldom or never read in our churches. Nor (which is much or more to be wished) have we any comment upon Scripture recommended by authority.[18]

The theatrical egotism of successful city–Church preachers, 'Fresh from a toilette of two hours' (256:548) and inclined to rely on poetical 'eloquence' rather than on the 'authority' desired by Jones, was notorious throughout the century, and Wordsworth does no more than add his own voice to a long line of critics.

The educational process Wordsworth is particularly concerned to trace in the development of his own mind, is the movement from love of nature to love of 'human-kind'; a knowledge that ensures the right application of habits of mind formed by communion with nature, 'The mountain's outline and its steady form', to human-kind in its imperfect state of social and political turmoil. The French Revolution was to expose the danger of forgetting, or setting aside, habits of mind rooted in nature. In Wordsworth's view, and he offers it as not untypical in this respect, his formal education was in no small way to blame for casting him unprepared into the confusion of a revolutionary situation. The moral to be drawn from the deceptively childlike poem 'Star Gazers', which appeared in the 1807 collection (composed 1806), makes the same point yet again. The telescope, representing the scientific quest for learning, is the property of a 'Show-man', selling the promise of greater knowledge to passers-by in Leicester Square. Wordsworth notes the disappointment evident on the faces of those who have used it: 'be their eyes in fault? / Their eyes, or minds? or, finally, is this resplendant Vault?' (ll. 11–12).[19] The belief that science, in this guise, can answer the deepest longings of the human soul is false, because real knowledge is 'not of this noisy world, but silent and divine!' (28).

The city is used primarily as an image of alienation, of morality and virtue perverted if not annihilated, of everything that community life represented by Grasmere Fair described at the beginning of Book VIII is not. Book VIII was written after Book IX and the first half of Book X had been composed, and serves primarily as a confirmation of the conviction that worthy political commitment and service must grow out of a love of nature. The French Revolution books show how the necessary wise passivity was lacking in the poet's education at the point at which he arrived in France for the second time. In Book VIII he illustrates his subsequent realisation that through 'Love of Nature' a 'Love of Mankind' based on moral rather than political foundations may be achieved. Once more he reverts to the image of the city to stress the universality of this 'feeling':

> Add also, that among the multitudes
> Of that great city oftentimes was seen
> Affectingly set forth, more than elsewhere

> Is possible, the unity of man,
> One spirit over ignorance and vice
> Predominant, in good and evil hearts
> One sense for moral judgments, as one eye
> For the sun's light. When strongly breathed upon
> By this sensation – whencesoe'er it comes,
> Of union or communion – doth the soul
> Rejoice as in her highest joy; for there,
> There chiefly, hath she feeling whence she is,
> And passing through all Nature rests with God.
>
> (308–10:824–36)

The scene is thus set for an account of the personal crisis around which everything in this poem had moved from the time of the composition of its earliest fragmentary passages; a crisis not resolved by Wordsworth in specifically Real Whig terms, but nevertheless analysed and argued for in ways which remind us of the pervasiveness of Real Whig and Commonwealthman rhetoric. The French Revolution exposed for the poet a profound ignorance in matters moral, social and political of a kind that had long been the substance of eighteenth-century political philosophy, and which Wordsworth, in the tradition of Commonwealthman propaganda, linked to the issue of picturesque perception:

> the place
> Was thronged with impregnations, like those wilds
> In which my early feelings had been nursed. (308:790–2)

The darkest period of his life is thus approached with an optimistic gleam of hindsight, even if in 1804 by no means all the battles had been fought and won.

9
The Prelude Books IX and X: legitimate radicalism

> I pursued
> A higher nature – wished that man should start
> Out of the worm-like state in which he is,
> And spread abroad the wings of Liberty,
> Lord of himself, in undisturbed delight.
> A noble aspiration! – yet I feel
> The aspiration – but with other thoughts
> And happier: for I was perplexed and sought
> To accomplish the transition by such means
> As did not lie in nature, sacrificed
> The exactness of a comprehensive mind
> To scrupulous and microscopic views
> That furnished out materials for a work
> Of false imagination, placed beyond
> The limits of experience and truth.
>
> (X, 404:834–48)

Books IX and X of the 1805 *Prelude* pose crucial questions of motivation. In the late 1790s Wordsworth's intentions seem to have been to write a poem that responded to a personal crisis of conviction and purpose, a crisis to which the Revolution had given dramatic political substance. He set about doing it by narrating and reflecting on a number of formative childhood experiences. The purpose of such a poem was to relocate political action in a subservient relationship to influences on the mind of a more permanent and universal kind derived from nature. In effect it would confirm the tradition of thought that conceived of the role of statesman as much in the light of a wise thinker or philosopher, as that of a politician engaged in day-to-day political activity.

Up until 1804 it seems clear that Wordsworth was determined to exclude anything like a specific account of the Revolution from the poem.[1] Having changed his mind at some point in the spring of that year, however, the ordering of the material may be seen as continuing in some degree the attempt to deflect the reader from engaging too closely with the event. The poet's motive is important to consider in this respect, and raises the issue of just how 'radical' Wordsworth had become between 1792 and his eventual arrival at Racedown.

Nicholas Roe has suggested that Wordsworth's commitment to Jacobin ideology was for a brief time significantly greater and more wholehearted than he was subsequently prepared to admit. Central to this thesis is Roe's belief that Godwin, and Godwin's circle, became far more influential after his return from France than Wordsworth ever indicates. The extent to which Beaupuy, the aristocrat turned revolutionary soldier, is written up as a mentor in Book IX signifies – according to Roe – the poet's effort to minimise the part played by Godwin in the history of his thinking.[2] Despite the difficulties evident in placing Wordsworth within the main-stream of 1790s political radicalism, Roe is not unsuccessful in suggesting that Wordsworth latterly seemed to have something to hide about the kind of political animal he became, and was seen to have become, by the mid 1790s when his brother urged him to be 'cautious in writing or expressing your political opinions'.[3]

But for all this, Wordsworth as an integral member of the radical political faction that endured imminent danger and persecution during this period remains slightly less than convincing. The nature of the problem is in fact established early on by Roe himself. Subscribers to the fund set up to help the families of London Corresponding Society members arrested for treason in 1794 included:

'Citizen Wordsworth 1s.–0d.' This donation was received by John Smith, a bookseller who lived in Portsmouth Street, Lincoln's Inn Fields ... who was 'Citizen Wordsworth' and was he in fact William Wordsworth?

As it turns out, no. 'Citizen Wordsworth' was Henry Wordsworth of Jewin Street, London, and a member of Bookseller Smith's 29th. Division.[4]

The reason for including this anecdote is interesting. We are expected to feel that if it was not William Wordsworth, it at least might have been, and a good deal is subsequently presented by Roe in terms of possibility and probability.[5]

The Government was prepared to listen to a report that Wordsworth was a potentially dangerous radical plotting treason;

but it is in the spirit of checking out a possibility, rather than providing proof of a certainty, that we must see the decision to monitor the activities of Wordsworth and Coleridge in Somerset in 1798. Roe presses the association with Thelwall in that respect as clear-cut evidence of both poets' continuing radical allegiance. To set against this, we have Coleridge's own account of Thelwall's frame of mind in the *Biographia Literaria*, and also Thelwall's own testimony. Together they imply that what he sought in his relationship with the poets was a fantasy of escape, of retirement from the political turmoil. In 1797 he composed *Lines, Written at Bridgewater* in which he celebrated his friendship with Coleridge and, in less intimate terms, his acquaintance with Wordsworth:

> Ah! let me then, far from the strifeful scenes
> Of public life (where Reason's warning voice
> Is heard no longer, and the trump of truth
> Who blows but wakes the Ruffian Crew of Power
> To deeds of maddest anarchy and blood)
> Ah! let me, far in some sequester'd dell,
> Build my low cot; most happy might it prove,
> My Samuel! near to thine ...
>   by our sides
> Thy Sara, and my Susan, and, perchance,
> Allfoxden's musing tenant, and the maid
> Of ardent eye, who, with fraternal love,
> Sweetens his solitude.[6]

Despite its obvious sub-Augustan cultural and stylistic debt, Thelwall is presumably giving us in this poem not only his idealised picture of how these poet–philosophers lived, but something of his actual knowledge of their lifestyle. He certainly does not associate them with a frame of mind anxious to incite rebellion.

It nevertheless remains valid to suspect that Wordsworth's own account of himself when he was at his most politically radical leaves something to be desired. Though Godwin is not mentioned by name in *The Prelude*, Roe finds evidence enough in Wordsworth's writing between 1794 and 1796 to suggest 'that Godwin was actually the immediate ancestor of Coleridge as Wordsworth's philosophic mentor and guide, and that this period of his life was a crucial precedent to his emergence as a poet'.[7] The matter of Wordsworth's political leanings is taken a step further by suggesting a preparedness on his part to support Robespierre: 'a number of later poems are not intelligible unless one admits the more sinister conjecture that Wordsworth's "devoted service" might have led to his making "a common cause" with Robespierre in prosecuting the Terror to save the Revolution in France.'[8] This would imply a very different position from that already referred to earlier by Peter Marshall and Mary Jacobus. We need to retain a clear sense of distinction, however, between a possible course of action seriously considered at the time, and what in the event evolved as Wordsworth's political stance. In presenting his engagement with revolutionary politics the way he did in 1804, Wordsworth had things not only to hide about the workings of his mind, he had a continuing creed of dissidence where his own Government was concerned to validate.

Much depends in the end on how genuinely politically innocent we believe the poet was through Cambridge and the subsequent months spent in France, 'Looking as from a distance on the World / That moved about me' (IX, 312: 24–5). He was capable of political enthusiasm, and indeed commitment, but both *Descriptive Sketches* and the *Letter to Llandaff* have been discussed here with a view to revealing Wordsworth's mind as politically unfocussed. The most celebrated concealment of these years, his love affair with Annette Vallon, is a reminder of the extent of the confusion and pain that was suffered.

Setting aside the immediate crisis of confidence in his own judgement, the fact remains that, if in the 1790s Wordsworth felt profoundly alienated from the political masters of his own country, in 1804 he still shows no inclination to conceal or indeed modify his memory of that disgust:

> Our shepherds (this say merely) at that time
> Thirsted to make the guardian crook of law
> A tool of murder ...
> Giants in their impiety alone,
> But in their weapons and their warfare base
> As vermin working out of reach, they leagued
> Their strength perfidiously to undermine
> Justice, and make an end of liberty. (X, 394:645–7, 652–6)

For all the comment and discussion that ensued about the poet's apostasy, there remains an important strand of consistency.

Wordsworth's poetry and prose of the late 1790s through to the latter years of the war against Napoleon suggests that earlier experiences (the Lowther debt included) established a cynicism with regard to the Government that lodged deep in his mind. In 1806 he wrote to Beaumont of Pitt:

I believe him, however, to have been as disinterested a Man, and as true a lover of his Country as it was possible for so ambitious a man to be. His first wish (though probably unknown to himself) was that his country should prosper under his administration; his next, that it should prosper; could the order of these wishes have been reversed, Mr. Pitt would have avoided many of the grevious mistakes into which, I think, he fell. (MY, 7)

The frustration he gave vent to in 1808 in *The Convention of Cintra* speaks of a long-held sense of grievance. In Books IX and X he set himself to speak frankly on that score, but equally he was concerned to avoid locating that disaffection with a political commitment he now viewed as misguided, especially as the basic critique he had of Pitt's policies remained unshaken with respect to the subsequent administration. Wordsworth sought to achieve the balance he needed by a scrupulous ordering of the material of these two books in particular. They were to contain an account both of political error, and of justified political discontent. He wanted to reveal a sound basis for dissent in the midst of misguided enthusiasm experienced during the formative years of that spirit of dissent. Using Beaupuy as a central influence on his political thought effectively does modify the 'radicalism' he espoused when in France; Beaupuy's position was that of a liberal aristocrat, a disciple of Rousseau and an enthusiast for the English republican theorists of the seventeenth century.[9] Before introducing Beaupuy, however, Wordsworth first describes his own 'Loose and disjointed' (IX, 318:107) frame of mind on arriving in France, and his instinctive rejection of the Royalist *emigré* position encountered at Orléans (312–22: 1–216). Following this, he gives his account of republican 'habits' of mind absorbed in his youth (322–4:218–30).

It is a passage which establishes an order of precedence. Wordsworth's radical instincts – subsequently to be influenced by the mêlée of French politics – are rooted in English history, and are at bottom a legitimate growth out of native political institutions. This is to differ substantially from the view of Jonathan Wordsworth who complains that, in the light of the subsequent sections on Beaupuy, 'the account of Wordsworth's inherent republicanism becomes rather pointless'.[10] The distinction Wordsworth makes is in fact crucial. It is to be noted that the strategy of deflection mentioned earlier leads him to abandon the critical tone in which Cambridge was earlier presented.[11] Though initially we may feel we have little more than a shift in emphasis from the earlier books, there is no doubt that his account is being significantly modified by the time we read of 'an equal ground' (324:231); as a sizar he knew differently.

A few lines further on he supplies us with what is probably the most fruitful clue of all when seeking the political context of Books IX and X:

> Add unto this, subservience from the first
> To God and Nature's single sovereignty
> (Familiar presences of awful power),
> And fellowship with venerable books
> To sanction the proud workings of the soul,
> And mountain liberty. It could not be
> But that one tutored thus, who had been formed
> To thought and moral feeling in the way
> This story hath described, should look with awe
> Upon the faculties of man, receive
> Gladly the highest promises, and hail
> As best the government of equal rights
> And individual worth. (324:237–49)

'Moral feelings' shaped by 'God and Nature's single sovereignty' is indicative of eighteenth-century rhetoric, linking the roots of Wordsworth's political habits of mind with those of the first poet of the Commonwealth, John Milton.

The account of Beaupuy's radicalism is therefore preceded by reference to fundamental republican virtues engendered by the circumstances of Wordsworth's upbringing in England. In 1804–05 Wordsworth sees this ordering of the material to be a correct reflection of the growth of his political consciousness. In the 1798–99 *Prelude* we found him describing his childhood as one where 'No delicate viands sapped our bodily strength', the consequence of which was to be 'A more than Roman confidence' (15:78, 29:489). The Roman, classical virtues were understood as implicit in the society in which he was brought up, and so the memory of 1804–05 that in 1792 he complacently understood the Revolution in France as 'A gift that rather was come late than soon' is not surprising (324:254). The 1798–99 text confirms the implications of the form which *Descriptive Sketches* took in revealing that from the first, Wordsworth understood the goal of the French Revolution to be the realisation of political principles already established and legitimised in Britain. In Thomsonian terms, this was a refined, perfected form of virtuous classical statecraft.

Central, therefore, to the way in which Wordsworth viewed his opposition to the Government was the idea that it was an historically legitimised position; he was every bit as concerned to argue this (and he did so at length in *The Convention of Cintra*), as were the Commonwealthmen and radical Whigs of the eighteenth century. Unlike the radicals of the 1790s who claimed with Paine that freedom required the severing of all links with the past (going as far back at least as the Norman Conquest), Wordsworth's position resembles far more closely the arguments of those who attacked the Government in the early 1760s. John Brewer has emphasised the significance of legitimacy for the followers of Wilkes and for the Society of Supporters of the Bill of Rights.[12] Reference to the Bill of Rights (1689) indicates how a justification for action with respect to grievances in the late eighteenth century was sought with reference to the political settlement at the accession of William III, calling to witness the 'martyredoms' of Russell and Sidney, and the writings of Molesworth, Moyle, Harrington and Nedham.

When, in 1775 on the eve of the American War, the London Association printed its 'Resolutions' for reform, it not only specifically referred its readers back to 1688 by way of legitimising its demands, it also offered Robert Molesworth's 'Preface' to his translation of Francis Hotoman's *Franco Gallia* as an introduction to its principles, promising a new edition of the complete work in the near future.[13] The Association urged like-minded persons to foster the habit of corresponding with one another on the state of liberty within the country. In all these things it was seeking to perpetuate the tradition of societies formed immediately after the Revolution to commemorate its achievements, not least of which was the Bill of Rights.

In the late 1780s, the Dissenters' Application Committee, a group particularly concerned to see the abolition of the Test and Corporation Acts, was instrumental in reinvigorating agitation for reform, and it took strength from the London Revolution Society, which met in 1788 to celebrate the centenary of the Glorious Revolution. The proceedings serve to confirm what Brewer has to say about the pervasive psychology of legitimisation through ritual and symbol: 'Ritualised conduct, the employment of symbols, or engagement in symbolic action can all be used to convey a political creed.'[14] When the Society met a year later, its members heard Richard Price claim that 1688 marked the beginning of 'that aura of light and liberty by which we have been made an example to other kingdoms, and become instructors of the world'. It was this *Discourse on the Love of our Country*, delivered just four months after the fall of the Bastille, that provoked Burke's *Reflections on the Revolution in France* (1790).[15]

Having established legitimacy as a major concern in the early part of Book IX of *The Prelude*, Wordsworth continues to use it as a recurring point of reference with respect to everything that follows.

When our attention is eventually drawn to Beaupuy, it is with an immediate and predictable emphasis on the moral and spiritual quality of his political commitment:

> By birth he ranked
> With the most noble, but unto the poor
> Among mankind he was in service bound,
> As by some tie invisible, oaths professed
> To a religious order. (328:309–13)

There is in these lines a direct reference back to the passage on English republicanism (322:219–31), for Beaupuy has renounced any claim to honour through 'wealth and titles' in favour of that 'tie invisible'. These observations are followed by a description of the more external consequences of his idealism, of 'a kind of radiant joy / That covered him about, when he was bent / On works of love or freedom' (328: 322–4). It is helpful here to recall the poet's ambivalent response to the faith of the pilgrims at Einsiedeln in *Descriptive Sketches*. Roman Catholicism is not to be countenanced; the tainted religion espoused by the British Establishment has become equally abhorrent, but a belief in God remains central to the concept of social and political virtue. The language of this passage therefore reveals an evangelical, 'born-again' excitement by way of explaining the trustworthiness of what this man stood for.

Eventually Wordsworth proceeds to a general description of the many conversations the two men had:

> Oft in solitude
> With him did I discourse about the end
> Of civil government, and its wisest forms;
> Of ancient prejudice, and chartered rights,
> Allegiance, faith, and law by time matured,
> Custom and habit, novelty and change;
> Of self-respect, and virtue in the few
> For patrimonial honour set apart,
> And ignorance in the labouring multitude. (328:328–36)

The major difference between Books IX and X and the rest of the poem, is of course the necessity to refer to specific political issues and matters of debate. In this passage, Wordsworth's pairing of 'ancient prejudice' and 'chartered rights' syntactically implies an antagonism between them; the connotations of 'prejudice' suggest that 'chartered rights' are viewed more sympathetically. 'Allegiance, faith, and law by time matured' all command respect, but are nevertheless listed as now in need of careful review. The potentially rival claims of 'Custom and habit', and 'novelty and change' are clearly implied, while the issue of how the ignorant 'labouring mutitude' are to be wisely led was one that we know exercised Wordsworth's mind a good deal.

Intriguing as it is to seek for Wordsworth's opinion in these lines, however, their main purpose to to set out an agenda. The passage goes on to indicate that, under Beaupuy's tutelage, and without as yet more radical influences to dull the sense he has of his own history and those 'habits' absorbed from 'books and common life', he was inclined to resolve the issues in a more balanced and tolerant way than would later be the case (328:44).

Still bearing in mind the fact that Wordsworth prefaced the appearance of Beaupuy with a reference to his own native 'republican' traditions, it would seem that he argues here that his ability to engage with Beaupuy in this discourse was as much due to his experience of 'common life' in England as it was to Beaupuy's eloquence. The French Revolution is in fact destined for a while to hamper his political vision, an object 'over near', pressing upon him, dazzling and misleading him with what was always that most dangerous of phenomena, 'the crowd' (328:345–7). Rather than

associating Beaupuy with the radical wing of the Revolution as it
was emerging in 1792, Wordsworth's instincts are to represent his
discourse in the tradition of English classical republicanism. This
again may be understood as a legitimising process, and in this respect
it is important to note how when describing Beaupuy's character he
implies a mind prepared for the rigours of adult life in a way very
similar to his own:

> He through the events
> Of that great change wandered in perfect faith,
> As through a book, an old romance, or tale
> Of Fairy, or some dream of actions wrought
> Behind the summer clouds. (326–8:305–9)

Whether conscious or not, the similarity of this to a passage already
quoted from Book V certainly reveals a very particular concern to
place Beaupuy within the context of the poet's own educational
experience:

> for my inner eye had seen
> Such sights before among the shining streams
> Of fairyland, the forests of romance –
> Thence came a spirit hallowing what I saw
> With decoration and ideal grace. (176:475–9)

This discussion has brought us to the tenth paragraph of Book IX.
Paragraph eleven (348–71) restates the balanced nature of the way
the two men attempted to review the existing state of political affairs,
but admits to the 'delight' they took in damning every aspect of
'royal courts', 'where dignity, / True personal dignity, abideth not'
(330:353–6). Paragraph twelve (372–96) describes how they used
history, 'the honorable deeds / Of ancient story' (330:372–3), to
confirm a sense of inevitable progress towards a fairer and politically
more just world. Again the appeal to history is undertaken to
legitimise their cause.

The two paragraphs that follow this (397–437 and 438–81) point
up the unresolved tension between a reasoned, 'academic' (332:397)
justification of revolution in the cause of liberty, 'of truth and error
passed away' (375), and the accompanying danger of thereby
destroying what is of value in the past, that which has received the
'reverential touch of Time' (471). Thus paragraph thirteen confines
us to 'academic groves', and 'interchange of talk, / On rational

liberty, and hope in man, / Justice and peace' (398–403). The function of the classical references to Dion and Plato, Eudemus and Timonedes, with their emphasis on 'philosophic war' (423), serves to confirm the moral and spiritual purpose involved, that of 'an authority Divine' (369–413). Beaupuy is to be reckoned among their number, and his death symbolises the failure of the French revolutionaries to realise the libertarian ideals of their classical mentors through the Revolution.

Paragraph fourteen, beginning at line 438, dramatically shifts the emphasis from theoretically reasoned, academic matter to a vivid description of the Loire valley, the sights and sounds of which, 'innocent yet / Of civil slaughter' (439–40), challenge an otherwise compelling conviction that there is a need for change. It is here that we may see how, though operating still within the political tradition that had nurtured William Crowe, Wordsworth is being confronted directly with its radical metamorphosis in a way which Crowe was never forced to experience. The pastoral 'solution' of *Lewesdon Hill* will not suffice, and the younger poet therefore faces a political dilemma which is not resolvable in his art by divesting his landscape of its inhabitants, or through the generalised moralising of Old Whig rhetoric. Unlike Crowe, Wordsworth is now forced to introduce into his poetry the challenge which political events and social conditions in the latter decades of the eighteenth century made to the pastoral politics of *Lewesdon Hill*. Regret for the loss of ancient wisdom and virtue had been the hallmark of poets like Akenside, Langhorne, Gray, Goldsmith and Crowe; but in *The Prelude*, set within the context of Wordsworth's experiences in France, his nostalgia has the effect of recasting the commonplace reflections of those poets in a significantly new mould.

Quite deliberately Wordsworth admits to a sense of regret for the changes which have taken place as a result of the Revolution; the poetry assumes a note of guilty stealth:

> Often in such a place
> From earnest dialogues I slipped in thought,
> And let remembrance steal to other times,
> When Hermits, from their sheds and caves forth-strayed,
> Walked by themselves, so met in shades like these ...
> Sometimes I saw, methought, a pair of knights
> Joust underneath the trees, that as in storm

> Did rock above their heads ...
> The width of those huge forests, unto me
> A novel scene, did often in this way
> Master my fancy, while I wandered on
> With that revered companion. And sometimes –
> When to a convent in a meadow green,
> By a brook-side, we came, a roofless pile,
> And not by reverential touch of Time
> Dismantled, but by violence abrupt –
> In spite of those heart-bracing colloquies,
> In spite of real fervour, and of that
> Less genuine and wrought up within myself –
> I could not but bewail a wrong so harsh,
> And for the Matin-bell to sound no more
> Grieved, and the evening taper, and the cross
> High on the topmost pinnacle, a sign
> Admonitory to the traveller,
> First seen above the woods. (334–6:445–9, 457–9, 465–81)

So it is that, his view actually being guided by Beaupuy:

> Imagination, potent to inflame
> At times with virtuous wrath and noble scorn,
> Did also often mitigate the force
> Of civic prejudice, the bigotry,
> So call it, of a youthful patriot's mind;
> And on these spots with many gleams I looked
> Of chivalrous delight. (336:497–503)

He is far more aware than any of his predecessors (he is given no choice) of the fact that, if the old chivalric world of virtue is to be preserved, it must itself be reordered and revised. One means whereby that might be achieved was already to hand, for throughout the century the Commonwealthman tradition had been using the cultural leaven of Gothic to sustain its political opposition to the Establishment. Classical academicism was thus augmented by its energetic Gothic counterpart.

The Commonwealthmen of the eighteenth century remained avid classicists, but they did not scruple to fashion Gothic history to suit the needs of their own times, that is to say where it aided a pragmatic justification of the need for a lasting settlement in 1688. Fanciful as this rendering could at times be, Samuel Kliger has argued that Gothic history nevertheless became 'a basic concept developing in the fiber of the nation'.[16] A complementary point has been made by Howard D. Weinbrot, who argues that the notion of a dominating Augustan culture in eighteenth-century England 'inhibits our seeing the major implications that the eighteenth century's rejection of Augustus had for literature, history, and politics'.[17]

The origin of the Gothic system of government was traced back to Asia, the common 'hive' of all races. Northern Europe, it was claimed, had subsequently fostered a morally purified and more robust version of the same system which had otherwise languished under a seductive, enervating Latin climate.[18] None of the political principles thus revealed were at odds with the republican strand of ideology that found its way into Commonwealthman political theory through Harrington, Neville, Molesworth and their successors. France in 1792, however, presented Wordsworth with a species of republicanism at odds with this, and potentially irreconcilable to his nostalgic picture of Cumberland society and university life.

In *The Prelude* the matin-bell, the evening taper and the cross of Gothic romance are symbols of a Christian tradition which the 'less genuine' fervour of the revolutionary spirit of the times is already destroying. The spiritual power for good in such 'Gothic' things is as real as that proffered by the classical ideal. In the former case, though, it is released through man's 'Imagination', stimulated by the mighty forests of the Loire valley, as surely as it is in the latter by the less immediately spectacular 'academic groves' of classical learning.

'History' has thus been summoned up as a guide to political judgement in paragraph twelve, has been presented in essentially classical terms in paragraph thirteen, only to be challenged in fourteen by what is specifically the poet's own tendency to indulge in a more Gothic vision of the past. Theresa M. Kelley has described Wordsworth's attachment to 'chivalric romance' as posing 'an irremedial conflict':

What Beaupuy says they are fighting against – the suffering and poverty of the French (especially the female French), the use of *lettres de cachet*, and the absence of a principle of *habeas corpus* – were all misuses of power practised by the *ancien régime*, whose authority derives from the chivalric past.[19]

Beaupuy's rational academicism is modified in these circumstances; the 'heart-bracing colloquies' and 'real fervour' of his companion for the revolutionary cause leave him still uneasy about the consequences of what threatens to be an imaginative diminishing, 'I could not but bewail a wrong so harsh' (336:476). The close affinity of this passage with the passage on the Grande Chartreuse in *Descriptive Sketches* should remind us once more of its affinity with the ambivalence of the Einsiedeln section in the earlier poem. One is also reminded yet again of the way Middleton presented Cicero's three villas and their complementary virtues. None of that, of course, was designed to cope with the atheism that now threatened France.

The sight of a 'hunger-bitten girl' enables Wordsworth to fashion a resolution of the debate of the previous verse paragraphs with twenty-three lines in praise of liberty which are contextualised politically not by France in 1792, but by the dissident Whig tradition we have already noted him using at the end of *Descriptive Sketches*. In effect, Wordsworth appropriates both the female vagrant motif of earlier eighteenth-century poetry, and Thomsonian political rhetoric; the most immediate and disturbing aspects of the French Revolution are set aside:

> I with him believed
> Devoutly that a spirit was abroad
> Which could not be withstood, that poverty
> At least like this would in a little time
> Be found no more, that we should see the earth
> Unthwarted in her wish to recompense
> The industrious, and the lowly child of toil,
> All institutes for ever blotted out
> That legalised exclusion, empty pomp
> Abolished, sensual state and cruel power,
> Whether by edict of the one or few;
> And finally, as sum and crown of all,
> Should see the people having a strong hand
> In making their own laws; whence better days
> To all mankind. (338:520–34)

The individual, human predicament remained Wordsworth's primary means of arriving at a political judgement. The subsequent failure of the Revolution to rescue the girl of Book IX undermines the fervour of the oration she inspires, and it is important to note how careful the poet is to locate this fervour initially with Beaupuy. Both the traditional moral of the female vagrant and the new radicalism of France are found wanting. It was, as we have seen, to

the task of refashioning the traditional vision of political justice with
the individual at its centre that Wordsworth set himself.

The political reforms demanded in this passage from *The Prelude*
may be shown to draw quite specifically on eighteenth-century
English traditions of political dissent. Reference has already been
made to Richard Price's *Discourse on the Love of our Country*, and its
ideological roots in the historically legitimised rhetoric of the
Dissenters' Committee, the London Association and the Society for
the Supporters of the Bill of Rights, and the widespread Common-
wealthman propaganda of the century. Wordsworth seems virtually
to be paraphrasing Price when the latter demanded:

First; the right to liberty of conscience in religious matters, secondly, the
right to resist power when abused; And thirdly, the right to choose our
governors; to cashier them for misconduct; and to frame a government for
ourselves.[20]

The 'right to liberty of conscience' referred to by Price is denied
through the process described by Wordsworth as having 'legalised
exclusion'; where the poet calls for the ending of 'sensual state and
cruel power', Price demands the 'right to resist power when abused',
and where Wordsworth wants to see the 'people having a strong
hand / In making their own laws' Price demands the 'right to choose'
(and dispose of) the 'governors', and to 'frame a government for
ourselves'. Wordsworth's reflections on the extent to which the
French Revolution was a legitimate movement, therefore, are
grounded in basic tenets of English classical republican ideology as it
had evolved from 1688, through the American War of Indepen-
dence, to his own time.

It will be helpful now to consider the structure of Books IX and X
taken together. We are clearly not given a consecutive narrative,
though the progression through Book IX is relatively orthodox. In
IX we reach the point in 1792 where Wordsworth's friendship and
admiration for Beaupuy is depicted as being at its height, along with
which went a passionate sense of the wrongs crying out to be righted
in society. The other major feature of Wordsworth's experience at
this time, his affair with Annette Vallon, is accounted for by the
story of Vaudracour and Julia with which the 1804 version of Book
IX ends.

But the debate in Book X between the value of tradition and the need for change encapsulated in lines 348–555, with its resolution in the hunger-bitten girl sequence, cannot be fully understood without reference to Book X. Initially Book X moves on with the narrative: Wordsworth leaves the Loire valley and travels to Paris, from thence he returns 'reluctantly' to England (368:176–201). We then hear of his frustration in England, his despair at the war, and we catch a glimpse of him on the Isle of Wight watching the fleet prepare to sail in the summer of 1793. A further reflection on his own despair at the course events were taking concludes this section at line 380. In the course of this the emphasis has been shifted significantly to his critical attitude towards his own government:

> Ere yet the fleet of Britain had gone forth
> On this unworthy service, whereunto
> The unhappy council of a few weak men
> Had doomed it, I beheld the vessels lie ...
>   In France, the men who for their desperate ends
> Had plucked up mercy by the roots were glad
> Of this new enemy. Tyrants, strong before
> In devilish pleas, were ten times stronger now.
>   (374–6:290–3, 306–9)

Of France and her fight againt the reactionary forces of Europe he writes:

> Meanwhile the invaders fared as they deserved:
> The herculean Commonwealth had put forth her arms,
> And throttled with an infant godhead's might
> The snakes about her cradle – that was well,
> And as it should be. (378:361–5)

There is no room here for paragraphs representing contending theories of political virtue; the theoretical discourse and idealism of Book IX gives way to a more direct account of the events themselves, and the stylistic change this occasions should inform our sense of the meaning of Book X: 'so preoccupied is this book with a stern "under"-countenance – the fear and terror of revolutionary France – that it cannot appropriate the language of the beautiful for a temporary, expressive shelter'.[21] Wordsworth himself certainly did not intend Book IX to be interpreted independently of Book X, its construction only confirms the relative arbitrariness of the break between them.

The narrative sequence that the first part of Book X follows terminates at line 380. The remainder of the book may then be described as twice retelling the story with which Book IX began, each time bringing it nearer the present, each time revisiting and reassessing the period of idealism associated with Beaupuy, and the subsequent agonising over French radicalism and British reactionism.

The first retelling takes us back to the early books of the poem. This is in fact a natural place for Wordsworth to reaffirm the interrelatedness of all his themes, and the childhood sequences are here set in their proper perspective, as having an immediate bearing on his understanding of what he learnt about himself and his fellow men and women in the 1790s. The passage with which this section begins marks a major attempt on the poet's part to expound his belief in a primary and secondary level of consciousness. It occurs at a pivotal moment in the structure of the two books; the orthodox chronology carried over from Book IX has been set aside, and the experiences thus far related are about to be reassessed twice with the intention of penetrating the experience more deeply using a heightened imaginative awareness.

It is a dense passage, and hardly rates as a success poetically or philsophically; but it is arguably a happier excursion into the field than Coleridge's attempt on what was fundamentally the same issue in Chapter XIII of the *Biographia Literaria*:

> When I began at first, in early youth,
> To yield myself to Nature – when that strong
> And holy passion overcame me first –
> Neither day nor night, evening or morn,
> Were free from the oppression, but, great God,
> Who send'st thyself into this breathing world
> Through Nature and through every kind of life,
> And mak'st man what he is, creature divine,
> In single or in social eminence,
> Above all these raised infinite ascents
> When reason, which enables him to be,
> Is not sequestered – what a change is here!
> How different ritual for this after-worship,
> What countenance to promote this second love!
> That first was service but to things which lie
> At rest, within the bosom of thy will:
> Therefore to serve was high beatitude;
> The tumult was a gladness, and the fear

> Ennobling, venerable; sleep secure,
> And waking thoughts more rich than happiest dreams.
>
> (380:381–400)

The opening lines tell of the dominance ('oppression') of that which informs the primary consciousness of man. This resides in the relationship between man and God mediated through nature, and it has been the function of the early books of *The Prelude* to record the poet's initiation into this 'holy passion'. The second level of perception arises from man's eventual entry into society, where he is given the opportunity to serve his fellow man; this is his 'second love', significantly described as 'this *after*-worship'. Wordsworth argues that the 'second love' which man evolves for matters of social concern (expressed through political conviction) is rightly understood as resting ultimately in the first, with love for and obedience to God conceived of here in unmistakably pantheistic terms: 'Who send'st thyself into this breathing world'.[22]

Danger threatens when the social and political role usurps the first 'holy passion' and becomes dominant, denying the 'unity of all' he had described in Part Two of the early *Prelude*, arguing there that it is alien to 'that false secondary power' when it stands alone (20:249–56). In consequence what is no more than 'this after-worship' controls the man who has denied the only trustworthy source of judgement and perception he has.

The Prelude in its early stages shows us Wordsworth turning his back on the current political events that dominated his life in the early 1790s to seek that which 'mak'st man what he is, creature divine'. For most of Book IX we witness an attempt to relive an experience of political enthusiasm that occurred before the full significance of the 'two consciousnesses' philosophy had matured. With the hunger-bitten girl sequence we consequently encounter an image that confirms an eighteenth-century tradition of political analysis, one which deflects us from confronting contemporary political radicalism, and introduces in its stead an imaginative appeal that convinces us 'a spirit was abroad' (338:521) capable of righting the social ills of the day. This was not the spirit of Jacobin populism, nor was it at that point capable of offering a convincing alternative to French radicalism as it was being fashioned by Robespierre.

What Wordsworth has done, therefore, in this passage from Book X is to challenge the ingenuous frame of mind represented in the preceding narration, and to provide a mature basis on which to review his experiences and political judgement. Interestingly, as we noted, he prefaces this process with a change of focus to the British political scene and the record of his own Government, a strategy similar to that used at the beginning of Book IX. His intention would still seem to be to imply that what he learns of value, he learns in the context of the British political tradition and the habits of mind it fosters, rather than the French.

Reflections arising from thoughts of 'early youth' take us on to line 439, and at 440 we are reminded of his first visit to France with Robert Jones. Wordsworth uses his memory of Arras, Robespierre's birthplace, as it was in 1790, to introduce his lengthy account of how he first heard of the death of Robespierre; the actual narrative coverage has thus been inched forward from the point we left it at in line 380 to July 1794. This passage constitutes one of Wordsworth's major expositions of his 'one life' theme; its use of landscape and of the memory of William Taylor have already been discussed. In its entirety the passage runs from line 466 to 566. What Wordsworth aims to achieve here is a revised formulation of the politics of pastoral which, in the form adherred to by Crowe, were inadequate to resolve the related political and aesthetic crises of the time. In this respect the Beaupuy passages of Book IX operate intentionally within the inadequate imaginative framework of eighteenth-century pastoral politics and its imagery, exposing the weakness of that position in the light of what follows. The key to a fresh vision of political virtue based upon the legitimate principles of liberty and freedom are achieved through imagery redolent of the 'one life', not Gothic romance and female vagrants.

The death of Robespierre is followed by a passage noting the cessation of the worst excesses of bloodshed in France, and confirming Wordsworth's continued disgust at his own country's attitude:

> Giants in their impiety alone,
> But in their weapons and their warfare base
> As vermin working out of reach, they leagued
> Their strength perfidiously to undermine
> Justice, and make an end of liberty. (394:652–6)

It is then at line 657 that he begins his second retelling of the story. The form this retelling takes is again all-important. Lines 657–756 are a reflection once more on his youthful ardour for change from the period of the poet's arrival in France and meeting with Beaupuy (though Beaupuy is not this time mentioned) to the outbreak of war between England and France. Line 689 is the beginning of the famous 'exercise of hope and joy' passage. Why is it necessary for him to go over yet again what the hunger-bitten girl passage has already told us? The style of these lines marks a return to the intense, poeticised imagery of Book IX, in contrast to the earlier part of Book X. But of course, the effect, when read with due regard to our experience of both books (and, indeed, of the preceeding eight books) is now altered. The passage which tells us that 'to be young was very heaven' (396–8:689–727) is generally quoted as an unambiguous account of the poet's feelings in 1792. In fact they are nothing of the sort.

The paragraph structure of Book IX has made it abundantly clear that Wordsworth wishes us to appreciate that his was a mind then beset by contending theories of the precise nature and virtue of events in France, couched in terms of tension between classical and Gothic traditions; in political terms the classical, 'commonsense' tradition was producing increasingly radical theories, the Gothic inclined to harbour a more conservative response. If he needed reminding, he – like us – only needed to look back to *Descriptive Sketches* to realise how mixed his feelings then were. The place for an undiluted outburst of enthusiasm in his own voice, rather than his own voice mediated through Beaupuy, is reserved for the point in his narrative where enough has been done through recalling events prior to and after the Beaupuy period to make it unavoidably ambivalent. The poet wishes to relive his enthusiasm as it at times no doubt enveloped him, but to relive it in a way that is as honest a recreation of it as he knows how to give; hedged about, that is to say, by doubts that were apparent to him from the first.

The lines which follow, taking up the story once more from February 1793, need equally careful interpretation:

> In the main outline, such it might be said
> Was my condition, till with open war
> Britain opposed the liberties of France. (400:757–9)

The reference here to his 'condition' is not only back as far as line 689 of Book X; it is in the first instance back to the beginning of

Book IX and the whole French Revolution narration. Ultimately it is a reference back to the beginning of the poem. Once more we are taken through an account of how the Revolution lost its way after 1793:

> And now, become oppressors in their turn,
> Frenchmen had changed a war of self-defence
> For one of conquest, losing sight of all
> Which they had struggled for. (400:791-4)

Throughout Book X Wordsworth is concerned to emphasise the way in which Britain's preparedness to go to war with France influenced his attitude. It points up the central place of the British political situation in shaping his own political views over against any imported radical tradition; the crisis was in essence a domestic one. In the brief paragraph, lines 791-804, he disowns French radical excesses only after indicating that the responsibility for them lay with his own and other reactionary European governments. When he goes on to say that he was 'not dismayed', therefore, we are to understand that his sustained opposition is based on an established 'radical' tradition which has long questioned the British Government's policies at home and abroad. The phrase he uses, 'I stuck / More firmly to old tenets' clearly implies a long-standing allegiance to political ideals which France had seemed to adopt and had attempted to realise. The pressures created by the situation, however, meant that even the 'old tenets' were destined to distortion. The circumstances were singularly unsuited to 'wise passiveness' and reflection; the 'opinions' (what should have been his 'second love' and 'after-worship') took pride of place over their source in his concept of a 'one life':

> But, rouzed up, I stuck
> More firmly to old tenets, and, to prove
> Their temper, strained them more; and thus, in heat
> Of contest, did opinions every day
> Grow into consequence, till round my mind
> They clung as if they were the life of it. (402:799-804)

Using the familiar philosophical and political rhetoric of eighteenth-century British writers, Wordsworth goes on to claim that Europe, and Britain in particular, followed a misguided course, abusing the time-honoured 'moral sentiments' and 'old opinions' of patriotism

which he, in common with his dissident Whig forebears, had come
so resolutely to believe in:

> Enough, no doubt, the advocates themselves
> Of ancient institutions had performed
> To bring disgrace upon their very names;
> Disgrace of which custom, and written law,
> And sundry moral sentiments, as props
> And emanations of these institutes,
> Too justly bore a part. A veil had been
> Uplifted. Why deceive ourselves? – 'twas so,
> 'Twas even so – and sorrow for the man
> Who either had not eyes wherewith to see,
> Or seeing hath forgotten. Let this pass,
> Suffice it that a shock had then been given
> To old opinions, and the minds of all men
> Had felt it – that my mind was both let loose,
> Let loose and goaded. (404:849–63)

The way is now clear for Wordsworth to proceed in his narrative
to the time where, through the companionship of Coleridge and
Dorothy, he began to come to terms with the apparent failure of his
life up to that point. Lines 931–40 contain a brief, caustic reference
to the instigation of Napoleon as Emperor, and from line 941 to the
end of the book (1005) Wordsworth occupies himself almost wholly
with an address to Coleridge, expressing his concern at his friend's
currently depressed state of mind:

> Thine be those motions strong and sanitive,
> A ladder for thy spirit to reascend
> To health and joy and pure contentedness:
> To me the grief confined that thou art gone
> From this last spot of earth where Freedom now
> Stands single in her only sanctuary –
> A lonely wanderer art gone, by pain
> Compelled and sickness, at this latter day,
> This heavy time of change for all mankind. (412:977–85)

Here then we have the proper context for the political debate of
Book IX, its romantic dreams of the past, its idealistic hopes for the
future, and its overall sense of dislocation from the realities of the
Revolution itself. Writing with a view to legitimising his continued
distrust of his own Government, Wordsworth appeals not to France,
but to Britain as 'this last spot of earth where Freedom now / Stands

single in her only sanctuary'. Whatever may have actually been his attachment to French or English Jacobinism, it is not now to be allowed to compromise his position as a critic of Pitt's war policy and the motives behind it, motives to be only too painfully illustrated by the Convention of Cintra a few years hence. As ever, Wordsworth wishes to legitimise his position. His meeting with the hunger-bitten girl does not mark a turning point for the poet, it is rather a dramatic confirmation of long-held views described in a way that should be tragically all too familiar.

The lost, destitute, wandering individual (as, for example, John Langhorne's female vagrant in *The Country Justice*) warns of time-honoured responsibilities not being fulfilled. It is a criticism based on a belief in the existing political system when brought to its full perfection. Mark Akenside's account in *The Pleasures of Imagination* is characteristic of this eighteenth-century view, while it also indicates its limitations for Wordsworth, grappling with the forces of emergent populism in revolutionary France:

> But now, behold! the radiant era dawns,
> When freedom's ample fabric, fixed at length
> For endless years on Albion's happy shore
> In full proportion, once more shall extend,
> To all the kindred powers of social bliss,
> A common mansion, a parental roof.
> There shall the Virtues, there shall Wisdom's train,
> Their long-lost friends rejoicing, as of old,
> Embrace the smiling family of arts . . .[23]

Akenside presents the picture of a society which has ceased to value the contribution 'the smiling family of arts' can make to its political life. For Wordsworth this comes to mean the loss of the imaginative faculty which he as a poet has suffered. In the Preface to *The Borderers*, therefore, he argued that 'works of Imagination' which enshrine and explain 'moral sentiments' are superior to 'real life'. A study of 'real life' unimaginatively conceived cannot see clearly 'the motive and the end'.[24] The omissions and deflections of which *The Prelude* appears to be guilty arise not from the poet's attempt to disavow his radicalism; Wordsworth certainly intended to reveal something of the error of his ways in the poem, but more importantly he was seeking to build a case for the continuing moral justification of his personal opposition to the political Establishment of his day.

10
'Our offences are unexpiated'[1]

I shall conclude with the words of a man of disciplined spirit, who withdrew from the too busy world – not out of indifference to its welfare, or to forget its concerns – but retired for wider compass of eye-sight, that he might comprehend and see in just proportions and relations; knowing above all that he, who hath not first made himself master of the horizon of his own mind, must look beyond it only to be deceived.

(The Convention of Cintra[2])

The impact of the French Revolution on the political life of Britain was such that there is a danger – especially for those looking at the Romantic movement in this country – of forgetting that a radical political tradition had been in existence throughout the century. Jacobinism was destined to define the term radical in the course of the 1790s, and what was there before is properly understood as degrees of dissidence emanating both from religious Dissent and from the Whig political interest, often expressing itself in extra-parliamentary groups and alliances. Whatever Wordsworth's engagement with Jacobinism might have been, his repudiation of the Revolution, of Godwin, Paine and Robespierre as political mentors did not impair his persistently dissident political habit of mind. The seeds of an eighteenth-century tradition of dissidence were sown in the literature he had encountered at Hawkshead by, among others, Thomson, Akenside, Beattie, and subsequently Crowe. A degree of dissidence is apparent in his early work, and a dissident frame of mind crucially informs *Lyrical Ballads*, while *The Prelude* confirms the legitimacy of the position of critical distrust he continued to hold, over against the Jacobinical radicalism he had rejected. It is worth remembering that when *The Prelude* was eventually published in 1850, Macaulay still found it 'to the last degree Jacobinical, indeed Socialist'.

It was certainly not until the latter years of the war, with the gradual evolution of a new era of political unrest in Britain and

Europe, that a significant modification of Wordsworth's political position began to take place. No reading of his poetry written during the war can therefore be complete without recognising the influence on his work of a continuing disaffection from the political Establishment. But from the late 1790s on, given the failure of revolution in France and the triumph of reactionary forces in Britain, his political position came to be defined by fears of being misconstrued, and by a sense of considerable isolation. Something of this can be deduced from Wordsworth's reply to a letter from John Thelwall of January 1804.

Thelwall had been heckled off the stage at a public lecture in Edinburgh, the result of a campaign orchestrated by Francis Jeffrey and William Erskine. In his attempt to hit back at Jeffrey, he looked to Wordsworth for support. Replying to Thelwall's letter, Wordsworth was happy to deal imperiously with Jeffrey and his views, but he went on to remind Thelwall that he had warned him against trying to lecture in Edinburgh in the first place, and where Thelwall requests constructive criticism of his own pamphlet in response to the outrage, he backs off completely:

As to the criticisms which you request of me, if I thought they would be of any value, I should be really sorry to say that I cannot at present find time to make them. I am now after a long sleep busily engaged in writing a Poem of considerable labour, and I am apprehensive least [*sic*] the fit should leave me, so that I wish to make the most of it while it is upon me. (EY, p. 432)

Having said this, he does go on to make a number of slighting criticisms of Thelwell's use of language. The letter ends with a clear and somewhat lofty indication of what their agenda for discussion ought most properly to be:

I have no more Room and am in a great hurry. Thank you again both for your Letter and Pamphlet. I shall be glad to see your remarks next summer, and to converse with you on Metre.

The fact that in Edinburgh and elsewhere Thelwall was being decried as a Jacobin traitor indicated only too plainly to Wordsworth the political isolation (if not persecution) that he himself was threatened with. In *The Prelude* he was even then engrossed in the task of establishing, at least to his own satisfaction, the honourable basis of his personal motives for dissent, the consequence of a habit of mind he could in no way abandon, nor write out of his poetry.

What was clearly needed, however, was a strategy marked by caution, a period of retirement perhaps, certainly of wise passiveness. Inevitably such a course of action was accompanied by feelings of guilt, but this might to some degree be expiated by looking forward to completing *The Recluse*, intended to be a comprehensive, public statement vindicating what in effect would be a contemporary rendering of the traditional radical Whig position.

The final books of the 1805 *Prelude* are not surprisingly therefore informed throughout by images of isolation, a state which the poem as a whole progressively exalts to the level of a solemn duty. A visionary poet must accept that the most profound wisdom is only attainable from contemplation in an 'individual state':

> Here must thou be, O man,
> Strength to thyself – no helper hast thou here –
> Here keepest thou thy individual state:
> No other can divide with thee this work,
> No secondary hand can intervene
> To fashion this ability. (XIII, 468:188–93)

In the 1805 text, Wordsworth reserves the narration of two crucial childhood experiences for Book XI. The incident where, separated from his companion, he comes to the site of a gibbet, and subsequently sees a girl carrying a pitcher; and the memory of waiting to be collected from school for the Christmas holidays (430–6:278–388). The first of these two incidents has already been discussed. In the general context of his situation in 1804–05, the import of both are plainly evident. The first incident (probably located on Penrith Beacon[3]) creates a mood of loneliness, fear and guilt, to some degree then mitigated by the sight of the girl who, though solitary, burdened and seemingly opposed by the elements, stoically struggles forward.

In the second incident Wordsworth describes himself as 'Feverish, and tired, and restless', awaiting the horses sent for himself and his brothers Richard and John for their homeward journey. Evidently anxious to be at home, he is forced to wait, and unwillingly endures this passivity in self-imposed isolation:

> Thither I repaired
> Up to the highest summit. 'Twas a day
> Stormy, and rough, and wild, and on the grass

> I sate half sheltered by a naked wall.
> Upon my right hand was a single sheep,
> A whistling hawthorn on my left, and there,
> With those companions at my side, I watched,
> Straining my eyes intently as the mist
> Gave intermitting prospect of the wood
> And plain beneath. (434:354–63)

In the course of the Christmas holidays his father died, and he remembers that at the time he could only understand what had happened as 'A chastisement', in some way a punishment visited on him for unspecified crimes. There are then two moments of isolation: waiting to return home, and the loss of his father. To cope with the trauma of the latter he discovers that the companionship of nature experienced in the former (bleak and significantly unpicturesque, 'The single sheep, and the one blasted tree') mysteriously provide the strength and the stoicism needed to cope with bereavement, and to be able to look to the future (436:375–84). The metaphorical application of this necessary aloneness to his present situation is made clear:

> And I do not doubt
> That in this later time, when storm and rain
> Beat on my roof at midnight, or by day
> When I am in the woods, unknown to me
> The workings of my spirit thence are brought. (436:384–8)

Wordsworth chose to terminate Book XII by recalling an experience of extreme solitariness, the period spent walking across Salisbury Plain in 1793. The theme of 'Imagination, How Impaired and Restored' therefore approaches its climax through a dramatic account of a visionary experience quite distinct in character from any previous examples. What he describes is not a moment of intense imaginative insight, it lays claim to an actual hallucination (or series of hallucinations over a period of three days), during which he witnesses both the barbaric cruelty and the serene beauty of the prehistoric world; the 'dismal flames' around the sacrificial altar, and the 'stillness' and 'pleasant sound' of music that accompanied the Druids' contemplative studies of 'the heavens' (454:330, 342–53).[4]

The significance of a recollection taken from this period of his life included the presence of specifically political concerns in a way recollections from childhood days did not. The year 1793 marked the time when the long and painful process of restoring his imaginative powers began, a restoration which required him to analyse and understand the relationship of his political self to his poetical self; it began in a state of utter loneliness with no clear sign of the path ahead:

> There on the pastoral downs without a track
> To guide me, or along the bare white roads
> Lengthening in solitude their dreary line,
> While through those vestiges of ancient times
> I ranged, and by the solitude o'ercome,
> I had a reverie. (454:315–20)

The importance of this passage is to be fully understood in the light of the way roads and tracks become regular points of reference in Books XI and XII. We remember the two roads the poet watched through the mist when waiting to go home from school (434:352), and the important passage in Book XII:

> I love a public road: few sights there are
> That please me more – such object hath had power
> O'er my imagination since the dawn
> Of childhood, when its disappearing line
> Seen daily afar off, on one bare steep
> Beyond the limits which my feet had trod,
> Was like a guide into eternity,
> At least to things unknown and without bound. (444:145–52)

It is by no means only Wordsworth's sense of continued political isolation and impotence that informs the structure of these final books. Wise passiveness was to some degree being explained and justified; but equally important to the Salisbury Plain passage is the vivid quality of the vision. The lines he added to the Penrith Beacon sequence (432:315–27) echo sentiments expressed also in the *Intimations Ode* (1804) and the *Ode to Duty* (1805), both poems which reveal urgent fears about the loss of visionary power. In the light of this his use of the 'spots of time' passage in Book XI takes on a particular significance in relation to the time when the later books were being composed:

> There are in our existence spots of time,
> Which with distinct preeminence retain
> A renovating virtue, whence, depressed

> By false opinion and contentious thought,
> Or aught of heavier or more deadly weight
> Of ordinary intercourse, our minds
> Are nourished and invisibly repaired. (428–30:257–64)

Stoicism is needed as much in order to retain his faith in himself as a poet, as it is in political convictions which continue to alienate him from the political Establishment.

Though perhaps never a pantheist in any formal sense, Wordsworth retained – over against a Coleridgean position deriving from Kant and expressed in the *Dejection Ode* – his belief in a 'voluntary power / Instinct' possessed by natural objects.[5] If the *Intimations Ode* challenged Coleridge's claim that 'we receive but what we give', in *The Prelude* we find him prepared – under the pressure of the moment in 1804 – to at least gesture towards a modification of his views in the general direction of the *Dejection Ode*:

> but this I feel,
> That from thyself it is that thou must give,
> Else never canst receive. (432:331–3)[6]

Other poems of this period show Wordsworth determined to maintain his political position and suffer the consequences of isolation in the process. Indeed the influence of the political factor becomes a crucial part of understanding the nature and form which much of the poetry took, as it does with *Lyrical Ballads*. An important example in this respect is the apparently light-hearted exercise in mock heroic first written in January 1806, *Benjamin the Waggoner*.

The earliest surviving complete manuscript of *Benjamin* dates from late March 1806, and there then followed the inevitable process of correcting and transcribing; it was not until 1819 that the poem was finally published. Paul F. Betz, in his introduction to the Cornell edition of *Benjamin*, argues that the poem's major interest lies in its mock heroic style:

Benjamin the Waggoner is his most extended effort in this vein. The poem parodies certain patterns in *Paradise Lost* and its sources in Genesis, and in classical tragedy and epic, while yet making a serious point: its story involves a trust given (by his master to Benjamin), a warning that the trust must be fulfilled, temptation, sin, a consequent fall, and suffering by others ... as well as by the sinner. And while not in form a ballad, the poem is suffused with the experimental approach and many of the dramatic and narrative techniques that caused the lyrical ballads to become the objects of intense critical interest. (Betz, p. 4)

Not only is it important to appreciate common stylistic ground with *Lyrical Ballads*; given a comparability of experimental dramatic and narrative techniques between the late 1790s and 1806, it is reasonable to suspect that the political themes – subject to a degree of 'displacement' – are basically consistent.

The story is about a wagoner who fulfils the essential qualities of a Wordsworthian hero; he is a solitary traveller, living a reflective life as he steers his wagon through the Lakeland passes. His life has not always been blameless, for he was once prone to drink; but all that has been put behind him, though not without an effort, and not without the occasional temptation to sample once more the sweets of dissoluteness. His altered fashion of life is closely identified with Wordsworth's own, and a passage in Book XII of *The Prelude* fits both Benjamin and Wordsworth equally well:

> seeing little worthy or sublime
> In what we blazon with the pompous names
> Of power and action, early tutored me
> To look with feelings of fraternal love
> Upon those unassuming things that hold
> A silent station in this beauteous world. (440:47–52)

The poet in fact lives in a cottage on Benjamin's route through Grasmere, a cottage that was suitably once the 'Dove and Olive Branch' tavern; it now houses 'A simple water drinking Bard':

> Then why need Ben be on his guard?
> He ambles by, secure and bold –
> Yet thinking on the times of old
> It seems that all looks wond'rous cold.
> He shrugs his shoulders, shakes his head,
> And for the honest Folks within
> It is a doubt with Benjamin
> Whether they be alive or dead.   (Betz, 48:61–8)

The state of purified solitary sobriety now attained by both the poet and Benjamin is being gently questioned – is 'retirement' and 'wise passiveness' in truth equivalent to being 'dead'? In *Lyrical Ballads* the 'wise passiveness' of 'Expostulation and Reply' is challenged at once by 'The Tables Turned'.

At the time he was writing these lines Wordsworth was under considerable pressure – self-inflicted, and from Dorothy and his wife Mary – to pursue his 'great work', *The Recluse*. But for all his determination and sobriety, he was finding it almost impossible to settle to what was in fact an impossible task.[7] To the puritanical side of his nature, the 'lively impulse of feeling' he described as having led to the composition of *Benjamin* must have seemed little better than blasphemous when he set the poem alongside the contribution he had intended to make to public life through active political commitment (Betz, p. 6); over against that, only *The Recluse* would do to justify his way of life. We need to remember these things when we read of the sober wagoner making his lonely way through the Lake District with his heavy, ponderous load, his mind engaged with the memory of an intoxicatingly exciting youth.

The wagoner passes Wordsworth's cottage, and comes next to 'The Swan', a tavern still very much in business. He resists temptation 'in despite / Of open door and shining light', and begins 'The long ascent of Dunmal-raise' (Betz, 52:92–104). While he is congratulating himself on his steadfastness, a storm breaks, in the midst of which he comes upon a terrified woman and her infant, by now a predictable enough development. Benjamin gets them into the shelter of his wagon, only to be hailed next by the woman's husband, a discharged sailor. The whole party, which includes an ass belonging to the sailor, battle on through the storm.

The sailor is Benjamin's downfall, for at the next village he tempts the wagoner into 'The Cherry Tree' where all his good intentions are forgotten, and along with the rest of the company, he gets very drunk. The consequence of the night's carousal is that Benjamin is late, and when his master eventually meets him he finds his wagoner and his wagon (and his dog which has been accompanying Benjamin) all considerably the worse for wear. Benjamin is sacked on the spot. The loss is twofold, 'both Waggoner and Wain', because no one can manage the wagon with Benjamin's skill (Betz, 108:751).

Explained thus briefly, there would seem to be only that initial identification of the 'water drinking Bard' with the wagoner to suggest that Wordsworth was engaged in anything more than a light-hearted exercise in parody. In fact, the political implications of the story are considerable, and would most certainly have had their part to play in Wordsworth's tardiness in publishing the poem.

In 1808, two years after completing the first version of *Benjamin*, Wordsworth was to read of the Convention of Cintra, and his consequent rage at what he saw as the hypocrisy, cynicism and immorality of the British Government's dealings with the Napoleonic armies in Portugal led him to write a pamphlet damning the Government, and Wellesly in particular, for their preparedness to treat with the French tyrant at the expense of the Spanish and Portuguese nations, both of whom were fighting for their liberty:

Again: independence and liberty were the blessings for which the people of the Peninsula were contending ... Now, liberty – healthy, matured, time-honoured liberty – this is the growth and peculiar boast of Britain; and nature herself, by encircling with the ocean the country which we inhabit, has proclaimed that this mighty, nation is for ever to be her own ruler, and that the land is set apart for the home of immortal independence. Judging then from these first fruits of British Friendship, what bewildering and depressing and hollow thoughts must the Spaniards and Portuguese have entertained concerning the real value of these blessings, if the people who have possessed them longest, and who ought to understand them best, could send forth an army capable of enacting the oppression and baseness of the Convention of Cintra; if the government of that people could sanction this treaty; and if, lastly, this distinguished and favoured people themselves could suffer it to be held forth to the eyes of men as expressing the sense of their hearts – as an image of their understanding. (&S I, 280:2381–98)

The sickening feeling of betrayal experienced in 1793, when, in the company of Calvert, Wordsworth stood on the Isle of Wight watching the British fleet prepare for War with France, had clearly not diminished. The basic principles of dissent remained unaltered, and in *The Convention of Cintra* as in *Salisbury Plain*, Wordsworth refers his readers unhesitatingly to Britain's shameful attack on the American colonies (a war 'waged against Liberty') as the major event in recent times which laid bare the central issues for debate (O&S I, 308–9:3572–605). It mattered not if the British Government's army defeated the French, here would be no lasting guarantee of liberty, for the war was still being waged for the basest materialistic motives, as had been the case in America where, against all the odds, the British were defeated.

Benjamin the Waggoner is as unqualified a statement of that conviction as *Salisbury Plain* or *The Convention of Cintra* ever was.

Indeed, what Wordsworth wrote in 1806 in *Benjamin* was arguably every bit as likely to get him into trouble had it been published then, as anything he said later in the pamphlet about Wellesley and the Government (and he did try, at the last minute, to modify the venom of *The Convention of Cintra*). To illustrate this claim for *Benjamin* we must look at the second canto (or 'Second Part' in the 1806 manuscript).

The action of the second canto is in effect the pivot upon which the whole poem turns, for it is there that Benjamin is tempted and falls. Following Betz's mock epic reading, there is no doubt about who the Satanic presence is, the devil in Wordsworth's Eden is played by the discharged sailor:

> A welcome greeting he can hear –
> It is a fiddle in its glee
> Dinning from the Cherry Tree.
>
> Thence the sound, the light is there,
> As Benjamin is now aware
> Who neither saw nor heard – no more
> Than if he had been deaf and blind –
> Till rouz'd up by the Sailor's roar
> He hears the sound and sees the light
> And in a moment calls to mind
> That 'tis the Village merry-night.
>
> (Betz, 68:290–300)

Before Benjamin has a chance to consider whether it is right or wrong, the sailor 'draws him to the door, "come in, / Come, come," cries he to Benjamin':

> And Benjamin – ah! woe is me! –
> Gave the word, the horses heard
> And halted, though reluctantly.
>
> (Betz, 70:315–17)

Wordsworth's enthusiasm for the poetry of Burns, and particularly for *Tam O' Shanter*, is evident in the spirited account he gives of the jollifications. Significantly, we are told that the woman and her child, still in the back of the wagon, have been forgotten; this in itself is an indication that Benjamin's social conscience has been dulled, and that the genuine impulse of 'patriotic and domestic love' is under threat. At this point Wordsworth makes a specific and unambiguous

connection between the evil represented by the sailor, and the spirit
in which the war with France was then being conducted. It is in the
context of a situation which tells of abandonment of duty, of
flippant, hedonistic pleasure, of the 'fall' of the honest wagoner, that
the sailor produces a large model, mounted upon a wheeled frame,
of a man-of-war:

> Surprize to all, but most surprize
> To Benjamin, who rubs his eyes,
> Not knowing that he had befriended
> A Man so gloriously attended.   (Betz, 74:378–81)

The irony of 'gloriously attended' is immediately evident; the
devil's toy which bewitches Benjamin and the rest of the drunken
company is no less than Nelson's flagship at the Battle of the Nile:

> So said, so done, the masts, sails, yards
> He names them all and interlards
> His speech, with uncouth terms of art,
> Accomplish'd in a Showman's part,
> And then as from a sudden check
> Cries out, ''tis there the Quarter deck
> On which brave Admiral Nelson stood –
> A sight that would have done you good.
> One eye he had which bright as ten
> Burnt like a fire among his men.
> Here lay the French and thus came we.'
> (Betz, 75–6:392–402)

Less than a year after his death and virtual beatification, we find
Wordsworth using Nelson's career as a focal point for his abhorrence
of a war he believed to be morally indefensible. The argument was
not – as it had been over the colonies and in the early 1790s – that
war was 'unnatural', but that the war, Nelson's war, was being
waged out of an unhealthy lust for power; men were going to their
deaths unworthily. The irony is inescapable when Benjamin – now
fallen irredeemably from grace – is moved to cry out:

> 'A bowl, a bowl of double measure,'
> Cries Benjamin, 'a draft of length
> To Nelson, England's pride and treasure,
> Her bulwark and her tower of strength?!'
> When Benjamin had siez'd the bowl
> The Mastiff gave a warning growl;

> The Mastiff from beneath the Waggon
> Where he lay watchful as the Dragon
> Rattled his chain – 'twas all in vain;
> For Benjamin, triumphant Soul!
> He heard the monitory growl –
> Heard, and in opposition quaff'd
> A deep, determin'd, desperate draft.
>
> (Betz, 76–8:413–25)

The 'monitory voice' looked for in *The Prelude* (14:18) is now become a 'monitory growl', a solemn warning not to be carried away by unthinking patriotism. Given the appearance of Wordsworth's tribute to Nelson in *Poems in Two Volumes* (1807), 'Character of the Happy Warrior', it will be helpful to look more closely for a moment at the way he responded – publicly and privately – to Trafalgar and its consequences.

Dorothy, in a letter to Lady Beaumont, tells of how she burst into tears on hearing of Nelson's death, while William, showing far less emotion, 'forced me to suspend my grief till he had made further enquiries' (EY, p. 650). When Wordsworth himself came to reflect on Nelson's death in a letter to Sir George Beaumont of February 1896, his views were guarded to say the least. He begins by surmising that Nelson's health being already in decline, the man would probably have died soon after his return from the battle anyway. The intention is clearly to suggest that the dramatic circumstances of his death are likely to distort an objective, balanced assessment of the man:

Few men have ever died under circumstances so likely to make their death of benefit to their Country: it is not easy to see what his life could have done comparable to it. The loss of such men as Lord Nelson is indeed great and real; but surely not for the reason which makes most people grieve, a supposition that no other such man is in the Country: the Old Ballad has taught us how to feel on these occasions:

> I trust I have within my realm
> Five hundred good as he.

But this is the evil that nowhere is merit so much under the power of what (to avoid a more serious expression) one may call that of fortune as in military and naval service; and it is five hundred to one that such men will [not] have attained situations where they can shew themselves so, that the Country may know in whom to trust. Lord Nelson had attained that situation; and therefore, I think, (and not for the other reason) ought we chiefly to lament that he is taken from us. (MY, p. 7)

He then moves on to give judgement on the career of Pitt, the passage already quoted in the previous chapter. The effect of that, of course, is to qualify profoundly any enthusiasm he might have for the war effort in which Nelson had figured so prominently. The principle adherred to here in matters of political judgement remains the same as that argued for poetry in the Preface to *Lyrical Ballads*: 'the feeling therein developed gives importance to the action and situation, and not the action and situation to the feeling'; the same point is implicit in the passage quoted earlier from *The Prelude* as relevant to an understanding of Benjamin's character, 'seeing little worthy or sublime / In what we blazon with the pompous names / Of power and action' (440:47–9).

An earlier letter to Beaumont further reveals Wordsworth's frame of mind:

I have just been reading two newspapers, full of fractious brawls about Lord Melville and his delinquencies, ravages of the French in the West Indies, victories of the English in the East, Fleets of ours roaming the sea in search of enemies they cannot find, &c &c &c, and I have asked myself more than once lately If my affections can be in the right place caring as I do so little about what the world seems to care so much for. All this seems to me 'a tale told by an Idiot full of sound and fury signifying nothing.' (EY, p. 593)

In 'Character of the Happy Warrior' there is no mention of Nelson whatever. The poem is a recital of all the classical republican virtues of the warrior statesman type, and if asked to put a name to the description, readers of Wordsworth could reasonably be expected to place this alongside the eulogy to Beaupuy in *The Prelude*, Book IX. Equally, of course, Wordsworth also has in mind the kind of warrior he himself would like to be, or has to some extent been forced to become; a leader who paradoxically holds back, whose natural instinct is to retire, whose central motive must be honest consistency:

> – Who, if he rise to station of command,
> Rises by open means; and there will stand
> On honourable terms, or else retire,
> And in himself possess his own desire;
> Who comprehends his trust, and to the same

> Keeps faithful with a singleness of aim;
> And therefore does not stoop, nor lie in wait
> For wealth, or honours, or for worldly state . . .[8]

The poem is wholly distinct from the genre of fulsome tributes that appeared over many weeks following Trafalgar. William Lisle Bowles's offering is a fair representative of the twenty poems addressing this subject printed in *The Gentleman's Magazine* for November 1805:

> Yet lift, brave Chief, thy dying eyes;
> Hark, loud huzzas around thee rise;
> Aloft the flag of Conquest flies!
>   The DAY IS WON.
>
> The Day is won – Peace to the Brave!
> But, whilst the joyous streamers wave,
> We'll think upon the Victor's grave:
>   PEACE TO THE BRAVE![9]

It is only through a note appended to 'The Happy Warrior' that we are invited to think of Nelson as an exemplar. Even here, the tone is revealing. The death of Nelson, Wordsworth writes, was the 'event' which 'directed the author's thoughts to the subject'. The 'event', then, rather than the man himself; and even this admission, it seems, has been unwillingly made, or 'induced':

His [Wordsworth's] respect for the memory of his great fellow-countryman induces him to mention this; though he is well aware that the verses must suffer from any connection in the Reader's mind with a Name so illustrious.[10]

Given Wordsworth's private correspondence, we must surely assume that a note of covert irony attends that final phrase. A democratic habit of thought informs the whole performance; a profound distrust of raising one individual above another, and of glorifying death by war.

As always, Wordsworth's political and aesthetic instincts are complementary. The 'peculiar grace' of the Happy Warrior is to be unaffected, 'a Soul whose master bias leans / To home-felt pleasures and to gentle scenes' (59–60). Simplicity and solitude of the same order are recurring themes in many of the 1807 *Poems*, where Wordsworth's own profession of a retired life in 'I am not One who much or oft delight' is echoed in poems like 'I Wandered Lonely as a

Cloud', 'The Small Celandine', 'To The Daisy', and in a narrative like
'The Blind Highland Boy':

> '*Lei-gha – Lei-gha*' – then did he cry
> '*Lei-gha – Lei-gha*' – most eagerly;
> Thus did he cry, and thus did pray,
> And what he meant was, 'Keep away,
> And leave me to myself!'[11]

In 'The Solitary Reaper' it is precisely the anonymity at the heart of
the experience described that gives it its worth. The girl sings 'by
herself', 'Alone she cuts, and binds the grain, / And sings a
melancholy strain.' There is no one to tell the listener what it is she
sings, and this lack of knowledge paradoxically renders the experience
all the more memorable:

> And, as I mounted up the hill,
> The music in my heart I bore,
> Long after it was heard no more.[12]

Everything that surrounded the death of Nelson, not least the
poetry, was ephemeral and untrustworthy, the very opposite of the
political and moral ideal of leadership and bravery laid out in 'The
Happy Warrior'. Benjamin's fall from grace in *The Cherry Tree*
brings together all Wordsworth's misgivings in this respect.

The moment when Benjamin drinks deep marks the point at
which the wagoner's reluctant sliding towards perdition becomes an
enthusiastic, 'determined' embracing of the evil which has been
beckoning to him. Nelson's ship 'in full apparel' becomes an image
of the sailor's showmanship and his seductive skills, just as
Benjamin's wagon was an image of his worthy, honest way of life,
reflecting for Wordsworth, no doubt, his own ungainly poetical
project, *The Recluse*. As they emerge from the tavern and make their
uncertain way into the night, Benjamin actually expresses a wish to
tart his wagon up and make it look more like a ship. Nothing could
mark his fallen state more; nothing could by implication be less
genuinely patriotic:

> 'I like,' said Ben, 'her make and stature
> And this of mine, this bulky Creature
> Of which I have the steering, this,
> Seen fairly, is not much amiss.
> We want your streamers, Friend! you know,

> But altogether as we go
> We make a kind of handsome show.'   (Betz, 86:550–6)

In Theresa Kelley's recent book, she draws attention to the subversive implications of the plot of both the first version, and the later published version of *Benjamin*: 'both versions minimize the value of the heroic sublime by having a drunken sailor and waggoner claim an heroic stature that neither exhibits'.[13] The considerable risk Wordsworth was contemplating in writing the poem has not been seriously considered, however, and indeed the assumption often is that by this time the poet's politics were far more conformist, or 'loyalist' than was clearly the case. When, for example, Donald Reiman reviewed the Cornell edition of the poem for *Studies in Romanticism*, he discussed in detail the genesis 'of the old sailor who plays so prominent a part in the poem'.[14] What Reiman did not do was to discuss in any detail the actual nature of the sailor's 'part' beyond the extraordinary assumption that he is the 'hero' of the piece even as Nelson must then have been a hero figure for Wordsworth.

Reiman is working from an assumed loyalist meaning for *Benjamin* to the point of ignoring the simple logic of the story, where surely no Wordsworth scholar familiar with the traits of the poet could miss Wordsworth's identification with the wagoner, rather than with the sailor who lures Benjamin to the demon drink, thereby bringing about his downfall. Reiman has evidently missed entirely a crucial political facet of the poem's ironic, mock epic moral. Such insensitivity arises from the still all too common assumption that in rejecting Jacobinism, Wordsworth's only alternative was total identification with the policies of his country's political leaders. A position of dissidence independent of Jacobinism, carried forward from an eighteenth-century English tradition, remains to be more widely recognised if poems such as this are to be properly understood.

Wordsworth, as he seldom fails in some way to do in his poetry, is addressing his own decision to live a life of 'retirement', where retirement meant not directly involving himself with political activity. His experience of the political world of action had been one of betrayal, and the moral is contained in the metaphor of *The Cherry Tree* as a place of thoughtless, literally inebriated activity. The political edge to that metaphor is insisted upon by the direct incorporation of Nelson, the hero of the hour, into the sailor's method of successfully getting Benjamin to betray his trust.

The specifically political turn of mind which Wordsworth had is as important here as in *Salisbury Plain*, and it is to be understood as rooted in eighteenth-century, Revolution Whig ideology, forever critical of Establishment political morality, though by this time increasingly anachronistic and isolated:

> A sad Catastrophe, say you –
> Adventure never worth a song?
> Be free to think so, for I too
> Have thought so many times and long.
> But what I have and what I miss
> I sing of these, it makes my bliss.
> Nor is it I who play the part,
> But a shy spirit in my heart
> That comes and goes, will sometimes leap
> From hiding-places ten years deep.
> Sometimes, as in the present case,
> Will show a more familiar face,
> Returning like a Ghost unlaid
> Until the debt I owe be paid.
>
> (Betz, 108–10:752–65)

He intended to make payment in full with the completion of *The Recluse*; when Wordsworth died in 1850, he was still in debt.

Epilogue

It was a solitary mound;
Which two spears' length of level ground
Did from all other graves divide:
As if in some respect of pride;
Or melancholy's sickly mood,
Still shy of human neighbourhood;
Or guilt, that humbly would express
A penitential loneliness.

(*The White Doe of Rylstone*[1])

Simply to equate Wordsworth's political position in his later years with that of the Tory party has for some time now been considered inadequate. After 1800, of course, he did become increasingly financially beholden to the Establishment, and to the new Lord Lonsdale in particular. Far from simplifying the situation, however, the circumstances that evolved rendered Wordsworth's position no less complex than it had been before:

we should never discount the economic facts of the poet's household, maintained as it was by the uneasy (even when unctuously acknowledged) sense of dependence upon the goodwill of the high and mighty. Like the archfiend himself, Wordsworth exercises freedom of choice under the eyes of an all-powerful, if not all-seeing, presence. Allowing him neither secure establishment nor unfettered freedom, it commits him to an uncomfortable and constantly adjusting vacillation between the two.[2]

The poetry discussed in the previous chapter begins to reveal the true, and lasting nature of Wordsworth's ambivalent position. Publicly he becomes increasingly identified with political conservatism, his developing friendships with Beaumont, Scott, and the new Lord Lonsdale indicate this, over against his awkwardness with friends from his 'radical' past like Thelwall. The embarrassment caused by Thelwall's application to him for active support in his campaign against Francis Jeffrey is discernible also in his correspondence with Francis Wrangham. Wrangham was a fellow member of Godwin's circle of friends in the early 1790s, and Wordsworth came to know him at the same time that he was introduced to Felix Vaughan, and to James Losh who drafted the petition of the Society of the Friends of the People in 1793.[3] But while in 1806 Wordsworth was resolutely refusing to become involved in Wrangham's scheme to publish a collection of satirical portraits in verse, in 1807 he was nevertheless happy to express full agreement with Wrangham's view that Nelson did not deserve the reputation of a truly great man, and added that he was in consequence going to withdraw the explanatory note to 'Character of the Happy Warrior' in future editions of the 1807 *Poems* (MY, p. 89 and 154).

The poetry of 1806–07 suggests a man anxious to avoid being named in public as committed to any specific political party or faction; 'my name would be mentioned in connection with the work', he wrote to Wrangham in 1806, 'which I would on no account should be'. His poetry is the work of an outsider, leaving a potentially controversial poem like *Benjamin the Waggoner* un-published, while making public a collection of poems likely only to arouse hostility because of their refusal to abide by Augustan tenets of poetic decorum. Yet the volume of 1807 indicates that he was evidently holding to the views expressed in the Preface to *Lyrical Ballads*, fostering still a belief in 'common life', and caring deeply for the lot of the 'labouring multitude' with whom he could only ever identify in a tenuous fashion.

We find him in *The Excursion* persisting with the use of a pedlar as his main mouthpiece; in the *Poems* of 1807 he claims serious poetic status for a sailor's mother, 'Majestic in her person, tall and straight', for beggars, for Alice Fell, for a solitary reaper, for a blind highland boy, and for the 'Spade of a Friend':

> Health, quiet, meekness, ardour, hope secure,
> And industry of body and of mind;
> And elegant enjoyments, that are pure
> As Nature is; too pure to be refined.[4]

He is rejecting on the one hand the world of polite, superficially 'refined' literary convention, and in doing so effecting to retire from the world of the rich and the mighty, insisting on his belief in 'simplicity', in 'Health, quiet, meekness, ardour, hope secure'; yet at the same time he finds himself by degrees becoming more and more dependent on patronage from the public world he variously seeks to avoid.

The task of reconciling the contradictions that beset Wordsworth in his situation as a poet in retirement was of course to be sought through the composition of *The Excursion*. The misanthropic Solitary was to be rescued by the wise discourse of the philosophic pedlar. What *The Excursion* achieved was a weighty and detailed analysis of the problems involved; it reached no clear resolution, and in that respect it reflects Wordsworth's integrity as a poet.

Walter Scott, writing with a far less compromising history of youthful political allegiances managed far more successfully to pursue the theme of reconciliation through the Waverley Novels. The contemporary political world required heroes like Guy Mannering, and Henry Morton in *Old Mortality*, men able to see clearly how the past might be reconciled to the present, and tradition to modernity. Wordsworth, rooted as firmly as he was in eighteenth-century traditions of thought, was never to achieve any comparable form of resolution. The solution he gradually evolved forced him to discard his all-embracing vision of the one life, turning instead to a more limited belief in the sanctity of domestic life and virtue:

At Alfoxden it had been possible to believe that love was general –

> The clouds were touched,
> And in their silent faces did he read
> Unutterable love.

– that creation was singing the song of the One Life, and singing it for all to hear (*Pedlar*, 99–101, 219). But now Cowper's moral, sentimental, personal God – the God of Victorian children and their pets – is called in ... as the means of justifying his decision to become a recluse ... After the initial confidence, *Home at Grasmere* shows him to be more and more aware that future blessedness, if it depends on human beings, may be a very long way off.[5]

At the heart of his sense of an integral aesthetic and political crisis, an issue informing his poetry from the early 1790s, lay a fundamental contradiction that continued to plague his creative life.

On the one hand there was a belief in 'individuality', a creed which demanded his 'aloneness'; on the other hand lay the persistent sense of the need to join with the crowd (potentially ever a 'mob') in order to make known and carry through great schemes of social and political improvement. In consequence of this, paradox and contradiction constantly underpin the manner of perception and exposition in Wordsworth's writing. In *Lyrical Ballads*, David Simpson finds evidence of 'a double vision projected to the point of schizophrenia' in 'There is an Eminence';[6] another example from the same source might be 'There was a Boy'.

In the 1805 *Prelude*, the most dramatic illustration of this tendency is reserved for the final book. The poet describes himself climbing Snowdon in expectation of an inspiring sunrise, but his experience is almost exactly the reverse of his expectations. He finds not the sun, but the moon, from whence his attention is drawn not heavenward, but earthward – seemingly into the very bowels of the earth – by the noise of a mighty waterfall below him. The effect of the clouds is such as to give him the impression, after all his exertions, that he stands on the sea-shore, and not on the top of a mountain. The experience seems to deny an escapist aesthetic; it is in one sense quite literally a bringing down to earth, just as the poet in 'Simon Lee', 'Resolution and Independence' or 'Point Rash Judgment', is brought down to earth. Everything promised by the ascent of Snowdon is denied; it is the crowning experience of reversal in a poem where so many of the most important narrative passages make their impact through an initial experience of anticlimax. The experience he seeks is one with which many, through a shared knowledge of contemporary aesthetic theory, might be expected to be able to identify. Paradoxically, though, it is an experience ideally to be had alone. The experience he actually has is one that does indeed set him apart, it is unique, unexpected, and complex. Yet it binds him to the earth, to what is real; the aloneness it offers is, however, all the more comprehensive.

There was to be no resolution of this paradox for Wordsworth. The child of 'There was a Boy' does not achieve manhood, the visionary oneness with nature terminates in death. The story of *Benjamin the Waggoner* ends in a judgement on Benjamin, and the consequences of his fall are absolute and irrevocable. In *The White Doe of Rylstone* (1807–08) Wordsworth pursues the same theme. Francis Norton refuses to ally himself with the cause of his father and his brothers, who are defending the old faith against the new

Protestant order of Elizabeth I. Towards the end of the poem he appears to have established himself as a successful mediator between the two conflicting sides; he is at once a lone voice, dissenting from the fanaticism of both factions, yet he is centrally involved in the action of the drama. Such impartiality, however, proves ultimately impossible to maintain. A pledge given to his father to safeguard the rebel standard, an act of filial love and sentiment, results in his brutal and unmerited murder at the hands of his father's enemies:

> The troop of horse have gained the height
> Where Francis stood in open sight.
> They hem him round – 'Behold the proof,'
> They cried, 'the Ensign in his hand!
> *He* did not arm, he walked aloof!
> For why? – to save his Father's land;
> Worst Traitor of them all is he,
> A Traitor dark and cowardly!' (PW III, 327–8:1462–9)

It is not difficult to trace here vestiges of Wordsworth's own anxieties about how successful he could be in preserving his own integrity under the pressure of changing times, increasing domestic responsibilities, and his continuing wish to be – for all his doubts – an active force in the political life of his country:

> Oh, who is he that hath his whole life long
> Preserved, enlarged, this freedom in himself? –
> For this alone is genuine liberty.
> Witness, ye solitudes, where I received
> My earliest visitations (careless then
> Of what was given to me), and where now I roam,
> A meditative, oft a suffering man,
> And yet I trust with undiminished powers . . .
> (*Prelude* XIII, 464:120–7)

Notes

1 Wordsworth and pastoral politics

1 Mark Akenside, *The Poetical Works*, ed. Rev. George Gilfillan, Edinburgh: James Nichol (1867), 220–1:1–10. Hereafter Akenside.

2 Sara Coleridge, *Memoirs*, quoted in Gordon Kent Thomas, *Wordsworth's Dirge and Promise*, Lincoln: University of Nebraska (1971), p. 36. Thomas's book is a study of Wordsworth's political pamphlet, *The Convention of Cintra* (1809).

3 John Barrell, *The Dark Side of the Landscape*, Cambridge University Press (1980). Other relevant studies by Barrell are: *The Idea of Landscape and the Sense of Place 1730–1840*, Cambridge University Press (1972); *An Equal, Wide Survey*, London: Hutchinson (1983); *The Political Theory of Painting from Reynolds to Hazlitt*, London: Yale University Press (1987).

4 See Mary Jacobus, *Tradition and Experiement in Wordsworth's Lyrical Ballads (1798)*, Oxford: Clarendon Press (1976), pp. 167–8. Hereafter Jacobus.

5 Oliver Goldsmith, *The Deserted Village*, in *The Poems of Gray, Collins and Goldsmith*, ed. Roger Lonsdale, London: Longman (1976), 678:59–62.

6 See Jonathan Wordsworth, *The Music of Humanity*, New York: Harper & Row (1969), p. 190. Hereafter *Music of Humanity*.

7 Vicesimus Knox, *Elegant Extracts: or Useful and Entertaining Pieces of Poetry*, London (1784).

8 Akenside: lines and passages quoted in the order in which they occur in the text: 6:78; 5:64; 6:81; 6:81; 17–18:476–480; 18:499–511; 15:409–10. *Pleasures* was first published in 1744, revised 1757. Knox used 1744, as here.

9 John Dixon Hunt, *The Figure in the Landscape*, Baltimore: John Hopkins University Press (1976), p. 219.

10 *Music of Humanity*, pp. 188–98. The phrase 'one life' is from *The Pedlar* (1798), reproduced in this book.

11 Albert Goodwin, *The Friends of Liberty*, London: Hutchinson (1979), p. 40. Hereafter Goodwin.

12 Goodwin, p. 34.

13 See Goodwin, pp. 36–7.

14 Goodwin, pp. 38–9.

15 Z. S. Fink, 'Wordsworth and the English Republican Tradition', in *Journal of English and Germanic Philosophy*, 47 (1948), pp. 107–26.

16 *Testaments of Radicalism*, ed. David Vincent, London: Europa (1977), p. 51.

17 Francis Blackburne, *Memoir of Thomas Hollis*, 2 vols., London (1780), I, iii–iv.

18 See H. T. Dickinson, *Liberty and Property*, London: Weidenfeld & Nicholson (1977), p. 103.

19 See Caroline Robbins, '"When It Is That Colonies May Turn Independent": An

Analysis of the Environment and Politics of Francis Hutcheson (1694–1746)', in *William and Mary Quarterly*, 11 (1954), pp. 214–51. See also Robbins', *The Eighteenth Century Commonwealthman*, New York: Atheneum (1968).

20 Algernon Sidney, *Discourses Concerning Government*, London (1704), p. 20.

21 Mary Moorman, *William Wordsworth, a Biography*, 2 vols., Oxford: Clarendon Press (1967), I, 290. Hereafter Moorman I and II.

22 Goodwin, p. 36.

23 In 'The Declaration of Independence', for example, issued by 'the thirteen United States of America' on 4 July 1776, the colonists appealed to 'the Laws of Nature and of Nature's God'.

24 Moorman I, 178–93.

25 William Crowe, *Lewesdon Hill, A Poem*, Oxford: Clarendon Press (1788). Line numbers are taken from this text.

26 The chief source of biographical detail for Crowe, with bibliography, is to be found in the *Dictionary of National Biography*.

27 See Ben Ross Schneider, *Wordsworth's Cambridge Education*, Cambridge University Press (1957). See also Heather Glen, *Vision and Disenchantment: Blake's Songs and Wordsworth's Lyrical Ballads*, Cambridge University Press (1983), pp. 86–7.

28 The MSS of 'Poems prepared for the installation of the Chancellor July 4–5, 1793' are to be found in the Bodleian Library, Oxford. Crowe's poem for this occasion was eventually printed in *Lewesdon Hill. Considerably Enlarged, With Other Poems*, London: Codell & W. Davis (1804).

29 'A Catalogue of Books in Race Down Lodge, May 1793', Bristol University Library MS.

30 See Peter Thrasher, *Pasquale Paoli, An Enlightened Hero, 1725–1807*, London: Constable (1970).

31 Caroline Robbins, 'Thomas Hollis in his Dorsetshire Retirement', in *Harvard Library Bulletin* 23, 4 (1975), pp. 411–28.

2 *An Evening Walk*: the pastoral tradition in early Wordsworth

1 *The Poetical Works of Beattie, Blair and Falconer*, ed. Rev. George Gilfillan, Edinburgh: James Nichol (1864), p. 22, stanza lxviii. Hereafter Beattie.

2 The text of the first version of *An Evening Walk* (1793) is used throughout.

3 *A Nocturnal Reverie* (1713) by Anne, Countess of Winchilsea, is often quoted as an early eighteenth-century precursor of this technique. It is reproduced in *Poetry of the Landscape and the Night*, ed. Charles Peake, London: Arnold (1967), pp. 38–40.

4 *Critical Review*, 2nd series, 8 (July 1793).

5 *The Deserted Village*, 677:37–8.

6 Richard Feingold, *Nature and Society*, Brighton: Harvester Press (1978), p. 115.

7 Raymond Williams, *The Country and the City*, London: Chatto & Windus (1973), p. 75.

8 Akenside, 137:1; 138:25–6.

9 For example: Dyer, *Grongar Hill* (1726); Jago, *Edge Hill* (1726); and of course Crowe's *Lewesdon Hill*. See R. A. Aubin, *Topographical Poetry in Eighteenth Century England*, New York: Modern Language Association of America (1936). See also Hunt, *op. cit.*

10 See R. W. Malcomson, *Life and Labour in England 1700–1780*, London: Hutchinson (1981), pp. 138–9; and Pamela Horn, *The Rural World 1780–1850*, London: Hutchinson (1980), pp. 30–5.

11 'Potters': 'In the dialect of the north, a hawker of earthenware is thus designated.' Wordsworth in his note to *Peter Bell* for the 1849–50 edition of PW.

12 For further discussion of the *Lyrical Ballads* poem, see Glen, *op. cit.*, pp. 310–15.

13 Gary Kelly, *The English Jacobin Novel*, Oxford: Clarendon Press (1976), pp. 3–6.

14 For a full discussion of this point, see John Barrell, *The Dark Side of the Landscape*, pp. 70–7.

15 *The Poems of Alexander Pope*, ed. John Butt, London: Methuen (1968) 148:169–74.

16 *Music of Humanity*, p. 53. See also Jacobus, p. 136.

17 John Langhorne, *The Country Justice*, in *The Late Augustans*, ed. Donald Davie, London: Heinemann (1977), 75–6:157–66. See also Jacobus, p. 144.

18 Davie, *op. cit.*, 89:60.

19 See Hollis *Memoir*, II, 714. On Wordsworth's reading in this area see Z. S. Fink, *The Early Wordsworthian Milieu*, Oxford University Press (1958), pp. 4–5, 24–5, 43.

20 See Barrell, *The Dark Side of the Landscape* pp. 118–19 for complementary evidence in the work of George Moreland and Thomas Rowlandson.

21 Davie, *op. cit.*, 84:145–62; pp. xxviii–xxxi. See stanzas I and XIV of Gray's *Elegy in a Country Churchyard*, in Lonsdale, *op. cit.*, pp. 117 and 127.

22 Williams, *op. cit.*, p. 82.

23 Alexander Pope, *Windsor Forest* (1712), in *The Poems of Alexander Pope*, 195:15.

3 *Descriptive Sketches* (1792–93): poetic and personal crises

1 See, for example, the letter to William Mathews, 23 November 1791, in EY, p. 36. For details of text referred to as Letters see Abbreviations.

2 Glen, *op. cit.*, p. 252. John Purkis, *A Preface to Wordsworth*, London: Longman (1982), pp. 50–3. Also of interest here is Paul Hamilton's discussion of 'Tintern Abbey' and poems in a similar vein in the 1800 *Lyrical Ballads* in *Wordsworth*, Brighton: Harvester (1986), pp. 61–8.

3 As with *An Evening Walk*, the influence of Beattie is important in this respect. See Jonathan Wordsworth, *The Borders of Vision*, Oxford: Clarendon Press (1982), pp. 310–12. Hereafter *Borders of Vision*. John Turner also notes Wordsworth's use of Goldsmith's *The Traveller* as a model, in *Wordsworth: Play and Politics*, London: Macmillan (1986), pp. 21–3.

4 See EY, p. 69, and Reed, p. 128.

5 Line numbers for *Descriptive Sketches* refer to the first version of 1793.

6 See George Lefebvre, 'Urban Society in the Orléanais in the Late Eighteenth Century', *Past and Present*, no. 19 (April 1961), pp. 46–75.

7 Thomas R. Edwards, *Imagination and Power*, Oxford University Press (1971), p. 119.

8 Purkis, *op. cit.*, p. 29.

9 Moorman I, 198–9.

10 Edward Duffy, *Rousseau in England*, London: University of California Press (1979), p. 30.

11 *Ibid.*, pp. 10–11.
12 *Ibid.*, pp. 19 and 20.
13 *Ibid.*, p. 30.
14 Goodwin, pp. 223–4.
15 Bernard Bailyn, *The Ideological Origins of the American Revolution*, Cambridge Mass.: Harvard University Press (1967), p. 49. See also John Derry, *English Politics and the American Revolution*, London: Dent (1976), pp. 3–5.
16 For Coleridge on Thomson see *Inquiring Spirit, A Coleridge Reader*, ed. Kathleen Coburn, New York: Minerva Press (1968), pp. 153 and 342.
17 *Music of Humanity*, p. 5.
18 *Memoir of Thomas Hollis*, I, 96.
19 James Thomson, *Liberty, The Castle of Indolence and other Poems*, ed. James Sambrook, Oxford: Clarendon Press (1986), 133–4:248–65; 131:156–60.
20 *Ibid.*, 142:558–9.
21 *Ibid.*, 143:597–8.
22 James Thomson, *The Seasons*, ed. James Sambrook, Oxford: Clarendon Press (1981), 220:365–75.
23 *Ibid.*, 222:414–23.
24 Thomson, *Liberty*, 147:717–20.

4 The *Letter to Llandaff*: a crisis of political allegiance

1 Watson's 'Appendix' is to be found in *Burke, Paine, Godwin and the Revolution Controversy*, ed. Marilyn Butler, Cambridge University Press (1984), pp. 142–8.
2 M. J. Syndenham, *The French Revolution*, London: Batsford (1965), p. 109.
3 J. M. Roberts, *The French Revolution*, Oxford University Press (1978), pp. 51–4. See also Alison Patrick, *The Men of the First French Republic*, Baltimore: Hopkins University Press (1973).
4 Moorman I, 206. Nicholas Roe, *Wordsworth and Coleridge, The Radical Years*, Oxford: Clarendon Press (1988), p. 45. Hereafter Roe.
5 Page and line numbers of the *Letter* from O&S I, 19–66.
6 T. W. Thompson, *Wordsworth's Hawkshead*, Oxford University Press (1970), p. 67. Roe, p. 72. David Simpson, *Wordsworth's Historical Imagination*, London: Methuen (1987), p. 61. Hamilton, *op. cit.*, p. 32.
7 *Ibid.*, p. 5.
8 See Roe, p. 133.
9 James Thomson, *Liberty*, 134:254–61.
10 Goodwin, pp. 174–5 and 483–5. *Borders of Vision*, p. 345. James K. Chandler, *Wordsworth's Second Nature: A Study of the Poetry and Politics*, University of Chicago Press (1984).
11 J. G. A. Pocock, *Politics, Language and Time*, London: Methuen (1972), p. 134. Caroline Robbins, *The Eighteenth Century Commonwealthman*, New York: Atheneum (1968), p. 263. John Almon, *A List of Books and Pamphlets printed for J. Almon, Bookseller and Stationer, opposite Burlington House, in Picadilly*, (1768).
12 Peter Brown, *The Chathamites*, London: Macmillan (1967), pp. 120–1 and 291–2. N.B. for 'Joshua Johnson' read 'Joseph Johnson'.
13 John Almon, *Anecdotes of the Life of the Right Honourable William Pitt, Earl of Chatham And of the Principle Events of His Time*, 3 vols., London (1810), II, 79.

14 *op cit*. Fink.
15 *Ibid.*, pp. 113–14. The passage from Wordsworth's *Letter* referred to in Fink's first paragraph is 36–7:215–47.
16 *Ibid.*, pp. 121 and 123.
17 Maynard Mack, *Alexander Pope: A Life*, London: Yale University Press (1985), pp. 532–4.
18 *The Political Works of James Harrington*, ed. J. G. A. Pocock, Cambridge University Press (1977), pp. 169–70.
19 W. A. Speck, *Stability and Strife: England 1714–1760*, London: Arnold (1977), pp. 223–4.
20 Thomas Paine, *Rights of Man*, ed. Henry Collins, Harmondsworth, Middx.: Penguin Books (1977), p. 64.
21 *Borders of Vision*, p. 264.
22 Turner, *op. cit.*, pp. 30 and 32–3.
23 See *Post-Structuralist Readings of English Poetry*, ed. Richard Machin and Christopher Norris, Cambridge University Press (1987).

5 Poetry of alienated radicalism

1 Beattie, p. 26 stanza xxii.
2 Marilyn Butler, *Romantics, Rebels, and Reactionaries*, Oxford University Press (1981), pp. 64–5.
3 See Robbins, '"When It is That Colonies May Turn Independent"'.
4 Francis Hotoman, *Franco Gallia translated by the Author of the Account of Denmark*, London (1721). The first quotation is from the section entitled 'The Bookseller to the Reader', p. A3. The second quotation is from p. 6 of the section entitled 'A Short Extract of the Life of Francis Hotoman'. See also Goodwin, p. 35; and J. A. Downie, *Robert Harley and the Press*, Cambridge University Press (1979), p. 21.
5 See Francis Burnaby, *Journal of a Tour through the Middle Settlements of America*, London (1775), p. 33.
6 Jacobus, p. 38.
7 See James Burgh, *Political Disquisitions*, 3 vols., London (1774–77), I, xvi–xviii. In the passage cited from Burgh's influential attack on Government policy and morality, he defends his 'republican' sympathies with reference to Gordon and Harrington; his definition of his position as a 'true independent Whig' closely parallels Molesworth's description of a True Whig in his Preface to *Franco Gallia*.
8 Turner, *op. cit.*, p. 50.
9 Agernon Sidney, *Discourses*, p. 13.
10 John Almon, *An Asylum for Fugitive Pieces*, London (1785), p. 146.
11 See Don Bialostosky, *Making Tales: The Poetics of Wordsworth's Narrative Experiments*, Chicago University Press (1984).
12 *The Prelude*, VI, 214–18:488–548.
13 Davie, *op. cit.*, 81:218.
14 Pocock, *op. cit.*, p. 133.
15 Davie, *op. cit.*, 85:171–7.
16 *Ibid.*, 86:213.
17 Butler *op. cit.*, p. 57.
18 *Ibid.*

19 *Ibid.*, p. 61.
20 *Ibid.*
21 Jacobus, p. 23. Peter Marshall, *William Godwin*, London: Yale University Press (1984), pp. 130–1. Turner, *op. cit.*, Chapter 6.
22 See Downie, *op. cit.*, p. 21.

6 The West Country years: 'wise passiveness'

1 See, for example, Turner, *op. cit.*, pp. 117–19.
2 Marjorie Levinson, *Wordsworth's Great Period Poems*, Cambridge University Press (1986), p. 18. Some indication of Wordsworth's frame of mind may be had from his letter of 21 March 1796 to William Mathews. EY, pp. 169–71.
3 *The Pedlar*, in *Music of Humanity*, 179:204–21.
4 *The Ruined Cottage and The Pedlar by William Wordsworth*, ed. James Butler, Brighton: Harvester Press (1979), pp. 461–2. Butler dates *Incipient Madness* a few months later than Gill and Reed, making it contemporaneous with *The Ruined Cottage*. See Moorman I, 286 and 313–14.
5 Reed, pp. 210 and 212.
6 *Ibid.*, pp. 202, 30 and 215.
7 Joseph Cottle, *Reminiscences of Samuel Taylor Coleridge and Robert Southey*, Highgate: Lime Tree Bower Press (1970), pp. 180–2. Coleridge, *Biographia Literaria*, London: J. M. Dent (1975), Chapter X.
8 Samuel Taylor Coleridge, *The Complete Poetical Works*, ed. E. H. Coleridge, Oxford: Clarendon Press (1912), 258:57–8.
9 See *Letter to Llandaff*, O&S I, 38:265–80, and letter to William Mathews, 23 May 1794, EY, p. 119.
10 See EY, pp. 210 and 166. Robbins, *The Eighteenh Century Commonwealthman*, pp. 156–66.
11 *The Complete Works of William Hazlitt*, ed. P. P. Howe, 21 vols., New York: AMS Press (1967), XI, 18–19.
12 William Godwin, *Enquiry Concerning Political Justice*, Harmondsworth, Middx.: Penguin Books (1985), p. 140.
13 Dickinson, *Liberty and Property*, p. 71.
14 James Sambrook, *The Eighteenth Century*, London: Longman (1986), p. 71.
15 *Ibid.*, p. 53.
16 Robert E. Sullivan, *John Toland and the Deist Controversy*, Cambridge Mass.: Harvard University Press (1982), pp. 182–3.
17 *Music of Humanity*, 179:209–12.
18 *Ibid.*, p. 245.
19 *Ibid.*, p. 179.
20 *Ibid.*, p. 184. See Jacobus, pp. 62 and 64–5.
21 Antonio Gramsci, 'The Formation of Intellectuals' in *The Modern Prince and Other Writings*, New York: International Publishers (1978), p. 119.
22 *Music of Humanity*, p. 245.
23 'Expostulation and Reply', LB, 104:24.
24 Jacobus, pp. 101–3.
25 E. P. Thompson, *The Making of the English Working Class*, London: Gollancz (1965), pp. 157–60.

26 In *Wordsworth's Historical Imagination*, pp. 222–3, David Simpson has a footnote in which he draws attention to the possible implications of the two locations cited in the poem. But he offers what may seem an overly elaborate explanation which contrasts the 'working economy' of Thelwall's farm to Wordsworth's residence in a rented manor house. In this reading the conclusion of the poem remains unsatisfactorily contradictory. I first published the straight forward political interpretation offered here in 'Salisbury Plain: Politics in Wordsworth's Poetry', *Literature and History*, 9, 2 (Autumn 1983) pp. 164–93.
27 *Borders of Vision*, p. 59; *Music of Humanity*, pp. 68–9, Jacobus, pp. 217–224.
28 Glen, *op. cit.*, p. 54.
29 Levinson, *op. cit.*, pp. 4–5.
30 *Ibid.*, p. 6. See Simpson, pp. 22–5.
31 Kelvin Everest, *Coleridge's Secret Ministry*, Brighton: Harvester Press (1979), p. 157.
32 Jacobus, pp. 188–94.
33 *Borders of Vision*, p. 122.
34 Levinson, *op. cit.*, p. 17.

7 Goslar: patriotic and domestic love

1 Purkis, *op. cit.*, p. 105.
2 Preface to *Lyrical Ballads* (1800), O&S I, 128:190.
3 'We plant cabbages, and if retirement, in its full perfection, be as powerful in working transformations as one of Ovid's Gods, you may perhaps suspect that into cabbages we shall be transformed.' Letter to William Mathews, 21 March 1796, EY, p. 169.
4 'Felt in the blood, and felt along the heart', LB, 114:29.
5 See Basil Willey, 'On Wordsworth and the Locke Tradition', in *English Romantic Poets*, ed. M. H. Abrams, Oxford University Press (1975), pp. 112–22. O&S I, 112.
6 Jonathan Wordsworth, 'The Two-Part Prelude of 1799', in The Norton Critical Edition, p. 570.
7 Levinson, *op. cit.*, p. 4. Simpson, pp. 191–2.
8 Basil Willey, *The Eighteenth Century Background*, Harmondsworth, Middx.: Penguin Books (1962), p. 134.
9 See Arthur Beatty, *William Wordsworth, His Doctrine and Art in Their Historical Relations*, Madison: University of Wisconsin Press (1922), pp. 100–7.
10 O&S I, 308–9:3572–622.
11 'A Poet's Epitaph', LB, 214:55–6.

8 The 1805 *Prelude*: retirement and education

1 Conyers Middleton, *The History of the life of M. Tullius Cicero*, 2 vols., London (1824), II, 467–8.
2 Robbins, *The Eighteenth Century Commonwealthman*, pp. 19, 282, 371.
3 Simpson, p. 126. The quotation is from *The Prelude*, 450:262–3.
4 Simpson, pp. 93–4.

5 John Thelwall, *The Peripatetic; or, Sketches of the Heart, of Nature and Society; in a Series of Politico-Sentimental Journals, in Verse and Prose, of the eccentric Excursions of Sylvanus Theophrastus, supposed to be written by himself*, 3 vols ., London (1793), I, 11.

6 Robbins, *The Eighteenth Century Commonwealthman*, pp. 301–8.

7 Robert Molesworth, *An Account of Denmark as It was in the Year 1692*, London (1693), Preface, pp. 15–16.

8 Robbins, *The Eighteenth Century Commonwealthman*, pp. 301–8.

9 Moorman I, 96.

10 Roe, pp. 93–6.

11 Burgh, *op. cit.*, III, 150.

12 *Letters from the Right Honorable the late Earl of Shaftesbury to Robert Molesworth Esq.*, London (1721), p. 20.

13 *Borders of Vision*, p. 194.

14 John Brewer, *Party Ideology and Popular Politics at the Accession of George III*, Cambridge University Press (1976), p. 259.

15 William Wordsworth to Dorothy Wordsworth, 6 and 16 September 1790. EY, p. 33.

16 John Brown, *Essays on the Characteristics of the Earl of Shaftesbury*, London (1751), pp. 232–3. See Francis Hutcheson, *An Essay on the Nature and Conduct of the Passions and Affections* (3rd edn, 1742), Florida: Scholars' Facsimiles & Reprints (1962), pp. 309–10.

17 Roe, pp. 23–7.

18 John Jones, *Free and Candid Disquisitions, Relating to the Church of England*, London (1749), p. 88. See Robbins, *The Eighteenth Century Commonwealthman*, pp. 300–1.

19 *Wordsworth's Poems of 1807*, ed. Alun R. Jones, London: Macmillan (1987), pp. 107–8. Hereafter Jones.

9 *The Prelude* Books IX and X: legitimate radicalism

1 *Borders of Vision*, p. 247.

2 Roe, p. 7.

3 *Ibid.*, p. 156.

4 *Ibid.*, p. vii.

5 *Ibid.*, pp. 9–10.

6 John Thelwall, *Poems Chiefly Written in Retirement*, London (1802), 126–32:8–7, 124–7.

7 Roe, pp. 7 and 176–7.

8 *Ibid.*, p. 39.

9 See Fink, *op. cit.*, pp. 107–10.

10 *Borders of Vision*, p. 250.

11 *Ibid.*, p. 249.

12 Brewer, *op. cit.*, pp. 21–3.

13 *The London Association, Letter and Resolutions of The London Association*, London (1775).

14 Brewer, *op. cit.*, p. 22.

15 Edmund Burke, *Reflections on the Revolution in France*, ed, Conor Cruise O'Brien, Harmondsworth: Penguin Books (1978), pp. 93–7; Goodwin, pp. 85–7.

16 Samuel Kliger, *The Goths in England*, New York: Octagon (1972), p. 208.
17 Howard D. Weinbrot, *Augustus Caesar in 'Augustan' England*, Princeton University Press (1978), p. 8.
18 Kliger, *op. cit.*, pp. 210–17.
19 Kelley, *op. cit.*, p. 116.
20 *Burke, Paine, Godwin and the Revolution Controversy*, ed. Marilyn Butler, Cambridge University Press (1984), p. 29.
21 Kelley, *op. cit.*, p. 117.
22 See *Borders of Vision*, pp. 352–3, and Anya Taylor, *Coleridge's Defense of the Human*, Ohio State University Press (1986), p. 136.
23 Akenside, 67–8:157–65.
24 *The Borderers by William Wordsworth*, ed. Robert Osborne, London: Cornell University Press (1982), 67–8:157–71.

10 'Our offences are unexpiated'

1 *The Convention of Cintra*, O&S I, 342:4941.
2 *Ibid.*, 342:4946–9.
3 Kelley, *op. cit.*, pp. 73–4.
4 Jacobus, p. 150.
5 1805 *Prelude*, I, 50:407.
6 See Taylor, *Op. cit.*, p. 164.
7 HG, p. 18. On the subject of sobriety, and Wordsworth's reference to himself as a 'water drinking bard', Schneider (op. cit.) refers to Wordsworth's reading of Horace: 'In these works he made his first acquaintance with those eighteenth century principles [of poetry] he was later to violate so deliberately.' Among the maxims of Horace Schneider quotes is, 'No poems can please long, nor live, which are written by water drinkers.'
8 Jones, 19–20:40–7.
9 *The Gentleman's Magazine*, November 1805, p. 1004.
10 Jones, p. 21.
11 *Ibid.*, 102:161–5. See also EY, p. 455; and *Essay Supplementary to the Preface* (1815), O&S III, 64:72–91.
12 Jones, 77:30–2.
13 Kelley, *op. cit.*, pp. 147–8.
14 'Benjamin the Waggoner by William Wordsworth, edited by Paul F. Betz', *Studies in Romanticism*, 21, 3, (Autumn 1982), p. 505.

Epilogue

1 PW, III, 288:170–7.
2 Simpson, p. 208.
3 Roe, pp. 192 and 225.
4 'To the Spade of a Friend (An Agriculturalist)', in Jones, 123–4:9–12. The other poems referred to in the volume are: 'The Sailor's Mother', pp. 14–15; 'Beggars', pp. 37–8; 'Alice Fell', pp. 39–41; 'The Solitary Reaper', p. 77; 'The Blind Highland Boy', pp. 98–104.
5 *Borders of Vision*, pp. 358–9.
6 Simpson, p. 214.

Bibliography

Akenside, Mark (1721–1805), *The Poetical Works*, ed. Rev. George Gilfillan, Edinburgh: James Nichol (1867).

Almon, John (1737–1805), *A List of Books and Pamphlets printed for J. Almon, Bookseller and Stationer, opposite Burlington House, in Picadilly* (1768). *An Asylum for Fugitive Pieces*, London (1785). *Anecdotes of the Life of the Right Honourable William Pitt, Earl of Chatham And of the Principle Events of his Time*, 3 Vols., London (1810). *Memoirs*, London (1790).

Andrews, Malcom, *The Search for the Picturesque*, London: The Scholar Press (1988).

Aubin R. A., *Topographical Poetry in Eighteenth Century England*, New York: Modern Language Association of America (1936).

Bailyn Bernard, *The Ideological Origins of the American Revolution*, Cambridge Mass.: Harvard University Press (1967).

Barrell John, *An Equal, Wide Survey*, London: Hutchinson (1983).
The Dark Side of the Landscape, Cambridge University Press (1980).
The Idea of Landscape and the Sense of Place, Cambridge University Press (1972).
An Equal, Wide Survey, London: Hutchinson (1983).
The Political Theory of Painting from Reynolds to Hazlitt, London: Yale University Press (1987).
Poetry Language and Politics, Manchester University Press (1988).

Beattie James (1735–1803) in *The Poetical Works of Beattie, Blair and Falconer*, ed. Rev. George Gilfillan, Edinburgh: James Nichol (1864).

Beatty, Arthur, *William Wordsworth, His Doctrine and Art in their Historical Relations*, Madison: University of Winsoncin Press (1922).

Bialostosky, Don, *Making Tales: The Poetics of Wordsworths Narrative Experiments*, Chicago University Press (1984).

Blackburne, Francis (1705–87), *Memoirs of Thomas Hollis*, 2 vols., London (1780). *Theological Works*, with an autobiography completed by his son, 7 vols., Cambridge (1805).

Bonwick, C., *English Radicals and the American Revolution*, Chapel Hill: University of North Carolina Press (1977).

Brewer, John, *Party Ideology and Popular Politics at the Accession of George III*, Cambridge University Press (1976).

Brooke, Henry (1703–83), *Gustavus Vasa*, London (1739).
The Poetical Works, Dublin (1792).

Brown, John (1715–66), *Athelstan*, London (1756).
Barbarossa, London (1755).
Essays on the Characteristics of the Earl of Shaftesbury, London (1751).

Brown, Peter, *The Chathamites*, London: Macmillan (1967).

Burgh, James (1714–75), *Political Disquisitions*, 3 vols., London (1777).

Burke, Edmund (1729–97), *Reflections on the Revolution in France*, ed. Conor Cruise O'Brien, Harmondsworth Middx.: Penguin Books (1978).

Burnaby, Andrew (1734?–1812), *Journal of a Tour through the Middle Settlements of America 1759–60*, London (1775).

Journal of a Tour to Corsica 1766, London (1804).

Butler, James (ed.), *The Ruined Cottage and The Pedlar by William Wordsworth*, Brighton: Harvester Press (1979).

Butler Marilyn, *Romantics, Rebels, and Reactionaries: English Literature and its Background, 1760–1830*, Oxford University Press (1982).

Burke, Paine, Godwin, and the Revolution Controversy, Cambridge University Press (1981).

Chandler, James K., *Wordsworth's Second Nature: A Study of the Poetry and Politics*, University of Chicago Press (1984).

Coburn, Kathleen (ed.), *Inquiring Spirit, A Coleridge Reader*, New York: Minerva Press (1968).

Cohen, Ralph, *The Art of Discrimination*, London: Routledge and Kegan Paul (1964).

Coleridge, Samuel Taylor (1772–1834), *The Complete Poetical Works*, ed. E. H. Coleridge, 2 vols., Oxford: Clarendon Press (1912).

Cottle, Joseph (1770–1853), *Reminiscences of Samuel Taylor Coleridge and Robert Southey*, Highgate: Lime Tree Bower Press (1970).

Crowe, William (1745–1829), *A Sermon Preached Before the University of Oxford at St. Mary's, Nov. 5 1781, by William Crowe, LL.B. Fellow of New College*, London: T. Cadell (1781).

Lewesdon Hill, A Poem, Oxford: Clarendon Press (1788).

Lewesdon Hill. Considerably Enlarged, With Other Poems, London: Codell and W. Davis (1804), contains *Verses: Intended to have been spoken in the theatre to the Duke of Portland, at his installation as Chancellor of the University of Oxford, in the year 1793*, pp. 58–62.

Cunningham, Hugh, 'The Language of Patriotism, 1750–1914', in *History Workshop*, 12 (Autumn 1981), pp. 8–33.

Derry, John, *English Politics and the American Revolution*, London: Dent (1976).

Dickinson, H. T., *Bolingbroke*, London: Constable (1970).

Liberty and Property, London: Weidenfeld & Nicholson (1977).

Politics and Literature in the Eighteenth Century, London: Dent (1974).

Downie John, *Robert Harley and the Press*, Cambridge University Press (1979).

Duffy, Edward, *Rousseau in England*, London: University of California Press (1979).

Edwards, Thomas R., *Imagination and Power*, Oxford University Press (1971).

Everest, Kelvin, *Coleridge's Secret Ministry*, Brighton: Harvester Press (1979).

Fawcett, Joseph (1758?–1804), *The Art of War*, in Arthur Beatty (ed.), *Joseph Fawcett: The Art of War*, Madison: University of Wisconsin Press (1918).

Feingold, Richard, *Nature and Society*, Brighton: Harvester Press (1978).

Fink Z. S., 'Dion and Wordsworth's Political Thought', in *Studies in Philology* (July 1953), pp. 510–14.

The Early Wordsworthian Milieu. A Notebook of Christopher Wordsworth with a few entries by William Wordsworth, Oxford University Press (1958).

'Wordsworth and the English Republican Tradition', in *Journal of English and Germanic Philosophy*, 47 (1948), pp. 107–26.

Gilpin, William (1724–1804), *Observations Relative Chiefly to Picturesque Beauty* ...

Particularly the Mountains and Lakes of Cumberland, and Westmoreland, 2nd edn, London (1788).

Glen, Heather, *Vision and Disenchantment: Blake's Songs and Wordsworth's Lyrical Ballads*, Cambridge University Press (1983).

Godwin, William (1756–1836), *Enquiry Concerning Political Justice*, Harmondsworth: Penguin Books (1985).

Goldsmith, Oliver (1730?–74), *Poems of Gray, Collins and Goldsmith*, ed. Roger Lonsdale, London: Longman (1969).

Goodwin, Albert, *The Friends of Liberty*, London: Hutchinson (1979).

Hamilton, Paul, *Wordsworth*, Brighton: Harvester (1986).

Harrington, James (1611–77), *The Political Works of James Harrington*, ed. J. G. A. Pocock, Cambridge University Press (1977).

Hartley, David (1705–57), *Observations on Man, His Frame, His Duty, and His Expectations*, 2 vols., London (1749).

Hazlitt, William, (1778–1830), *The Complete Works of William Hazlitt*, ed. P. P. Howe, New York: AMS Press (1967).

Hipple, Walter John, *The Beautiful, The Sublime and the Picturesque in Eighteenth Century British Aesthetic Theory*, London: Scholar Press (1988).

Hollis, Thomas (1720–74), among the works edited by Hollis were Neville, *Plato Redevivus* (1763); Sidney, *Discourses Concerning Government* (1763); Toland, *Life of Milton* (1761).

Horn, Pamela, *The Rural World, 1780–1850*, London: Hutchinson (1980).

Hunt, John Dixon, *The Figure in the Landscape*, Baltimore: John Hopkins University Press (1976).

Hutcheson, Francis (1694–1746), *An Essay on the Nature and Conduct of the Passions and Affections with Illustrations on the Moral Sense* (3rd edn, 1742), Florida: Scholars' Facsimile and Reprints (1969).

Jacobus, Mary, *Tradition and Experiment in Wordsworth's Lyrical Ballads 1798*, Oxford: Clarendon Press (1976).

Jones, John, *Free and Candid Disquisitions, Relating to the Church of England*, London (1749).

Kelley, Theresa, *Wordsworth's Revisionary Aesthetics*, Cambridge University Press (1988).

Kelly, Gary, *The English Jacobin Novel*, Oxford: Clarendon Press (1976).

Kliger, Samuel, *The Goths in England*, New York: Octagon (1972).

Knox, Vicesimus (1752–1821), *Elegant Extracts: or Useful and Entertaining Pieces of Poetry*, London (1784).

Langhorne, John (1735–79), *Poetical Works, with Life*, London (1798).
The Country Justice, in *The Late Augustans*, ed. Donald Davie, London: Heinemann (1977).

Lefebvre, Georges, 'Urban Society in the Orléanais in the Late Eighteenth Century', *Past and Present*, no. 19 (April 1961), pp. 46–75.

Levinson, Marjorie, *Wordsworth's Great Period Poems*, Cambridge University Press (1986).

Lipking, Lawrence, *The Ordering of the Arts in Eighteenth Century England*, Princeton University Press (1970).

Locke, John (1632–1704), *An Essay Concerning Human Understanding* (1689). The text was repeatedly revised in the author's lifetime, appearing in a definitive edition in 1706.

London Association, *The London Association, Letter and Resolutions of the London Association*, London (1775).

Machin, R. and Norris, C., *Post-Structuralist Readings of English Poetry*, Cambridge University Press (1987).

Mack, Maynard, *Alexander Pope, A Life*, London: Yale University Press (1985).
The Garden and the City, London: Oxford University Press (1969).

Malcomson, R. W., *Life and Labour in England 1700–1780*, London: Hutchinson (1981).

Marshall, Peter, *William Godwin*, London: Yale University Press (1984).

Mason, William (1724–97), *Caractacus, A Dramatic Poem. Written on the Model of the Ancient Greek Tragedy, first published in the Year 1759*, York (1777).

Middleton, Conyers (1638–1750), *The History of the life of M. Tullius Cicero*, London (1741, edn quoted 1824).

Molesworth, Robert (1656–1725), *An Account of Denmark, as It was in the Year 1692*, the Third Edition corrected, London (1694).
A Short Narrative of the Life and Death of John Rhindholt, translated and published by Molesworth, London (1717).
Franco-Gallia: or, an Account of the Ancient Free State of France and Most other Parts of Europe, before the Loss of their Liberties. Written Originally in Latin by the Famous Civilian Francis Hotoman, In the Year 1574. And Translated into English by the Author of the Account of Denmark. The Second Edition, with Additions and a New Preface by the Translator, London: Edward Valentine (1721).
Marinda, Poems and Translations by M. Monk, ed. with an Introduction by Robert Molesworth, London (1716).

Moore, C. A., 'Whig Panygeric Verse, 1700–1760', in *PMLA*, 41, 2 (1926), pp. 362–401.

Moorman, Mary, *William Wordsworth, a Biography*, 2 vols., Oxford: Clarendon Press, (1967).

Morse, David, *Perspectives on Romanticism*, London: Macmillan (1981).

Murrin, John M., 'The Great Inversion, or Court versus Country: A Comparison of the Revolution Settlements in England (1688–1721) and America (1776–1816)', in *Three British Revolutions: 1641, 1688, 1776*, ed. J. G. A. Pocock, Princeton University Press (1980).

McFarland, Thomas, *Coleridge and the Pantheist Tradition*, Oxford: Clarendon Press (1969).

Osborne, Robert (ed.), *The Borderers by William Wordsworth*, London: Cornell University Press (1982).

Paine, Thomas (1737–1809), *Rights of Man*, ed. Henry Collins, Harmondsworth: Middx.: Penguin Books (1977).

Patrick, Alison, *The Men of the First French Republic*, Baltimore: Hopkins University Press (1973).

Pinney, 'A Catalogue of Books in the Library at Racedown Lodge, County of Dorset, Property of J. Pinney Esq. Taken this day of May 1793', MS Bristol University Library.

Pocock J. G. A., *Politics, Language and Time*, London: Methuen (1972).

Pope, Alexander (1688–1744), *The Poems of Alexander Pope*, ed. John Butt, London: Methuen (1968).

Prickett, Stephen, *England and the French Revolution*, London: Macmillan (1988).

Priestley, Joseph (1733–1804), *An Essay on the First Principles of Government and on the Nature of Political, Civil, and Religious Liberty*, London (1768).

Purkis, John, *A Preface to Wordsworth*, London: Longman (1982).

Reiman Donald, 'Benjamin the Waggoner by William Wordsworth, edited by Paul F. Betz', *Studies in Romanticism*, 21, 3 (Autumn 1982).

Rivers, Isabel, *The Poetry of Conservatism*, Cambridge University Press (1973).

Robbins, Caroline, 'Honest Heretic: Joseph Priestley in America, 1794–1804', in *Proceedings of the American Philosophical Society*, 106 (1962), pp. 60–76.

'Library of Liberty – Assembled for Harvard College by Thomas Hollis of Lincoln's Inn', in *Harvard Library Bulletin*, 5 (1951), pp. 5–23, & 181–196.

The Eighteenth Century Commonwealthman, New York: Atheneum (1968).

'The Strenuous Whig, Thomas Hollis of Lincoln's Inn', in *William and Mary Quarterly*, 3rd series, 7, 3 (July 1950), pp. 406–53.

'Thomas Hollis in his Dorsetshire Retirement', in *Harvard Library Bulletin*, 23, 4 (1975), pp. 411–28.

'"When It Is That Colonies May Turn Independent": An Analysis of the Environment and Politics of Francis Hutcheson (1694–1746)', in *William and Mary Quarterly* 11 (1954), pp. 214–51.

Roberts, Charles W., 'The Influence of Godwin on Wordsworth's Letter to the Bishop of Llandaff', in *Studies in Philology*, 22 (1932), pp. 588–606.

Roberts, J. M., *The French Revolution*, Oxford University Press (1978).

Roe, Nicholas, *Wordsworth and Coleridge, The Radical Years*, Oxford: Clarendon Press (1988).

Royle and Walvin *English Radicals and Reformers 1760–1848*, Brighton: Harvester Press (1982).

Sambrook, James, *The Eighteenth Century*, London: Longman (1986).

Schneider, Ben Ross, *Wordsworth's Cambridge Education*, Cambridge University Press (1957).

Shaftesbury, Earl of (1671–1713), *Characteristics of Men, Manners, Opinions, Times*, 3 vols., London (1714). This is a second corrected edition of the 'revised' edition published in 1713, the work was first published in 1711.

Letters from the Right Honourable the Late Earl of Shaftesbury to Robert Molesworth, Esq., Now the Lord Viscount of that Name. With Two Letters written by the late Sir John Cropley, London (1721).

Sidney, Algernon (1622–83), *Discourses Concerning Government*, London (1698, edn quoted 1704).

Simpson, David, *Wordsworth's Historical Imagination*, London: Methuen (1987).

Speck, W. A., *Stability and Strife: England 1714–1760*, London: Arnold (1977).

Sperry, Willard L., *Wordsworth's Anti-Climax*, Cambridge University Press (1935).

Sullivan, E., *John Toland and the Deist Controversy*, New Haven, Conn.: Harvard University Press (1981).

Sydenham, M. J., *The French Revolution*, London: Batsford (1965).

Taylor, Anya, *Coleridge's Defense of the Human*, Ohio State University Press (1968).

Thelwall, John (1764–1834), *The Rights of Nature against the Usurpations of Establishments*, Norwich (1796).

Poems Written in Close Confinement, London (1795).

The Peripatetic; or, Sketches of the Heart, of Nature and Society; in a Series of Politico-Sentimental Journals, in Verse and Prose, of the eccentric Excursions of Sylvanus Theophrastus, supposed to be written by himself, 3 vols., London (1793).

Poems Chiefly Written in Retirement, London (1802).

Thomas, D. O., *The Honest Mind: The Thought and Work of Richard Price*, Oxford University Press (1977).

Thomas Gordon Kent, *Wordsworth's Dirge and Promise*, Lincoln: University of Nebraska Press (1971).

Thompson, E. P., 'Eighteenth Century English Society: Class Struggle Without Class', in *Social History* (May 1978), pp. 133–65.

The Making of the English Working Class, London: Gollancz (1965).

Whigs and Hunters, Harmondsworth, Middx.: Penguin Books (1977).

Thompson, T. W., *Wordsworth's Hawkshead*, Oxford University Press (1970).

Thomson, James (1700–48), *Poetical Works*, ed. J. Logie Robertson, London: Oxford University Press (1961).

The Seasons, ed. J. Sambrook, Oxford: Clarendon Press (1981).

Liberty, The Castle of Indolence and Other Poems, ed. J. Sambrook, Oxford: Clarendon Press (1986).

Tancred and Sigismunda. A Tragedy, London: A. Millar (1745).

Thrasher, Peter, *Pasquale Paoli, An Enlightened Hero, 1725–1807*, London: Constable (1970).

Turner, James, *The Politics of Landscape*, Oxford: Basil Blackwell (1979).

Turner, John, *Wordsworth: Play and Politics*, London: Macmillan (1986).

Vincent, David (ed.), *Testaments of Radicalism*, London: Europa (1977).

Weinbrot, Howard D., *Augustus Caesar in 'Augustan' England*, Princeton University Press (1978).

Wildi, Max, 'Wordsworth and the Simplon Pass', in *English Studies*, 40 (August 1959), pp. 224–32.

Willey, Basil, *The Eighteenth Century Background*, Harmondsworth: Penguin Books (1962).

'On Wordsworth and the Locke Tradition', in *English Romantic Poets*, ed. M. H. Abrams, Oxford University Press (1975).

Williams, Raymond, *The Country and the City*, London: Chatto & Windus (1973).

Wordsworth Jonathan, *The Borders of Vision*, Oxford: Clarendon Press (1982).

The Music of Humanity, New York: Harper & Row (1969).

'The Two Part Prelude of 1799' in *The Prelude 1799, 1805, 1850*, ed. Jonathan Wordsworth, M. H. Abrams, and Stephen Gill, London: Norton (1979), pp. 567–85.

Index